PRENTICE HALL
LITERATURE

PENGUIN 🐧 EDITION

Reading Kit

Grade Seven

PEARSON

Prentice
Hall

Upper Saddle River, New Jersey
Boston, Massachusetts

ISBN 0-13-165402-0

2 3 4 5 6 7 8 9 10   10 09 08 07 06

Contents

ALPHABETICAL LIST OF SKILLS PAGES

VOCABULARY

GRAMMAR

© Pearson Education, Inc., publishing as Pearson Prentice Hall.

	Practice	Assess

The *Reading Kit* has four parts, each designed to help you address the needs of students with varying ability levels.

- Use Part 1 to reteach and reassess unmastered skills
- Use Part 2 to develop independent application of active reading strategies
- Use Part 3 to ensure that students of all ability levels actively participate in learning activities and class discussions.
- Use Part 4 to devise strategies for addressing the special needs of diverse learners.

Part 1 Practice and Assess

Part 1 is organized around the skills taught in the student edition and is organized in the order in which the skills are taught and assessed. These *Practice* pages are designed to reteach skills targeted by the benchmark, but you can use them at any time that you feel reteaching is needed. All *Practice* and *Assess* pages are also available electronically on Success Tracker.

- After administering a benchmark test, use the Interpretation Chart that accompanies the tests to determine which *Practice* pages should be assigned to students.
- After students complete the *Practice* assignments, use the *Assess* pages to check mastery of the specific skills that have been retaught.

Part 2 Everyday Reading Strategies

Part 2 provides teacher and student pages for teaching reading strategies that develop active, thoughtful reading practices in *all* students. In addition, by giving direct instruction in these strategies, you will provide struggling readers with the tools they need to improve their comprehension and interpretation. These strategies can be used with any literature selection.

- Introduce the strategy, using the strategy plan and the graphic organizer.
- Once students are familiar with the strategy, encourage them to use the strategy independently with other selections.

Part 3 Classroom Management for Differentiated Instruction

Part 3 describes practical, effective strategies for engaging students of all ability levels in learning activities and class discussions. These research-based, classroom-tested techniques allow you to support your struggling students and challenge your advanced students in the same discussion or activity. These frameworks can be used with any literature selection or discussion topic.

Part 4 Language Arts Instruction—Professional Articles

Part 4 gives an overview of the diverse classroom. It also provides an analysis of the reading process, identifying the four aspects that need to be addressed to fully support diverse learners. Sections dedicated to specific characteristics of and challenges posed by three groups follow, along with discussion of strategies and resources for each: English language learners, less proficient learners, and special needs students.

Practice and Assess

Reading: Context Clues

Practice

You can often figure out the meaning of an unfamiliar word by using the other information in the sentence in which it appears. This information is called the **context** of the word.

In the paragraph below, some words have been left out. Read the entire paragraph. Then, go back and write on each blank a word that makes sense to you.

With only about 40,000 men and women, the United States Coast

Guard is **1.** _____ than any of the other Armed Forces.

However, this little group is very important to the nation. Every year they

save many **2.** _____ and millions of **3.** _____

worth of goods and ships. They also rescue people during hurricanes,

floods, and other **4.** _____. The Coast Guard is a seagoing

police force that can arrest anyone who breaks the **5.** _____.

They watch for oil **6.** _____ and make safety rules. They

protect fish and other sea **7.** _____. Coast Guard

icebreakers help ships that become trapped in frozen lakes and rivers

during the **8.** _____. The Coast Guard uses radio,

lighthouses, and markers to help captains **9.** _____ their

ships. They also broadcast weather information to warn ships about

dangerous **10.** _____.

How do you know that *smaller* is the word that belongs on the first blank? You know because the rest of the sentence provides clues.

First, it is clear that the Coast Guard is being compared with the other Armed Forces—the Army, the Navy, and so on.

Second, because the number of Coast Guard personnel is given, the comparison probably deals with the number of people in the different services.

Third, since the word *only* is used about the number Coast Guard personnel, it is probably *smaller* than other Armed Forces.

Reading: Context Clues

Assess

A   Use context clues to choose the best meaning for the underlined word.

1. Dan often <u>flies</u> to Florida in the summer.

    A. insects   **B.** travels by airplane   **C.** flaps his wings

2. Jane pressed the flowers between the <u>leaves</u> of an old book.

    A. part of a tree   **B.** goes away   **C.** pages

3. The clerk gave Pete a handful of <u>change</u>.

    A. put on other clothes   **B.** to make different   **C.** coins

4. The math teacher reports that her new students are very <u>sharp</u>.

    A. pointed   **B.** smart   **C.** good-looking

5. Tom <u>polished</u> off the last piece of pie.

    A. ate up   **B.** made shiny   **C.** made perfect

6. The queen greeted all the guests at the grand <u>ball</u>.

    A. part of the foot   **B.** round toy   **C.** fancy party

B   Match each underlined word to its definition. Use context clues to help you.

1. _____ In winter, the colonists traveled by <u>pod</u> because the snow was so deep.

2. _____ Delia spread blueberry <u>preserves</u> on her toast.

3. _____ A <u>post rider</u> delivered their packages.

4. _____ Mom <u>arranged</u> to give a party for the new teacher.

5. _____ Looking across the vast <u>plain</u>, we saw nothing but miles and miles of wheat.

6. _____ Reen's great grandparents, and other <u>ancestors</u>, all came from Ireland.

7. _____ After a long day at work, Dad was <u>beat</u>.

> a. planned
> b. family members
> c. kind of sled
> d. large area of flat land
> e. jam
> f. very tired
> g. mail carrier on horseback

Literary Analysis: Narration

The act or process of telling a story is **narration.** A narrative tells a story or a part of a story. The person telling the story is the narrator and can be someone in the story or an outside observer. A narrative presents a series of events in time order and often uses words and phrases such as *first, then,* and *after that* to make the order clearer.

Transition Words and Phrases	
after	meanwhile
at first	next
eventually	second
finally	soon
later	then

Read the following paragraph and fill in each blank with a transition word or phrase that makes the sequence of events clear. Use the words in the box on this page.

Noni grabbed his warmest boots and sealskin hat. **1.** _____

he put on his heaviest coat because the trip ahead would be a long one.

Outside, his two faithful dogs, Nikki and Rikki, greeted him. The dogs

were **2.** _____ hitched to the sled, and they all set off.

However, **3.** _____ traveling only a short distance, the sled

overturned on a steep slope. Noni tumbled down the snowy slope and was

shaken but not hurt. **4.** _____ he wanted to continue the

trip, but **5.** _____ he decided to put it off a day.

6. _____ the dogs barked loudly, wanting to be unhooked

from the sled. **7.** _____ they were freed and ran on ahead of

Noni back to home, happy the journey was over so soon.

Literary Analysis: Narration

Read each sentence below. Then, rearrange them in time order. Use the transition words and phrases and other clues to help you. Finally, rewrite the sentences as a narrative paragraph on the lines provided.

1. _____ Immediately he rushed past the dogs and stormed into the cabin.

2. _____ Then, as Noni came close to the cabin, he panicked.

3. _____ At last, he rushed out the front door with them, flinging them into the snow.

4. _____ After a while, Noni neared home, dragging the sled.

5. _____ Smoke was coming from a side window near the stove.

6. _____ Even before he arrived, he could hear the sled dogs barking.

7. _____ Then he ripped flaming curtains from the wall.

_____

_____

_____

_____

_____

_____

Literary Analysis: Point of View

Practice

Point of view is the view from which the **narrator,** or storyteller, speaks. In **first-person point of view,** the story is told by a character who is in the story and is part of the action. The reader sees and knows only what the narrator sees and knows. In **third-person point of view,** the story is told by someone outside the action. This narrator can describe the thoughts and actions of any or all of the characters in the story.

Read the story excerpts. Write **F-P** if the excerpt is told from the first-person point of view. Write **T-P** if the excerpt is told from third-person point of view.

1. _____ Ernie says that being a good magician is not easy. He and Gert practice their tricks for hours a day. Sometimes they watch themselves in the mirror as they do the tricks. Sometimes they might invite an audience to watch. "The hand is quicker than the eye!" Ernie always says.

2. _____ Laura and I were completely silent. We crouched down behind the garbage cans afraid to even breathe. Who was that masked figure sneaking through the garage? Suddenly my nose started tingling. "Ah, ah, ah-choo!" I sneezed.

3. _____ I watched Jason as he took his time putting on the roller skates. Why had he told LeTeena he could really skate? I noticed that she had not been that impressed. Why did Jason always have to make up stories? I could tell that Jason was feeling nervous. He looked at me with a weak smile and sighed.

4. _____ Identical twins Manu and Mico used to dress the same way, speak the same way, and go everywhere together. However, ever since they met Sylvia, the twins look quite different. Manu dresses in khakis and button-down shirts. Mico nearly always wears jeans and T-shirts.

5. _____ "A storm is coming," said Cassie. "We better pack up and get off the beach." Dark clouds were forming, and the wind was getting stronger. Cassie, Tina, and Jake quickly folded the towels, while Deena used her cell phone to call her dad. When Mr. Jackson heard the phone ring, he was already about to leave to pick up the kids at the lake.

Literary Analysis: Point of View

Assess

A Circle the letter of the answer choice that correctly completes each sentence.

1. In the first-person point of view, the person telling the story is a ____.

    A. character in the story   **B.** person outside the action of the story

2. In the third-person point of view, the person telling the story is a ____.

    A. character in the story   **B.** person outside the action of the story

3. If the reader cannot be sure whether to believe the person telling the story, the story is probably being told from the ____.

    A. first-person point of view   **B.** third-person point of view

4. When a story is told from the third-person point of view, readers know ____.

    A. only what the narrator experiences   **B.** what many of the characters do and say

B Read each passage. Then, answer the questions.

I really do not like Daniel. He is the meanest kid on the block. Plus, he is always showing off. There he goes again. He might as well wear a sign that says, "Look at me! I am the greatest!" Oh, no. He is heading this way! I am going to get out of here fast.

1. What is the point of view? _____

2. Do readers know whether the narrator's view of Daniel is correct? Why or why not?

_____

Sasha and Arnie volunteer at the Humane Society after school three days a week. First, they check to make sure that all the dogs' cages are clean and that every dog has fresh water. Then, the boys see which dogs are scheduled for a walk. They may walk as many as eight dogs before Arnie's mom comes to pick them up at 5:30.

3. What is the point of view? _____

Literary Analysis: Fiction and Nonfiction

Practice

Fiction: literary works that describe made-up people and events.

Nonfiction: literary works that describe real people and events or ideas.

A Read the following examples and decide if each is fiction or not. Write *yes* if the example is fiction and *no* if it is not.

1. _____ A man sleeps for twenty years. When he awakes, everything has changed. His children are grown, and his house has been torn down.

2. _____ Lou Gehrig was a famous baseball player who faced a serious illness with courage. The disease ALS is today referred to as Lou Gehrig's disease.

B Read each description. Write *fiction* or *nonfiction* to identify each one.

1. _____ This is a story about a group of fifteen-year-old girls who enjoy ice-skating. They have been taking lessons together for three years. Now one of them is moving away. As the story unfolds, we learn about the adventures they have had together. We also learn about some experiences they have had apart in the three years since they first met.

2. _____ This is an account of a real scientist's year in the African jungle studying gorillas. The work opens as the scientist imagines all the things that can go wrong when he begins his observations in the jungle. It ends a year later with the scientist presenting his findings at a wildlife biology seminar.

C Read each description. Write *fiction* or *nonfiction* to identify each one.

1. _____ The time is the reign of Queen Elizabeth I. England is at war with France. The events and descriptions of the soldiers are accurate and supported by historical accounts.

2. _____ In this story, Juanita and her stepbrother Luis are on vacation. They have gone off to a faraway part of the beach in search of shells. Suddenly, the tide comes in and cuts off the path back to the cottage.

3. _____ In this story, Clyde lives on the planet Venus and wants to learn to play the saxophone. His music teacher turns out to be a robot with six hands. The robot automatically knows every song that Clyde is interested in playing.

Literary Analysis: Fiction and Nonfiction

Assess

A Write *fiction* on the line if you expect the selection will be about imaginary people and events. Write *nonfiction* if you think it will be about real people and events.

1. _____ a story about a boy who sails across the Atlantic Ocean alone on a raft

2. _____ the life story of Abraham Lincoln

3. _____ a book about the rain forests of South America

B Read each selection and write what it is—fiction or nonfiction. Then, tell one clue that helped you decide.

1. Among the Iroquois, the basic unit of society was the "fireside," or family, made up of a woman and all her children. A group of two or more families was known as a clan. Everyone in a clan considered the others in the clan to be relatives. Several clans lived together in a village.

_____

2. Once upon a time, in a city beneath the sea, a beautiful mermaid was kept captive by Gustaf, ruler of the oceans, and his cruel wife, Astrid. The mermaid lived in a magnificent palace and was served all the food she could eat. Yet she longed to be free.

_____

3. At 21 stories high, the Cape Hatteras lighthouse in North Carolina is the tallest one in the United States and is one of our nation's most prominent landmarks. The lighthouse was built in 1870 on a barrier island, 457 m from the shoreline, to warn sailors of dangerous water.

_____

4. Sally awoke one morning to find that it had snowed the night before. Looking out her bedroom window, she saw that the plow had not yet cleared her street. Was it possible that school would be canceled?

_____

Vocabulary: Word Origins

Practice

The **origin** of a word is the word's history. Many English words come from languages such as Latin, Greek, or French. Understanding a word's history can help you remember the word's meaning.

Word	Comes from	Means
significance	Latin word meaning "sign"	meaning, importance
reveal	Latin word meaning "to pull back the veil"	to tell or make known; to show
revelation	Latin word meaning "to pull back the veil"	something shown or made known
context	Latin word meaning "to weave together"	connection between a word and its surroundings
verify	Latin word meaning "true"	to prove something to be true

Fill in each blank with the correct word from the chart. Make sure the word fits the meaning of the sentence.

1. I promised not to _____ the secret of who won the contest.

2. A good driver knows the _____ of every traffic sign she sees on the highway.

3. I can _____ that I was sick by bringing a note from my doctor.

4. The meaning of a word depends on the _____ of the sentence in which it is used.

5. At the end of the movie, there was a surprising _____ of the main character's secret.

Name _____ Date _____

Vocabulary: Word Origins

A Next to each word, write the letter of the choice that describes the word's origin.

1. _____ reveal   **A.** Latin word meaning "sign"

2. _____ verify   **B.** Latin word meaning "pull back the veil"

3. _____ context   **C.** Latin word meaning "true"

4. _____ significance   **D.** Latin word meaning "to weave together"

B Use one word from Exercise A to replace the underlined word or words in each sentence. Write the correct words on the lines.

1. _____ My teacher asked me to <u>prove</u> that the facts in my report were true.

2. _____ You can figure out the meaning of a new word by noticing its <u>nearby words in the sentence</u>.

3. _____ If you remove the paint from that old table, you will <u>show</u> the beautiful wood that is underneath.

4. _____ The <u>meaning</u> of his urgent message was very clear.

Grammar: Common and Proper Nouns

Practice

A **common noun** is the general name of a person, place, or thing. A **proper noun** names a particular person, place, or thing. Proper nouns always begin with a capital letter.

A Write *common noun* or *proper noun* to describe the underlined word.

1. Thomas Alva Edison was born in <u>Ohio</u> in 1847. _____

2. He was educated at <u>home</u> by his mother. _____

3. At age twelve he was a <u>newsboy</u>. _____

4. Edison later worked on a train in <u>Michigan</u>. _____

B Underline the common nouns and proper nouns in each sentence.

5. Edison patented over one thousand inventions.

6. Where did the busy inventor work in America?

7. The laboratory was in New Jersey.

8. His phonograph was famous in Europe.

9. Thomas Edison helped to invent movies.

C Copy the nouns you underlined in Exercise B. Write them in the correct column.

Common Nouns	Proper Nouns
10. _____	15. _____
11. _____	16. _____
12. _____	17. _____
13. _____	18. _____
14. _____	19. _____

Grammar: Common and Proper Nouns

A Read each sentence. Write *common noun* or *proper noun* to describe each underlined word.

1. Many tourists enjoy visiting <u>England</u>. _____

2. The <u>country</u> has many historic sites. _____

3. The town where <u>Shakespeare</u> was born is famous. _____

4. Shakespeare's <u>plays</u> are still performed there today. _____

5. <u>The Royal Shakespeare Company</u> entertains audiences. _____

6. The <u>company</u> often performs in Stratford-on-Avon and in London.

   _____

7. On one <u>occasion</u> we saw a great English actor onstage. _____

B Underline each common noun. Circle each proper noun.

8. Many people watch the boats on the river.

9. The home of the royal family is Buckingham Palace.

10. Queen Elizabeth sometimes stays at Windsor Castle with her family.

11. There are many ancient castles located throughout England.

12. One of the busiest stations for trains is Victoria Station.

13. Fleet Street is the destination of some business travelers.

14. People often drink tea in the afternoon.

15. Many citizens of other nations respect the traditions of the English.

Grammar: Possessive Nouns

Practice

A **possessive noun** shows ownership. It always has an apostrophe. Use a possessive noun to show that something belongs to someone.

Singular Possessive Add an apostrophe and *s* ('s) to the singular noun.	the cat John	the cat's bed John's baseball
Plural Possessive Add only an apostrophe (') to a plural noun that ends in *s*.	cats boys	cats' bed boys' baseball
Add an apostrophe and an *s* ('s) to a plural noun that does not end in *s*.	children women	children's toy women's shoes

A   Underline the possessive noun in the sentence. Then, write *singular* or *plural*.

1. The library's three rooms are full of people. _____

2. The children's story hour had just begun. _____

3. Maria browsed in the young adults' section. _____

4. Some books' covers were old and worn. _____

5. Her favorite book's title is *The Runner*. _____

6. The author's name is Cynthia Voigt. _____

7. The town's library is a busy place on Saturday. _____

B   Write the possessive form of each underlined noun.

8. The <u>laboratory</u> environment is very organized. _____

9. The two <u>chemists</u> goal was to create a new product. _____

10. The <u>computer</u> screen showed several formulas. _____

11. The <u>men</u> experiments were a success. _____

12. Each <u>day</u> work brings some rewards. _____

13. A <u>chemist</u> lab is an interesting place. _____

Grammar: Possessive Nouns

A   Replace each word in parentheses with a plural or possessive form.

1. For many (year) _____ gold was (Alaska)

_____ most important product.

2. Most (mine) _____ yields were not as great as the

(miner) _____ expected.

3. However, many (miner) _____ stayed to become permanent

(inhabitant) _____ of Alaska, and the (territory)

_____ population doubled in a ten-year period.

4. Alaska was one of the last two (state) _____ to join the
Union.

B   Underline the correct form of the noun for each sentence.

5. The (oceans, ocean's) waters became choppy.

6. Then (wave's, waves) washed over the deck.

7. Deck (chairs, chair's) were blown about.

8. The (passengers, passengers') faces showed worry.

9. The (ships, ship's) captain was not alarmed.

10. He asked people to go to their (cabins, cabin's).

11. Everyone followed Captain (Jones, Jones's) orders.

12. The (engine's, engines) hummed through the night.

13. The (navigators, navigator's) kept the ship on course.

14. By dawn the (sun's, suns) rays began to shine through clouds.

Grammar: Forms of Plural Nouns

Practice

A **plural noun** names more than one person, place, thing, or idea. Most nouns add -s to form the plural. Some nouns change their spelling in the plural. A few have the same singular and plural spelling.

A Write the plural form of each noun.

1. girl _____

2. glass _____

3. pony _____

4. tomato _____

5. elf _____

6. tooth _____

7. birch _____

8. fox _____

9. lash _____

10. monkey _____

11. sheep _____

12. hobby _____

B Rewrite the following sentences, changing the nouns in parentheses to their plural forms.

13. Many (person) observed their (shadow).

_____

14. (Century) ago Egyptian (child) used shadow clocks.

_____

15. Later (man) and (woman) used sundials.

_____

16. (Guess) were made on stormy (day).

_____

17. (Clock) and (watch) are timepieces.

_____

Grammar: Forms of Plural Nouns

Assess

A Write the plurals of these nouns.

1. potato _____

2. chief _____

3. branch _____

4. valley _____

5. box _____

B Write the plural of each noun.

1. book _____

2. bunch _____

3. foot _____

4. allergy _____

5. thief _____

6. aluminum _____

7. half _____

8. spaghetti _____

9. lunchbox _____

10. hero _____

C Rewrite the following sentences, changing the nouns in parentheses to their plural forms.

1. (Zoo) give people in (city) a chance to see wild (animal).

_____

2. (Fox) lie by their dens, and (monkey) play on (rope).

_____

3. (Sea lion) and (seal) frolic and splash in two (pool).

_____

Writing: Comparison-and-Contrast Essay

Practice

A **comparison-and-contrast essay** discusses the similarities and differences between two subjects. A comparison-and-contrast essay should include the following:

- a topic involving two or more subjects that are alike and different
- details about each subject

You may gather details for your essay in a Venn diagram or two-column chart like this one:

Similarities	Differences

A Read the example. Then, answer the questions.

Many people love to play baseball. Tennis is also extremely popular. Both sports are usually played outdoors, though tennis can be played indoors. Tennis is usually played by individuals, and baseball is played by teams. Both sports provide great exercise. Professional baseball players are often seen as heroes by young fans, and so are professional tennis players.

1. What are the things being compared in the example?

_____

_____

2. What could be another point of comparison between tennis and baseball?

_____

B Begin a comparison-and-contrast essay. Pick two things that you would like to compare to each other and list at least two similarities and two differences.

1. My topic is _____ compared to _____.

2. Two similarities are _____ and _____.

3. Two differences are _____ and _____.

Writing: Comparison-and-Contrast Essay

Assess

Choose one of the following topics. Then, complete the activities that follow.

two characters in a movie you have seen   two people you know

two sports or activities   two seasons or times of day

two places you have visited   other

1. Write your specific topic on the line.

_____

2. List facts and details about each subject.

_____   _____

_____   _____

_____   _____

_____   _____

3. List three similarities and/or differences that you will write about.

_____

_____

_____

4. Write the first paragraph of your comparison-and-contrast essay on the
following lines.

_____

_____

_____

_____

_____

_____

Writing: Hyperbole

Practice

Hyperbole [pronounced hy PER boh lee] is an exaggerated, and often amusing, way of describing something. Authors use hyperbole for effect, to make sure they get their point across. For example, this is a hyperbole: "I was running so fast that the soles of my sneakers practically burst into flame. Smoke was coming out from under my feet."

A   Circle the letter of the word or phrase that best completes the hyperbole.

1. My frog jumped so high that

    A. he jumped right over a stick.
    B. he made a big splash when he landed.
    C. he caught a fly on the moon.
    D. his legs stretched out behind him.

2. The pepperoni pizza was delicious, and we

    A. could have eaten a whole room full of it.
    B. finished the whole thing.
    C. wanted to order another one.
    D. had a salad, too.

B   Decide whether the following statements are true or false. Circle *T* or *F*.

1. T / F Hyperbole is not used mainly for effect.

2. T / F Hyperbole makes writing more entertaining.

3. T / F Hyperbole would be good to use in a serious research paper.

4. T / F Authors use hyperbole when they want their readers to get a vivid impression.

Writing: Hyperbole

Assess

Write three examples of hyperbole on the lines provided. You may describe items that are listed in the box, or you may think of your own examples.

| a bee sting | noisy fireworks | a long test |
| a parade | a scary watchdog | a delicious sundae |

1. _____

_____

2. _____

_____

3. _____

_____

4. Explain why you would use hyperbole in your writing. What sorts of writing do you think are best suited to hyperbole?

_____

_____

_____

_____

Writing: Descriptive Essay

Practice

A **descriptive essay** creates a vivid image of a person, thing, or place. A descriptive essay paints pictures with words. In a good description, the reader will be able to do more than see the scene, however. He or she will be able to hear, taste, smell, and feel it as well. Your choice of words helps create the picture you want the reader to visualize. That is why it is important to use a thesaurus and to classify your details so they can be presented in an organized way. Good descriptive essays create very vivid impressions.

A Complete this exercise on your own paper. List six or seven details that describe a place. Include details that appeal to at least three senses. Some of the details should also reflect your feelings about the place. Choose one of the following subjects or think of another place that is special to you.

1. a room in a house

2. a landscape through which you have traveled by plane, car, train, or boat

3. a place associated with a holiday

4. an imaginary place you would like to visit

5. the inside of a closet

B Complete the following activities as preparation for writing a descriptive essay. Use the place you chose in Exercise A.

1. Classify the details so that you will be able to present them in a clear and organized way.

2. Add appropriate adjectives and adverbs to your details.

3. Write down your feelings about this place. Try to reflect these feelings with vivid adverbs and adjectives.

4. Write two possible topic sentences that could be supported by your details.

5. Decide on a spatial order for your description. For example, will you order your details from near to far, outside to inside, or left to right?

Writing: Descriptive Essay

Assess

A Write the sense that each of the following words goes with.

1. glowing _____

2. icy _____

3. booming _____

4. sour _____

5. gas fumes _____

6. cushioned _____

B For a paragraph describing a calm, beautiful lake, which of the following details would you NOT include? Write your answer on the lines and explain it in a sentence.

1. the reflection of soft, fluffy clouds in the water

2. the loud music from a nearby car radio

3. a soft, gentle breeze in the late afternoon

4. ripples on the water caused by a fish

_____

_____

_____

_____

C Read the following list of subjects for a description. On the line opposite each subject, write how the details might be arranged.

1. a tree _____

2. a telephone conversation _____

3. a bottle of soda _____

Reading: Author's Purpose

Practice

An **author's purpose** is his or her main reason for writing. The most common purposes for writing are to inform, to persuade, and to entertain. To determine an author's purpose, notice the types of details included in the work. Writers may use facts and statistics to inform or persuade. They may use stories about personal experiences to inform or entertain. Often, authors will have more than one purpose—to inform while entertaining, for example.

Read each paragraph. Then, answer the questions.

When you buy a bicycle helmet, make sure it fits you well. The foam pads should touch your head all around, and the helmet should sit level. Tighten the straps so that they are snug but comfortable. You must not be able to pull off the helmet, no matter how hard you try.

1. Is the author's *main* purpose to entertain, to inform, or to persuade?

_____

_____

2. List two details from the paragraph to support your answer to #1.

_____

_____

It was a beautiful day. Ramona put on her helmet, hopped on her bike, and headed to bike path near her house. She was peddling merrily along, when suddenly she heard a loud, hissing sound. "Oh, no," she thought, "not a snake!" She peddled faster but noticed that her bike was bouncing badly. When she looked back, she saw that her rear tire was flat. "So that was the hissing!" No snake, after all—just a flat tire and a ruined bike ride.

3. Is the author's *main* purpose to entertain, to inform, or to persuade?

_____

_____

4. List two details from the paragraph to support your answer to #3.

_____

_____

Reading: Author's Purpose

A Read the paragraph. Then answer the questions.

   Wherever and whenever you ride your bicycle, you should wear a helmet. You may not know it, but statistics show that a bike rider can expect to crash within 4,500 miles of riding. Every year, more than 600 people die in bicycle crashes, mostly from head injuries. Your bicycle helmet can protect you. Do not go biking without it!

1. Is the author's *main* purpose to entertain, to inform, or to persuade?

   _____

2. List two details from the paragraph to support your answer to #1.

   _____

B Circle the letter of the choice that best answers the question. Then, explain your choice.

1. In an article about a new movie, a writer briefly describes the story, names the main actors and the director, and tells the movie's rating. What is the writer's purpose?

   A. to persuade   **B.** to inform   **C.** to entertain   **D.** all three

   Explain: _____

2. In an article about the same movie, another writer tells the story in detail. He describes a slow-moving plot, actors who are not right for their roles, and dull background music. He ends with the line, "If you need to catch up on your sleep, this is the movie for you." What is the writer's purpose?

   A. to persuade   **B.** to inform   **C.** to entertain   **D.** all three

   Explain: _____

3. Another writer describes the same movie in glowing terms—exciting story, great acting, terrific special effects. He ends his article with the line, "Do not miss it!" What is this writer's *main* purpose?

   A. to persuade   **B.** to inform   **C.** to entertain   **D.** all three

   Explain: _____

Reading: Web Site's Purpose

Practice

A **Web site** is a specific location on the Internet. Like authors of text documents, the creators of Web sites usually have a specific **purpose** for what they write or present. Knowing who sponsors and maintains a Web site can help you determine that purpose. Often, the URL ending indicates the source of a site. The following chart explains some common URL endings.

URL Ending	Description	Usual Intent
.edu or .gov	Site is maintained by an educational institution or a government agency.	to provide reliable information
.org	Site is probably maintained by a nonprofit organization.	to provide information about an issue or cause
.com	Site is maintained commercially or personally.	to sell or promote something
.net	Site is maintained by a network.	varies

Write the letter of the best answer for each of the following questions.

1. _____ If the purpose of a Web site is to sell or promote something, what would be the URL ending?

   A. .edu   **B.** .com   **C.** .gov   **D.** .net

2. _____ If a Web site has an .org URL ending, what is its intent?

   A. to provide information about an issue or a cause
   B. to sell or promote something
   C. to provide government information
   D. to provide information for educational purposes

3. _____ If a site is maintained by a government agency, what would be the URL ending?

   A. .edu   **B.** .org   **C.** .net   **D.** .gov

Reading: Web Site's Purpose

Assess

Write the letter of the best answer for each of the following questions.

1. _____ If a site is maintained by a network, what would be the URL ending?

   A. .org   **B.** .gov   **C.** .net   **D.** .com

2. _____ Who would maintain a Web site with the URL ending .edu?

   A. a government agency
   B. a nonprofit organization
   C. a network
   D. an educational institution

3. _____ If a site is maintained commercially or personally, what would be its intent?

   A. to provide information about a cause
   B. to sell or promote something
   C. to provide information about an issue
   D. to provide reliable information

4. _____ If a site is maintained by a nonprofit organization, what would be its URL ending?

   A. .org   **B.** .net   **C.** .gov   **D.** .com

Literary Analysis: Setting

Practice

The **setting** of a story is the time and place of the action.

A Choose the best answer for each question. Circle the letter.

1. What does the setting of a story include?

   A. the time and place   **B.** only the time   **C.** only the place

2. Which of these words tells where a story happens?

   A. time   **B.** beginning   **C.** place

3. Which of these words tells when a story happens?

   A. time   **B.** beginning   **C.** place

B Read the description of each problem. Match it with the most likely setting.

1. A colony of tourists has lost communication with Earth.

   A. the past in New York   **B.** the future on the   **C.** the present in
                                      moon   San Diego

2. A group of men in America want to be free of England.

   A. the future in Boston   **B.** the present in Detroit   **C.** the past in Boston

3. A sixteen-year-old wants to work at a computer store, but his parents say no.

   A. ancient Egypt   **B.** Florida now   **C.** Illinois in 1900

C Match each problem in Column 1 with a resolution in Column 2.

Column 1   **Column 2**

1. _____ A ship hits an iceberg.   **A.** A child is saved by modern
                                                    medicine.

2. _____ A child is lost in a snowstorm.   **B.** Two countries agree to keep peace.

3. _____ A man invests his money badly.   **C.** A family resolves to live more
                                                    simply.

4. _____ A plane goes down in enemy   **D.** Some people are lost at sea.
   territory.

Literary Analysis: Setting

A   Read the description. Circle the two answers that fit the setting.

1. Two friends are at a street fair. The mood is happy.

    A. heartbreaking sobs   **B.** the smell of hot dogs   **C.** sounds of music

2. An elevator has stopped between floors. It is late at night.

    A. an alarm ringing   **B.** the lights go out   **C.** sunshine

3. Twelve people are on a river raft. They are laughing and paddling.

    A. animated conversation   **B.** sound of trucks on a road   **C.** life jackets

B   Circle the answer that best describes the tone of each setting.

1. The green meadow was covered with beautiful purple wildflowers. Just then, a graceful deer bounded across the meadow. Nearby, a robin was looking for worms.

    A. appreciation of nature   **B.** dislike of animals   **C.** fear of animals

2. Rain pounded the ground. Thunder rumbled, and lightning streaked across the sky. It seemed that all the forces of cruel nature were at work today.

    A. fondness for storms   **B.** fear of storms   **C.** admiration for nature

C   Read the paragraph. Then write *true* or *false* for each of the following statements.

    The black ocean was cold and ugly. All around were pieces of ice that had broken off icebergs. The temperature was twenty degrees below zero. Would the crew survive this Arctic expedition?

1. _____ The setting points to a story of adventure.

2. _____ The setting points to a story about the beauty of nature.

3. _____ The setting points to a story about a father's love for his son.

4. _____ The setting points to a story of survival.

Literary Analysis: Historical Context

Practice

Historical context—the actual political and social events and trends of the time—can explain why characters act and think the way they do.

Read the two passages. Then, complete the Venn diagram. Describe Marly's situation and reactions in the *Then* section. Describe Carla's situation and reactions in the *Now* section.

Marly knew that it was her responsibility to do the laundry. Her mother had three smaller children to care for, and she needed help with some of the housework. In the small Western town where they lived, everyone in a family had to pitch in to get the household work done.

Doing the laundry was an all-day event. Clothes had to be scrubbed by hand down at the stream, using homemade soap. Then, they had to be rinsed and hung outdoors to dry.

By evening, Marly was exhausted. Sometimes, if she was lucky, there would be a community meeting where she could socialize with other girls her age for a few hours.

****

Carla usually came home from school on Thursday and did the laundry for her mother. Some of her friends' mothers had cleaning ladies, but Carla's mother couldn't spare the money for such a luxury. She worked in a small office, and she did not get paid that much.

Carla did not mind doing the laundry, though. There were machines in the basement of her building. She could sit down there and do her homework while she waited for the washer and dryer to finish, and she could go out later. The whole job took maybe two hours. Sometimes, while she worked, she talked on the phone to one of her friends.

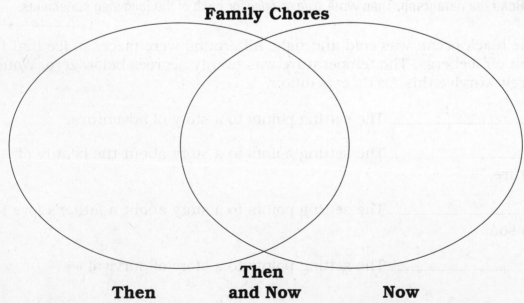

Family Chores

Then

Then and Now

Now

Literary Analysis: Historical Context

Assess

A   Read the journal entry, and write whether the statements that follow it are *true* or *false*.

(August 12, 1521, the day before Tenochtitlán fell to the Spaniards.)

The white men have been attacking our city for three months now. We Aztecs are fighters, and we fought back, but they brought diseases. Thousands of us have already died. More will die soon, as we have little food to eat.

I remember when I first laid eyes on these strange men. They were dressed from head to toe in gleaming iron. They tore down the pictures of our gods. Now, the end of our city is near. I wonder what will become of our markets and our temples, of the great pyramid. What will become of our people?

1. _____ The Aztecs are a cowardly people.

2. _____ Tenochtitlán will get back its earlier strength.

3. _____ The Aztecs follow certain religious practices.

4. _____ The writer is a white man.

B   Read the paragraph. For the questions that follow, circle the correct response or write your answer on the blank.

(Jane Smith, Massachusetts Bay Colony, 1640)

This year, my brother Samuel will go to Harvard College. He is the first in our family to go. Harvard will train Samuel to become a minister. I would like to go too, but I can't because I am a girl. I will remain on the farm. I will help my mother make soap and sew clothing. There are six children younger than I. I must help raise them as well. I have no choice but to stay home until I am old enough to get married and take care of my own family.

1. **A.** Jane is (happy, unhappy) because she can't go to Harvard.

   B. What words tell you this? _____

2. Jane would MOST like to

   A. get an education   **B.** watch the children

3. Which of these statements is something that Jane would agree with?

   A. The farm is an exciting place.
   B. She will lead the same life as her mother.

Literary Analysis: Comparing Authors' Purposes

Practice

An **author's purpose** is his or her main reason for writing. The most common purposes for writing are to inform, to persuade, and to entertain. Different authors might write on similar topics with different purposes for writing.

General Purpose	Specific Purpose	Details That Show Purpose
To Inform	to inform readers about how children played in the past	serious words; includes many facts
To Entertain	to entertain readers with funny stories about his childhood	silly stories; fun language
To Persuade	to persuade readers that today's children are too restricted	asks readers to share opinions

Read each passage. Then, answer the questions.

I When I was growing up in the tiny town of Bellsville, we had Postmistress Perkins. Postmistress Perkins seemed to run the town. One April Fool's Day, Uncle Al put a bullfrog in a box and took it to the P.O. When the box started hopping around on the postal scale, Miss Perkins chased Uncle Al out of the Post Office, waving a yardstick.

II When I was growing up in the tiny town of Montville, we children played outside after school every day. We didn't have a lot of money, but we did have a lot of fun. I think we learned a lot during that playing time. We learned how to negotiate and how to compete. We learned how to manage bullies and how to take care of our friends. We learned real life lessons.

1. What is the author's main purpose in passage I?

   A. to entertain   **B.** to persuade   **C.** to inform   **D.** to teach a lesson

2. Underline some of the details in the passage that support your answer to question 1.

3. What is the author's main purpose in passage II?

   A. to entertain   **B.** to persuade   **C.** to inform   **D.** to argue

4. Underline some of the clues in the passage that support your answer to question 3.

Literary Analysis: Comparing Authors' Purposes

Assess

Read the two passages. Then, answer the questions that follow.

I Walking is easily the most popular form of exercise. . . . Walking burns approximately the same amount of calories per mile as does running. . . . Briskly walking one mile in 15 minutes burns just about the same number of calories as jogging an equal distance in 8½ minutes.

—*The President's Council on Physical Fitness and Sports*

II Come on, everybody, put down your remotes and your game controllers and start moving! You don't have to take kickboxing or join the cross-country team to get in shape—walking is great exercise! Join the Middleschool Walking Club as we hit the pavement each morning at 6:30 A.M. Believe it or not, you'll be glad you did!

1. What is the main difference between the details in these two passages? Circle the letter of the best answer.

   A. Passage I gives details about walking, and Passage II gives details about exercise.

   B. Passage I is serious and uses a lot of facts. Passage II uses more playful word choices.

   C. Passage I includes fun language, and Passage II includes facts about calories.

   D. Passage I is filled with made-up details, while Passage II contains only facts.

2. Is the author's purpose in passage I to entertain, to inform, or to persuade?

   _____

3. List at least two details from the passage to support your answer to question 1.

   _____

   _____

4. Is the author's purpose in passage II to entertain, to inform, or to persuade?

   _____

5. List at least two details from the passage to support your answer to question 3.

   _____

   _____

Name _____ Date _____

Vocabulary: Prefixes *re-* and *pre-*

Practice

A **prefix** is a word part that is added to the beginning of a base word. A prefix changes the meaning of a word.

Example: The prefix *re-* has different meanings. Sometimes it means "again." It can also mean "back or backward." Adding *re-* to the root *peal*, which means "to call," makes *repeal*, which means "to take back officially" or "to recall." The prefix *pre-* means "before" or "earlier in time."

A Add a prefix to each of the following words. Write a word that means "before" or "earlier in time" for each word given.

1. arrange _____   **4.** pay _____

2. cook _____   **5.** test _____

3. school _____

B Think about the meanings of each prefix and base word. Then, write a definition for the word in bold type. Check your definitions in a dictionary.

1. *re-* (back or backward) + *gress* (to go) = **regress**

Definition _____

2. *re-* (back) + *imburse* (to pay) = **reimburse**

Definition _____

3. *re-* (back) + *instating* (legal putting back) = **reinstating**

Definition _____

4. *re-* (back/again) + *trieve* (to find) = **retrieve**

Definition _____

34 Reading Kit

© Pearson Education, Inc., publishing as Pearson Prentice Hall.

Name _____ Date _____

Vocabulary: Prefixes *re-* and *pre-*

Assess

A Read the definition in the first column. Then add the prefix *re-* or *pre-* to the base word in the second column to form a word that matches the definition. Write the word in the last column.

	Definition	Base Word	Base Word with Prefix
1.	to judge beforehand, prematurely	judge	1.
2.	something you do to prevent something bad from happening	caution	2.
3.	to package materials before selling	package	3.
4.	happening too soon	mature	4.
5.	built in advance	fabricated	5.

B Read the sentences. Use context clues and the prefix in the underlined word to help you determine the word's meaning. Then, write a definition for each underlined word.

1. Our Constitution begins with a <u>preamble</u> that explains its purpose.

Definition of *preamble:* _____

2. As he stepped onto the icy sidewalk, he had a <u>premonition</u> that he might fall.

Definition of *premonition:* _____

3. The recipe required that the meat be <u>precooked</u>.

Definition of *precooked:* _____

4. As you are usually on time, I <u>presume</u> you have an excuse for being late.

Definition of *presume:* _____

Grammar: Personal Pronouns

Practice

A **personal pronoun** takes the place of one or more nouns. An **antecedent** is the word or words to which the pronoun refers.

A Underline the personal pronouns in each sentence.

1. I asked my friends, "Have you found the calculator today?"

2. "Oh, so the strange object we found is yours?" Ben kidded me.

3. "Why isn't your name on the back?" his brother Jack said.

4. I said it was not mine; my brother Julio owned the calculator.

5. "You should feel lucky it was found by us," Mara said.

6. "Its case is ripped, but I bet your father could repair it."

7. Later, she and we boys discussed our summer plans.

8. "Are you going to try out for our community play?" Ben asked.

9. They said they would rather try their luck as villains.

B Write all of the personal pronouns and their antecedents in the following sentences.

1. The class saw Denise do her first magic trick.

_____

2. She started it by borrowing Carmen's straw hat.

_____

3. "What are you going to do with my hat?" she asked.

_____

4. Denise took off the ribbon and cut it into several pieces.

_____

5. She told Carmen to put them into the hat and shake it.

_____

Grammar: Personal Pronouns

A Underline the personal pronoun in each sentence.

1. The explorers sailed their ship across the Pacific Ocean.

2. Bill left his homework on the bus.

3. Where are you going, Bob?

4. The champion skater always performed on his newest skates.

5. The woman washed her car every week.

6. The actors practiced their parts at the rehearsal.

7. Two deer led their young to the river.

8. The bicycle is yours, Martha.

9. When the astronaut landed his spaceship, the sun had already set.

10. A large sheepdog buried its bones behind the barn.

B Fill in each blank with a personal pronoun.

1. Albert Einstein devoted _____ life to science.

2. "Where are _____ gloves?" I asked myself.

3. Carol came forward to receive _____ award.

4. The Mississippi River empties _____ waters into the Gulf of Mexico.

5. Because _____ canoe was the fastest, they won the race.

6. Colin lost _____ wallet at the bus station.

7. The hikers cleared the fallen brush off the trail using _____ hands.

8. Jamie drove _____ car to the fair.

9. Tommy was late to _____ first soccer game.

10. Betsy has just written _____ first book.

Grammar: Possessive Pronouns

Practice

A **possessive pronoun** shows ownership. Some possessive pronouns are used alone. Some possessive pronouns are used before nouns.

A   Write the correct possessive pronoun to complete each sentence.

Example: My brother's gloves are thick. _____His_____ hands stay warm.

Robert's new suit is gray. **1.** _____ shoes match

the suit perfectly. He got the suit at a relative's shop. You can see

many different styles of suits in **2.** _____ showcase.

Robert's mother is a tailor in the shop. **3.** _____ job is to

make each suit fit perfectly. A dog sits at the shop door. The dog wags

4. _____ tail when it sees Robert.

B   Write each sentence. Replace the underlined word or words with a possessive pronoun.

1. I like the twins' knitted hats.

_____

2. Have you ever seen hats as unusual as the twins'?

_____

3. The pink scarf is Jenny's, too.

_____

4. Which hat in that pile is Maria's?

_____

C   Use a possessive pronoun to complete each sentence. Write it on the line.

1. Dan hung _____ jacket in the closet.

2. Tina put _____ jacket on the chair.

3. The players keep _____ jackets in the locker room.

4. Which jacket is _____?

38 Reading Kit

Grammar: Possessive Pronouns

Assess

A In each sentence circle the possessive pronoun.

1. It is their own party that they're planning.

2. I hear you're taking your new album to the party.

3. It's important that the album remains in its jacket.

4. There's no chance they will think the album is theirs.

5. They're Barbara and Joe; this is their party.

B Circle the word in parentheses that correctly completes each sentence.

6. Barbara and Joe like (their, they're) home.

7. Joe complains that Barbara's room is bigger than (his, him).

8. It's much bigger than (mine, my).

9. (His, Him) collections take up half the room.

10. Barbara does not clutter (her, hers) room with collections.

11. However, this collection of glass animals is (her, hers).

12. Is it as nice as (your, yours) collection?

13. I believe that (their, they're) interested in coin collecting.

14. Wouldn't you prefer to start a collection of (your, you're) own?

15. (Theirs, There's) a probability that I will start one someday.

16. I understand (you, you're) going to visit Joe and Barbara.

Grammar: Pronoun-Antecedent Agreement

Practice

A **pronoun** takes the place of a noun or nouns. An **antecedent** is the word or words to which a pronoun refers. An antecedent may appear before or after the pronoun. Sometimes the antecedent is not in the same sentence as the pronoun.

A Circle the antecedent of the underlined pronoun.

Example: (Vermont) and <u>its</u> climate attract many visitors.

1. Visitors like natural beauty, so <u>they</u> bring cameras.

2. The government of Vermont said <u>it</u> would encourage visitors.

3. Most states maintain <u>their</u> highways for safe driving.

4. "<u>I</u> like paved roads," one woman told the tourist board.

5. Many Vermonters work in the tourist industry; <u>they</u> support their state.

6. On <u>their</u> arrival, Tim and Joel were offered hot apple juice.

7. The mountains with <u>their</u> natural beauty attract visitors.

8. Ms. Brockman does not ski, but <u>she</u> works at a ski lodge.

B Draw an arrow from each pronoun to its antecedent.

Example: The artist comes every October because he enjoys autumn.

1. Visitors to the mountains can hike on their beautiful old trails.

2. The tallest monument is 406 feet high; it honors colonial soldiers.

3. A tourist asked if she could take pictures.

4. A tourist said he saw the birthplace of President Coolidge.

5. Vermonters are proud of their state.

6. "I went to school in Peacham," a visitor offered.

7. "It has a wonderful history," said one man about the state.

Name _____ Date _____

Grammar: Pronoun-Antecedent Agreement

A An antecedent is circled in each sentence below. Underline the pronoun that refers to it.

1. (Mr. Garcia) had spent all winter planning his garden.

2. He had studied seed (catalogues) and had ordered seeds from them.

3. Mrs. Suzuki's (children) were curious. They wondered what he would plant.

4. (My friend and I) also had questions about Mr. Garcia's plans.

5. The (neighbors) all took their turns glancing over Mr. Garcia's fence.

6. His polished and sharpened tools were (Mr. Garcia's) particular pride and joy.

B The pronouns are underlined in the following sentences. Circle the antecedent to which each pronoun refers.

7. Mr. Garcia turned the soil with <u>his</u> shovel.

8. Mr. Garcia took seeds from a packet and scattered <u>them</u> in rows.

9. As soon as <u>they</u> saw the seeds, birds flocked over the garden.

10. Mrs. Suzuki waved <u>her</u> arms to frighten away the birds.

11. Mr. Garcia nodded gratefully. Mrs. Suzuki spoke to <u>him</u>.

C Write the correct pronoun for each circled antecedent.

12. Mrs. Suzuki said that _____ would be a beautiful (garden.)

13. (Mr. Garcia) stopped and wiped _____ forehead.

14. Then Mr. Garcia turned on the (hose) and drank water from

_____.

15. When _____ was finished, (Mr. Garcia) invited Mrs. Suzuki to visit.

16. The two (neighbors) had _____ first good opportunity to chat.

© Pearson Education, Inc., publishing as Pearson Prentice Hall. Reading Kit **41**

Spelling: Homophones

Practice

A **homophone** is a word that sounds exactly like another word but has a different spelling and meaning.

A Use the words in the box. Write the homophone for each word. Remember, the two words must sound the same.

hours	write	sun	rows	tow	sail

1. rose _____   **2.** toe _____   **3.** right _____

4. sale _____   **5.** ours _____   **6.** son _____

B Underline the correct homophone for each sentence.

1. She ran to (warn, worn) us that the river was flooding.

2. It was so foggy that we almost (missed, mist) the turnoff.

3. The day started out sunny, but then it started to (rain, reign, rein).

4. The traffic was bad, and it took two hours to get (their, there, they're).

5. His friend (seas, sees, seize) him in the restaurant and comes over to talk.

6. There are wildflowers and old barns on the country (road, rode, rowed).

C The underlined words are not correct. Cross out each one, and replace it with a homophone.

horse	mane	mooed	fowl	reins
deer	through	herd	neighs	tails

1. As I walked <u>threw</u> the field, cows <u>mood</u> and swatted their <u>tales</u>.

2. My <u>hoarse</u> Pinto sees me coming and <u>nays</u> in welcome.

3. I pat his <u>main</u> to say hello and grab his <u>reigns</u>.

4. I saw three <u>dear</u>, a <u>heard</u> of sheep, and some wild <u>foul</u>.

Spelling: Homophones

A Underline the correct homophone. Check your answers in a dictionary.

1. Sixty minutes is an (our, hour).

2. One plus one equals (to, two, too).

3. Seven days make one (weak, week).

4. In this place means it is (here, hear).

5. Those who claimed victory have (won, one).

6. An aircraft is a (plain, plane).

7. The contraction for *they are* is (their, they're).

B Complete each sentence by writing the correct homophone on the line.

1. A. Keisha tied her _____ back with a ribbon.   hair, hare

   B. A _____ is larger than a rabbit.   hair, hare

2. A. My dog has a long _____.   tale, tail

   B. Ray told a scary campfire _____.   tale, tail

3. A. We read a book written _____ a famous author.   by, buy

   B. She stopped at the mall to _____ a present.   by, buy

4. A. The _____ building was torn down.   hole, whole

   B. The workers are digging a large _____.   hole, whole

C Edit the following grocery store sign. Cross out the three misspelled words. Then spell the words correctly in the space above or below the crossed-out words.

> Their is know fish today.
> Try again next weak.

Name _____ Date _____

Writing: News Report

Practice

A **news report** supplies the basic, important facts about an event. It usually answers the questions *Who? What? Where? When? Why?* and *How?* Before you begin to write a news report, you should make a list of specific questions that need to be answered. If you were writing about the school play, for example, you might want to know what play is being presented, who is playing in the lead roles, when and where it will be put on, and how the rehearsals are going. In a news report, you put the most important information in the first paragraph of the story. In the rest of the story you provide further details.

Imagine you have been given an assignment to write a news report about the swim team for the school newsletter. Each numbered item has two questions. Circle the letter of the question that would be most helpful in writing a news report.

1. **A.** Who is the funniest member of the swim team?
   B. Who is the captain of the swim team?

2. **A.** What do the swimmers do while they are on the bus?
   B. What is the record for the season so far?

3. **A.** Does the coach like indoor pools better than outdoor pools?
   B. Where is the next meet to be held?

4. **A.** When did most of the swimmers learn how to swim?
   B. When is the next meet to be held?

5. **A.** Why is this year's team so successful?
   B. Why do some people like to swim?

6. **A.** How does the coach feel about this season so far?
   B. How do swimmers stay warm while they are waiting to race?

Writing: News Report

Imagine that you are writing a news report for the school newspaper. The event you will be reporting on is a special assembly—a popular author is visiting the school. You will have a chance to talk to the author. List six questions that you would ask to gain the facts for your report. Remember to include the basics: who, what, where, when, why, and how.

Question 1 _____

_____

Question 2 _____

_____

Question 3 _____

_____

Question 4 _____

_____

Question 5 _____

_____

Question 6 _____

_____

Writing: Letter/Letter of Proposal

Practice

The letter you write to a friend is different from the letter you write to a company asking for a refund. A friendly letter is casual and chatty. A business letter is formal. When you write a letter, write in the way that is appropriate to your audience and purpose.

A **letter of proposal** is one type of business letter. In a letter of proposal, you present an idea for a project that requires assistance or funding. The company or person to whom you send a letter of proposal should be interested in your topic. You would send a proposal for a new miniature golf course to the town recreation department, for example, and not to an animal rescue group. A letter of proposal requires these elements:

- Formal and polite language
- A clear statement of the proposal that is being made
- An appropriate formal greeting, such as "Dear Ms. Smith" or "To Whom It May Concern," followed by a colon.
- An appropriate closing, such as "Sincerely," or "Respectfully," followed by a comma

A Match the greetings in the left column with the closings on the right. Write the letter of the answer on the line.

1. _____ Dear Reverend Leonard: **A.** Your pal,

2. _____ Dear Uncle Paul,   **B.** Sincerely,

3. _____ Hi, Mike   **C.** Your loving nephew,

B Choose the topic that is most likely to interest each of the following people. Write the letter of the answer on the line.

1. _____ a twelve-year-old boy who loves football

    A. a recipe for nachos   **C.** a book on garden design
    B. a history of the Detroit Lions

2. _____ a woman with a beautiful garden

    A. a book on growing roses   **C.** photographs of old cars
    B. a pamphlet on collecting glass

C On a separate sheet of paper, write a letter of proposal to a mayor for a town wide cleanup.

Name _____ Date _____

Writing: Letter/Letter of Proposal

A The first column lists examples of types of letters. The second column lists greetings and closings. Match the correct greeting and closing with each type of letter described.

1. _____ Business letter. You read about a job as a camp counselor. You want to persuade the employer to hire you.

2. _____ Friendly letter. You are on vacation and want to write to your best friends

3. _____ Letter of Proposal. You write to your senator hoping to raise funds to improve state parklands

A. Dear Senator:
Sincerely,

B. Dear Sir or Madam:
Respectfully,

C. Hi there!
Love,

B Choose one of the following topics for a proposal. Then, complete the activities that follow.

a new hologram video-game system

a documentary film about baton twirling

a series of articles about life in middle school

a play based on your own life

1. Write your topic on the line. _____

2. To what sort of organization, company, or individual would you send your letter of proposal? _____

_____

3. On the lines provided, write a brief letter of proposal about your topic.

_____
_____
_____
_____
_____
_____

Writing: Autobiographical Narrative

An **autobiographical narrative** is a story that tells of real events in a writer's life.

A Select an exciting event that has happened to you. Complete the following items to help you organize details.

1. Identify the time and place in which your story is set.

Time: _____ Place: _____

2. Use the following word web to establish and describe your main character. In the center oval, write his or her name. In the outer ovals, write words that describe this person. Your central character need not be yourself.

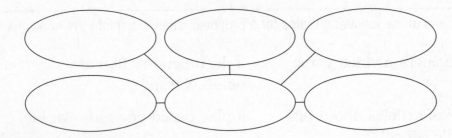

3. Briefly list the event or events that will occur in each stage of your plot.

Exposition: _____

Rising Action: _____

Climax: _____

Falling Action: _____

Resolution: _____

B Use the following lines to draft your autobiographical narrative. Continue on the back of your paper.

_____

_____

_____

Writing: Autobiographical Narrative

Assess

A Arrange these story events in a logical order with a beginning, a middle, and an ending. Write a brief description of each event on the timeline in the part of the story where it belongs.

- All day, we checked the apartment, the hall, and the street.
- That night, we found Boots cuddled in my new white scarf!
- In the morning, we could not find my white cat Boots.

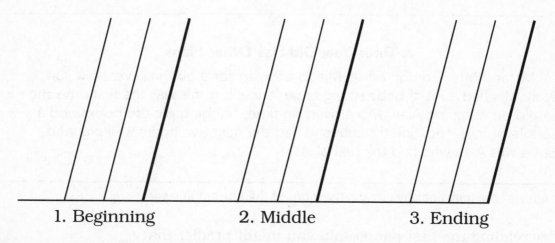

1. Beginning   2. Middle   3. Ending

B Recall a personal experience that you think would make an interesting story. Write a narrative about your experience. Be sure to include a beginning, a middle, and an ending. Use details about characters, setting, problems, and dialogue to make your narrative more interesting. You may continue your narrative on the back of your paper.

_____

_____

_____

_____

_____

_____

_____

_____

Reading: Predicting

Practice

Predicting means making a guess about what will probably happen next in a story. You can predict based on what you have already read. You can also predict based on background knowledge—things you already know.

A Read the title of the following passage. What does the title lead you to predict about the

story? _____

_____

A Three-Year-Old Has Other Plans

Mr. and Mrs. Gordon asked Mia to baby-sit for their three-year-old son, Alan. Mia had a lot of baby-sitting experience, but this was the first time she would be watching Alan. Mia arrived on time, bringing picture books and a couple of toys, too. She thought she had the next two hours well planned. But it was Alan who had the real plans.

B Answer the questions by circling the letter of the correct answer.

1. After reading the first paragraph, you might predict that

    A. Mia will read a story to Alan.   **B.** Alan will spoil Mia's baby-sitting plans.

While Mia waved goodbye to the Gordons, Alan took apart the TV remote. After much searching, Mia found the batteries under the couch and snapped the remote together again. While she was busy with the remote, Alan wandered into the kitchen, opened a box of cereal, and dumped it on the floor. Mia found a broom and began to sweep.

Mia was beginning to think that she never wanted to baby-sit again when Alan smiled sweetly and gave her a hug. Mia hugged him back and thought, "Maybe baby-sitting is not so bad after all."

2. Finish reading the passage. Which event might happen next in this story?

    A. Alan calls his parents and cries.   **B.** Mia reads a story to Alan.

3. Which prediction for the future is most likely to be true?

    A. Mia will baby-sit for Alan again.   **B.** Mia will quit baby-sitting forever.

Reading: Predicting

Answer the following questions and circle the letter of the best answer.

1. Read the title of the following passage. What do you think the story is about?

   A. battles that soldiers fought in
   B. other elements of soldiers' lives besides battles

2. Read the passage. Which sentence best expresses the major point of this passage?

   A. Soldiers ate hard bread and cornmeal.
   B. A soldier had enough to eat, but the food was not tasty.

Hardtack and Music: The Life of a Civil War Soldier

At noon, the Civil War soldier had his big meal for the day. It was called dinner. There was generally enough to eat, but the food was not very tasty. One day's rations might include pork, beef, soft or hard bread, and flour or cornmeal. Potatoes, onions, beans, rice, sugar, pepper, salt, and coffee were served only if they were available. The hard bread, called hardtack, was the main dish at most meals. A soldier was given ten of these small, hard biscuits. Hardtack was so hard that it had to be pounded to break it into pieces.

3. What do you predict the next paragraph will be about?

   _____

   _____

4. What clues are you using to make your prediction?

   _____

   _____

Literary Analysis: Plot

Plot is what happens in a story—the sequence of events that makes up the story. Plot includes rising action, events that show conflict; climax, the high point of the story; falling action, events that follow the climax; and resolution, the final outcome of the story.

A Number the events in the order they would probably happen in a story.

_____ A small team works to clean up the neighborhood.

_____ The neighborhood changes for the better.

_____ Dana's parents buy a house.

_____ Dana plans a Saturday cleanup party.

_____ People plant gardens.

B Read each event before you begin. Decide which event has to be the first, which has to be second, and so on. Then, number the events in the order they would happen.

A. _____ After what seems like a very long time, the police and paramedics arrive on the scene. People are freed from the wreckage. Luckily, no one was seriously hurt.

B. _____ Juan and Carlos board the train in Chicago bound for a good time in Denver.

C. _____ In the morning, a bus arrives to take the passengers to the nearest town. Juan and Carlos then can catch another train to Denver.

D. _____ Juan and Carlos spend the night in the gym of a high school on cots set up by the Red Cross.

E. _____ They are enjoying a meal in the diner when suddenly there is a crashing sound. The train lurches forward and then comes to a complete stop.

Literary Analysis: Plot

Assess

A Read each statement. Write *true* or *false* on the line.

1. _____ The plot of a story centers on a conflict.

2. _____ The conflict usually is introduced near the end of a story.

3. _____ The words *conflict* and *climax* describe different parts of a plot.

4. _____ The rising action is where the conflict of a plot is resolved.

B Read the following events. Put them in order from 1 to 4 to show how they lead to the climax. The problem will be 1, and the climax will be 4.

_____ At first, the biggest problem is that Roland and the aliens speak different languages.

_____ Roland is captured by aliens and taken to another planet.

_____ After months have gone by, Roland is all skin and bones. He has nothing to lose, so he decides to try to escape.

_____ After several weeks on a strange diet, Roland's energy weakens, and he loses weight.

C Match each term in Column 1 with its description in Column 2.

Column 1	Column 2
1. _____ conflict	A. The story develops with more problems.
2. _____ rising action	B. Everything comes to a conclusion.
3. _____ climax	C. The problem must be faced.
4. _____ resolution	D. A problem is described.

Literary Analysis: Character

Practice

Each **character** in a story has character traits: attitudes and behaviors that define him or her. Different types of characters will do and say different types of things.

A Several character traits are listed in the following box. Write the word that best describes each character next to the description of the character's actions.

kind	clever	shy	brave	reckless

1. _____ Dana stood at the edge of the crowd of kids, saying nothing.

2. _____ Ali raced around the corner on his in-line skates. He hardly noticed the cars whizzing around him.

3. _____ Nilda rigged up a motion detector that sounded an alarm when anyone entered her room.

4. _____ Tony helped his little sister fix her broken scooter.

5. _____ The park ranger moved slowly toward the rattlesnake, holding the snake-catching pole. Swiftly, she caught the snake by the neck and put it safely in a bag.

B Use these words to compare the characters in each pair of sentences below:

friendly	calm	lonely	restless

1. A. _____ "I took some cookies over to the new neighbors. They seem like nice people."

B. _____ "I wish I had more friends, but I don't know how to talk to people."

2. A. _____ "When I meditate, I imagine the sound of the wind in the trees."

B. _____ "Each morning I can't get my shoes on and get out the door fast enough. Then, I jog in place while I wait for my bus. Sometimes it is hard to sit through a whole class."

Name _____ Date _____

Literary Analysis: Character

Read this passage. Then, fill in the chart.

O'Malley, the president of the company, dressed like an executive. He enjoyed looking good, for he had gotten his job the hard way, starting at the lowest level of the company and working his way up. O'Malley had never gone to school beyond high school, but his experience at the company helped him fill in the gaps in his education. Because he had done just about every job there, he was truly familiar with every part of the company. He often stopped to chat with employees who held jobs he once had filled.

Now, however, O'Malley found his job being threatened. McSwain, the owner of the company, had always promised the president's job to his son. It was almost time for Junior to take over. Junior had a fine education, but he had only worked in the high-paying jobs in the company. He knew no one in the mailroom or the factory. In fact, he never even visited there. Junior liked to dress as "one of the guys," usually wearing casual work shirts and blue jeans.

	O'Malley	**Junior**
1. How the character looks		
2. What the character does		
3. Character traits of each (name at least two)		

© Pearson Education, Inc., publishing as Pearson Prentice Hall.

Vocabulary: Word Roots -*dict*- and -*ver*-

Practice

A **word root** forms the basic part of the word and gives it its primary meaning. If you know the meaning of a root, you can often figure out the meaning of a whole word. For example, the root -*dict*- means "to speak, talk, or say," as in *dictionary* and *diction*. The root -*ver*- means "truth." Words such as *verdict* and *verify* contain this root.

Choose the word that best completes each of the following sentences. Write the word in the blank.

aver: state firmly, swear   **predict:** see coming, guess

dictate: say aloud, speak   **veracity:** truth

dictator: strict ruler   **verify:** prove, confirm

edict: order, law   **veritable:** real

1. Looking at the sky full of dark clouds, she was able to _____ that it would soon rain.

2. The details in the child's account of the accident added to its

   _____.

3. A government led by a _____ does not allow citizens to make political choices.

4. The health officer issued an _____ that did not allow the use of untreated drinking water.

5. I will _____ the words to the song as you type.

6. She knew so many of her friends' numbers that she was a _____ phone book.

7. The witness was able to _____ the incidents leading up to the crime.

8. She will _____ that she was at home all evening, but will the jury believe her?

Vocabulary: Word Roots -dict- and -ver-

Assess

A Circle the letter of the word that best completes each sentence.

1. The queen issued a(n) _____ allowing her subjects to have more holidays.

    A. dictionary   **C.** verdict
    B. edict   **D.** contradiction

2. The coach could not begin to _____ who would win the game on Saturday.

    A. verify   **C.** predict
    B. indicate   **D.** avert

3. The _____ of her statements was never doubted.

    A. veracity   **C.** prediction
    B. indication   **D.** aversion

4. Raise your hand to _____ when you have finished your test.

    A. predict   **C.** indicate
    B. verify   **D.** dictate

5. Use a(n) _____ to determine the meaning of the word.

    A. dictionary   **C.** edict
    B. verdict   **D.** dictator

6. The skaters had to wait for the judges to _____.

    A. dictate   **C.** avert
    B. contradict   **D.** verify

B Use each of the following words in a complete sentence.

1. verify _____

2. dictate _____

3. veracity _____

4. indicate _____

5. predict _____

Grammar: Action Verbs and Linking Verbs

Practice

A **verb** expresses action or being. Verbs that express a state of being are called **linking verbs.** Common linking verbs are forms of the verb *be* (am, is, was were), *appear, become, feel, grow, look, remain, seem, smell, sound, stay, taste,* and *turn.* **Action verbs** show actions that can be seen (*run, catch*) or not seen (*think, see*).

Action Verbs	Linking Verbs
Some scientists <u>work</u> with plants.	Some scientists <u>are</u> botanists.
John often <u>thinks</u> about careers.	Science <u>seems</u> important to John.

Identify each underlined verb as *action* or *linking.*

Example: Many botanists <u>help</u> farmers with their crops. _____action_____

1. These scientists <u>develop</u> stronger types of plants. _____

2. Strong plants <u>fight</u> disease with good results. _____

3. Healthy plants certainly <u>are</u> a great benefit to farmers. _____

4. They rapidly <u>grow</u> large. _____

5. These crops <u>increase</u> the yield at harvest time. _____

6. Some new strains of plants <u>taste</u> delicious. _____

7. In many ways agriculture <u>benefits</u> from scientific improvements.

   _____

8. For amateur gardeners, the new plants <u>seem</u> impressive.

   _____

9. They often <u>look</u> beautiful, as well. _____

10. They often <u>collect</u> plants for study. _____

Grammar: Action Verbs and Linking Verbs

Assess

Identify each underlined verb as *action* or *linking*.

1. They <u>run</u> with energy. _____

2. They <u>build</u> nests on the ground. _____

3. Some <u>make</u> their homes along the seashore. _____

4. The nests <u>seem</u> safe. _____

5. The golden plover <u>migrates</u> long distances. _____

6. It <u>breeds</u> in Arctic regions. _____

7. Some plovers <u>stay</u> in Florida during the winter months. _____

8. The bird <u>flies</u> about 2,400 miles over open ocean. _____

9. A picture of a plover <u>is</u> on our living room wall. _____

10. They <u>are</u> small birds with long legs. _____

11. All plovers <u>migrate</u> from place to place. _____

12. People <u>recognize</u> its shrill cry of "killdeer." _____

13. Two black bands <u>mark</u> its white breast. _____

14. The feathers on its back <u>are</u> grayish-brown. _____

15. The female <u>lays</u> four black-spotted eggs. _____

16. The killdeer <u>is</u> a type of plover. _____

Grammar: Regular and Irregular Verbs

Practice

Regular verbs form their tenses in a predictable way.
Irregular verbs do not follow a predictable pattern.

A Sort these words according to the sound made by the ending *-ed.*

landed	rained	called	shifted
looked	named	crushed	turned
helped	planted	pushed	sorted

/t/	/d/	/ed/

B Complete each sentence with the correct irregular verb.

| thought | caught | built | knew | flew |

1. The pig _____ a wonderful house close to the pasture.

2. I _____ all the answers, so I got an A on the test.

3. Ann _____ about the book all day, even when she did her chores.

4. The man _____ the cow that had left the pasture.

5. The spaceship _____ back toward Earth.

Grammar: Regular and Irregular Verbs

Assess

A Write the present participle, past, and past participle of each regular and irregular verb in the following chart.

Present	Present Participle	Past	Past Participle
1. climb	_____	_____	_____
2. buy	_____	_____	_____
3. cook	_____	_____	_____
4. drive	_____	_____	_____
5. grow	_____	_____	_____

B Circle the correct form of the verb in parentheses.

1. Anna had (wrote, written) a letter to the newspaper.

2. She had (spoke, spoken) about pollution near her home.

3. She (thunk, thought) it was a bad thing.

4. She (said, say) something must be done.

5. The city has finally (began, begun) a cleanup.

C Complete each sentence by writing the form of the verb shown in parentheses.

1. We _____ a skunk in our backyard. (past of *spot*)

2. The daily temperature had _____ below 32 degrees. (past participle of *fall*)

3. Our cat has _____ himself on my pant legs. (past participle of *rub*)

4. We _____ to the lake one chilly morning. (past of *go*)

5. Sally had _____ her thick mittens. (past participle of *wear*)

Grammar: Verb Tenses

Practice

The **tense** of a verb shows time.

A Study the table. Complete the table by writing examples for the verb <u>act</u>.

Tenses	Expresses Action	Helping Verbs	Principal Parts	Examples
Present	taking place now		present	I _____
Past	took place in the past		past	I _____
Future	will occur in the future	will, shall	present	I _____
Present Perfect	happened at an indefinite time in the past and may still be happening	have, has	past participle	I _____
Past Perfect	happened before another past action	had	past participle	I _____
Future Perfect	will be finished before a stated time in the future	will have, shall have	past participle	I _____ _____

B Draw a line to show the tense of each underlined verb. The first one is done for you.

Tense

1. We <u>will learn</u> about the southwestern Native Americans.

2. Navajo and Apaches <u>live</u> in the Southwest.

3. Early people of the Southwest <u>hunted</u> with spears.

4. Arrowheads and other relics <u>tell</u> about this early life.

5. You <u>will enjoy</u> this film on Navajo art.

6. Spaniards <u>have played</u> a part in Native American life.

7. Native Americans <u>had left</u> many villages before the Spaniards came.

present

past

future

present perfect

past perfect

future perfect

Name _____ Date _____

Grammar: Verb Tenses

A For each sentence, circle whether the underlined verb is in the present, past, or future tense.

1. My brother Gary <u>helped</u> me with my project.   present   past   future

2. He <u>built</u> the box for my ant farm.   present   past   future

3. An ant farm <u>shows</u> a community of ants.   present   past   future

4. Through the glass you <u>see</u> their actions.   present   past   future

5. Tomorrow I <u>will display</u> my ant farm at the   present   past   future
   science fair.

B Complete each sentence by writing the form of the verb shown in parentheses.

1. Last Saturday we _____ cars for charity. (past tense of *wash*)

2. We _____ just over a thousand dollars. (past tense of *raise*)

3. The charity _____ our help. (present tense of *need*)

4. It _____ a worthy cause. (present tense of *be*)

5. Next week we _____ it again. (future tense of *do*)

C On the line, rewrite each sentence using the verb tense indicated.

1. The trumpet played loudly.

   Present tense: _____

2. The flute whistles sweetly.

   Past tense: _____

3. The musicians tune their instruments.

   Future tense: _____

4. The piano player runs his hands across the keys.

   Past tense: _____

Writing: Informative Article

Practice

An **informative article** explains something. When writing an informative article, you will begin with a factual main idea and develop it with specific factual support.

Suggestions for Writing an Informative Article

1. Choose a topic that you know about.

2. Organize your information logically. Start with a topic sentence that tells what your article is about.

3. Use specific examples, details, and facts.

4. Use clear and precise language. Define or explain terms that your readers may not know.

5. Keep your audience in mind and write in an appropriate way.

Read the following paragraph and then answer the questions.

By the mid 1700s, several changes had taken place in the American colonies. For one thing, the colonies were growing in population. In addition, they were becoming experienced in governing themselves and taking care of local affairs. They were also producing more products than ever before. Therefore, they did not need to rely on England for goods and supplies. Most of all, the colonists needed England less and less for protection from the French and Spanish.

1. What is this article about? _____

2. For what kind of audience do you think this was written? _____

3. What kind of supporting information is given? Underline three pieces of supporting information.

4. How is the paragraph organized? _____

5. How could the language in sentence 4 be improved? _____

_____

Name _____ Date _____

 Circle one of the following topics or choose one of your own. Then, fill in the information requested below.

How to plan a vacation	Making a pizza
Working out for health	The basics of cheering
How to build a campfire	Playing the guitar

1. Identify your audience. _____

2. Write a topic sentence. _____

_____

3. Write three supporting ideas/pieces of information.

_____

_____

_____

4. Tell the order in which you would use the ideas.

_____

_____

5. Write definitions for unfamiliar terms. There should be *at least two words* that are specific to your topic and that might need explanation for your readers.

_____

_____

Writing: Journal Entry

Practice

A **journal** is used to record events, observations, and ideas from your own experience.

Planning Your Journal

1. Decide on the purpose of your journal.
2. Decide how often you will write entries. Consider your purpose and your own habits: How much time do you want to commit to keeping a journal?
3. Take notes about the things that happen to you. Jot down as many answers as you can to the following questions: Who? When? Where? and Why?
4. Brainstorm for descriptive details about the people, places, and things you will write about and add them to your notes.

Choose one of the following topics or a topic of your own. Then, plan your journal entry by answering these questions.

a funny misunderstanding	a disappointment
a quarrel	a lucky accident

1. When? _____

2. Who? _____

3. Where? _____

4. What? _____

_____

_____

5. Your reaction? _____

_____

_____

Writing: Journal Entry

Read the following two journal entries. Then, complete the activity.

Monday, December 12
    I can't believe how nervous I am! It is two days before the All-County chorus tryouts. I have been practicing two pieces, a classical aria and a folk song. My music teacher said that my voice is sounding strong. But I found out that I have to practice without my CD playing background music. Part of the audition is singing with no accompaniment. That worries me.

Tuesday, December 13
    I tried singing with no musical backup today, and I think I sounded like a cat or maybe a chicken. What am I going to do? My mother said that I sounded fine to her, but I think she just says things like that because she loves me. I am in a panic, and it feels like my throat is tightening up. Wish me luck tomorrow.

Now, write the journal entry for the next day. Try to imagine how this character thinks and feels.

Wednesday, December 14

_____

_____

_____

_____

_____

Writing: Review of a Short Story

When you write a **review of a short story,** you explain what you liked and did not like about a story. You should refer to the setting, scenes, characters, plot elements, and the author's style to support your opinion. Before you write a review of a short story, reread it and take notes in a chart like the one shown here:

What I liked about this story	What I did not like about this story

A Answer the following questions.

1. Circle the letters of *all* the elements of plot and style that you could possibly discuss in a short story review:

   A. plot   **D.** summary   **G.** tone   **J.** sensory details
   B. conflict **E.** character   **H.** point of view **K.** fact and opinion
   C. setting   **F.** dialogue   **I.** cause and effect **L.** word roots

2. A review of a short story is based on which of the following?

   A. well-known facts
   B. advanced literary theories
   C. one reader's thoughtful opinion
   D. one reader's random mood

3. When you review a short story, what is most important?

   A. It is most important to really like the story that you review.
   B. It is most important to have read the story carefully and to have thought about it.
   C. It is most important to find something wrong with the story.
   D. It is most important to get other people to read the story.

Writing: Review of a Short Story

Assess

Answer the following questions.

1. What is the purpose in reviewing a short story?

   A. to express the main ideas about the story and how you felt about them
   B. to show readers how well you can write a review
   C. to show readers how to recognize plot devices and the author's purpose
   D. to develop a dance or play about the story

2. What would be most important to discuss in a short story review?

   A. when the author was born
   B. how long it took you to read the story and take notes
   C. what you liked about the plot and characters
   D. what you liked about the book jacket

3. Do you have to say only good and positive things about a short story when you review one? T / F

   Explain your answer. _____

   _____

4. Think of a short story that you have read. Write two things that you like about it and two things that you do not like as much.

   _____

   _____

   _____

   _____

   _____

   _____

Reading: Make Inferences

Practice

Readers often have to **make inferences,** or logical guesses, about characters, the setting, and events by recognizing and using details in the story.

A Read the paragraph. Then, answer the questions.

As Rebecca turned away from the window, she was frowning deeply. She walked quickly across the room toward the door to the kitchen and to the back stairs. Then she stopped and turned back into the living room. A loud knock sounded at the front door. Hearing it, Rebecca jumped slightly and grabbed the back of a chair. The knock came again. Biting her knuckle, Rebecca glanced toward the kitchen door and then back toward the front door. A third knock sounded. Rebecca could hear her mother calling her name. But still she stood, nervously holding the back of the chair.

1. How do you think Rebecca feels?

_____

2. Underline the words and phrases that helped you figure out Rebecca's feelings.

3. What do you think Rebecca would like to do?

_____

B Read each of the following passages. Then, answer each question.

You ask your sister how she did on her history test. She replies by slamming her books down on a table and snapping, "I don't even want to talk about it."

1. What would you guess happened?

_____

It is Sunday afternoon, and the back tire of your bike suddenly goes flat. A friend, who says she knows tires, patches the leak and promises that your tire is as good as new. Then, on the way to school on Monday morning, you feel a thumping from the back tire.

2. What can you infer about your tire and your friend?

_____

Reading: Make Inferences

Read each of the following passages. Then, for each question either circle the letter of the correct answer or write your answer on the line provided.

As Sam walked through the doorway, he fiddled with the zipper on his jacket. The room was filled with kids. They all looked like they had known each other forever. Sam found an empty desk at the back of the room. He sat down and glued his eyes to the desk.

1. Who is Sam?

A. a new student in the class   **B.** a substitute teacher

2. What words in the paragraph support your answer?

_____

3. How does Sam feel?

A. nervous   **B.** bored

4. What words in the paragraph support your answer?

_____

Above all, Paul loved the color of the glass. There were sheets of the deepest red. Some sheets were pale green and other light colors. Many of the clear pieces had bumps or ridges to give them texture. With so much to pick from, Paul thought, I can certainly create my masterpiece.

Just then, Mrs. Laurenti came into the shop. She looked around in a bored way. "Still picking up scraps of useless glass, eh, Paulie?" she remarked. Then she strolled out the door.

1. What is Paul's plan?

A. to pick pieces of glass to   **B.** to make a beautiful window
put on sale

2. What words in the passage support your answer?

_____

3. How does Mrs. Laurenti feel about Paul's work?

A. She does not appreciate his work.   **B.** She is impressed with it.

4. What words in the passage support your answer?

_____

Reading: Generalization

Practice

A **generalization** is a broad statement that applies to many examples and is supported by evidence. For example, a person with several well-behaved dogs might make the generalization that dogs are excellent pets. A person who has eaten many tasty apples might make the generalization that apples taste good.

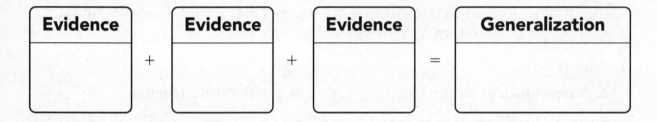

Evidence		Evidence		Evidence		Generalization
	+		+		=	

Read the following examples. Then, make a generalization for each.

1. Jan had a great time at her friend Luis's Halloween party in fifth grade. She had a terrific time at Luis's Halloween party in sixth grade. She also had a wonderful time at Luis's Halloween party in seventh grade.

Generalization: _____

2. Mark ordered a fish fillet sandwich for lunch, but he did not like it. Months later, he tried a bite of his brother's fish fillet sandwich, but he still did not like it. His grandmother made him a fish fillet sandwich for lunch one day, and he did not like it.

Generalization: _____

3. Anna and Luke worked together on a science project and earned a good grade. They were chosen as a team the next year and again worked well together. For the science fair they did a project together and won a prize.

Generalization: _____

4. Robert, Alex, and Marcia are all in Mr. Donner's math class. It takes Robert 30 minutes to do his math homework. It takes Alex about 25 minutes to do his math homework. It takes Marcia a little over half an hour to do her math homework.

Generalization: _____

Reading: Generalization

Read the following passages. Then, make a generalization based on what you have read.

Walking for Fitness and Fun

Walking Is for Everyone

Walking is a popular form of exercise, and it is growing more popular each year. Walking is good for every age group: The rate of participation does not decline in the middle and later years. In a national survey, the highest percentage of regular walkers for any group was among men 65 years of age and older.

Walking: The Slow and Sure Way to Fitness

People walk for many reasons: for exercise, for enjoyment, for solitude, or simply for transportation. No matter the reason, though, people who are walking are getting great exercise. When walkers maintain a good brisk pace and walk on a regular basis, there are definite health advantages. Some of these include lowered resting heart rate, gradual weight loss, and reduced blood pressure. Briskly walking one mile in fifteen minutes burns as many calories as jogging the same distance in eight and one-half minutes.

Walking: Convenient and Inexpensive

Walking is an easy exercise regimen. You can do it almost anytime. You can do it almost anywhere. There is no special equipment needed. And it does not cost anything. No matter what your age or condition, walking can make you healthier and happier.

1. Make a generalization about what you have read. _____

_____

_____

_____

2. Underline three facts or ideas in the passage that you used as evidence to support your generalization.

Literary Analysis: Conflict and Resolution

Practice

Many stories revolve around a main **conflict,** a struggle between opposing forces. A conflict can be either internal or external. In an **external conflict,** a character struggles with an outside force such as nature or another character. An **internal conflict** happens when a character struggles with clashing emotions, feelings, beliefs, or desires. The **resolution** of the story occurs when the conflict or problem is solved.

Identify what type of conflict exists in the following excerpts. Write the answer on the line provided. Then, write a resolution for the conflict.

1. Hernan and Juan are best friends who go to the same school. The baseball coach at their school recently put up a sign-up sheet for pitching tryouts. Both boys have signed up to try out. Juan feels that if Hernan is selected as a pitcher and he is not, Hernan will not want to be on the team. Juan wants his friend to be the pitcher but does not know if he should say anything to Hernan.

   Type of conflict: _____

   Resolution: _____

   _____

   _____

   _____

2. Elise decided to take her dog Max to the park for a long walk in the afternoon sunshine. Once at the park, Max was busy sniffing the ground and following the scent of something. All of a sudden, Max began to bark as a large bear lumbered across their path. Terror filled Elise as she began to shout.

   Type of conflict: _____

   Resolution: _____

   _____

   _____

   _____

Name _____ Date _____

Read the questions and circle the letter of the best answer.

1. Sari is a girl who is not very organized. She becomes chairperson of a food drive in her school. What conflict will probably occur?

   A. Sari will have a hard time getting the food drive to work.
   B. Sari will get angry at her friends for not helping her more.

2. Sari's mother helps her with the food drive. She makes lists, puts labels on packages, and keeps records of people she has called. What is a likely resolution?

   A. The food drive fails.
   B. Sari learns some organizational skills.

3. Antonio's girlfriend badly wants to go to an expensive party, but Antonio has little money. He is proud and hates to ask for help from anyone. What conflict will probably occur?

   A. Antonio will ask his girlfriend to share expenses, and she will refuse.
   B. Antonio will have a hard time figuring out how to pay for the party.

4. Antonio's girlfriend figures out a way to make money by washing cars. What is a likely resolution?

   A. Antonio will borrow money from his girlfriend to pay for the party.
   B. Antonio will still try to find a way to make money on his own.

5. Suppose you were reading a story about a track star who was vain about his running skills and his good looks. Which of these actions would he most likely take?

   A. spend time making sure he looked perfect before a race
   B. try to help a runner who was not as skilled

Literary Analysis: Theme

Practice

A story's **theme** is its central idea, message, or insight into life. It can be implied or stated directly.

A Read about the characters and their goals. Circle the letter of the theme that best matches the goal.

1. Miss Emily has worked hard for thirty years. She wants to retire and travel around the world.

   A. People of all ages need change in their lives.
   B. Everyone should retire and travel around the world.

2. Joey loves to be on stage. He acts in school plays. His dream is to become a famous actor.

   A. Being in a school play can be fun.
   B. People like to think about what they can do to be successful.

B Circle the letter of the theme that best matches the actions of the character.

1. Sam is a pilot. His plane was in a midair accident over a large city. He was in danger of losing his own life, his copilot's life, and perhaps the lives of others on the ground. He grabbed the controls and headed for an open area he saw below him. Carefully, he landed the plane.

   A. A small plane should never be allowed to fly over a city.
   B. Sometimes, a person must remain calm to survive in a crisis.

2. A new girl named Lola came into Kerri's class. Some of the kids laughed at her because she dressed a little funny. Kerri started wondering how she would feel if she were in Lola's place. She invited Lola to her home and discovered that Lola was a great storyteller. Kerri and Lola had a great time laughing together.

   A. We need to look beyond outward appearances to see the real person.
   B. The right clothes and hairstyle are really important.

Literary Analysis: Theme

Assess

A Write *true* or *false* in front of each statement.

1. _____ The theme always tells exactly what happens.

2. _____ The theme is the meaning of a selection and can be implied or directly stated.

3. _____ Sayings that express something about life in general are often themes.

B Read the following example. Then, circle the best answer for each question.

Wilma Rudolph was an athlete who had a difficult childhood. After she contracted scarlet fever and double pneumonia at the age of four, she could not use her left leg. She learned to walk again at age seven and ran in races when she was twelve. Later, she won gold medals running in the Olympics. Wilma's life is proof that if people try hard enough, they can often overcome great handicaps.

1. What is the message, or theme, in this paragraph?

   A. Wilma Rudolph got pneumonia when she was four.
   B. You can overcome many difficulties if you try.

2. Which sentence from the paragraph states the theme?

   A. Wilma's life is proof that if people try hard enough, they can often overcome great handicaps.
   B. Wilma Rudolph was an athlete who had a difficult childhood.

3. Is the theme implied or directly stated?

   A. implied   **B.** directly stated

Literary Analysis: Irony

Irony is a literary device that uses contrast or contradiction to surprise, amuse, or shock readers. There are different types of irony. In *situational irony*, there is a contrast between what an author leads readers to expect and what actually happens. In *verbal irony*, there is a contrast between what a character or person says and what that speaker really means.

Type of Irony	Example
Situational irony	People would note the irony if the fire house burned down.
Verbal irony	To say that a very bad plan is "an outstanding plan," when you mean to show that you do not approve of it.

Answer the following questions by circling the letter of your choice.

1. Which of these is an example of situational irony?

   A. A little brother or sister who is always a brat brightens the day for some nursing-home residents.
   B. A fat, lazy, and friendly cat turns out to be a very good pet.
   C. Grandparents get together with their grandchildren and enjoy an outing.
   D. A gymnast trains so hard for a meet that he wins a medal.

2. Which of the following is an example of verbal irony?

   A. "Good morning!" said Luisa brightly. "It's a beautiful day!"
   B. "I hope you're feeling better," said the nurse as she took my temperature.
   C. "Please call me if you need anything," said the guidance counselor.
   D. "Nice ride," said Bob as the muffler fell off my uncle's old car.

3. How might an author use irony in a short story?

   A. He or she might use lots of dialogue so that the action moves quickly.
   B. He or she might include lots of description so that readers can get a good sense of the story's setting.
   C. He or she might lead readers to expect a certain outcome and then make the plot shift in an unexpected way.
   D. He or she might choose a serious theme to make the story believable.

Literary Analysis: Irony

Read the following selection. Then, answer the questions that follow.

In a small, rural town lived a young boy named Leon who longed to live in the city. All his life he dreamed and planned for the day when he would be living in a modern apartment building, working in sleek office tower, and being part of the excitement of city life. Leon studied hard and went to a good college. He became an architect. He applied for a job with the city's best-known architectural firm. People said he would never be hired by such a big firm, that it was impossible to get a job there, but he proved them all wrong: He was hired.

The life he had always dreamed of had begun. He could not believe his good fortune. On the first day of his new job, he was handed a memo about his first assignment, which read:

"We are pleased to assign you to an exciting two-year project working with our most important client. The client, whose identity will remain secret for now, requests that a new place of business be designed for him and his closest advisors. He has grown tired of the city and wishes to move his offices to the peacefulness of the countryside. We are pleased to tell you that for the next two years you will be living and working in a lovely country setting."

1. What outcome did you expect?

_____

2. List at least three details from the story that supported the outcome you expected.

_____

_____

_____

3. What is the actual ending of the story?

_____

4. Is this story an example of situational irony or verbal irony?

_____

Vocabulary: Prefixes *con-*, *sub-*, and *ob-*

Practice

A **prefix** is a syllable or group of syllables added to the beginning of a word. A prefix changes the meaning of a word or makes a new word. Every prefix has a meaning.

Prefix	Meaning	Examples
con-	with, together	concert, convention
sub-	under, below	subheading, subject
ob-	against, blocking	objection, obstacle

A Read each definition. Then, write *con-*, *sub-*, or *ob-* on the line to form a word that fits the definition. The underlined words will help you.

1. _____ **ordinate:** someone who ranks <u>below</u> others

2. _____ **clusion:** answer found by putting all the clues <u>together</u>

3. _____ **struction:** something that <u>blocks</u> your way

4. _____ **struction:** the act of building or putting something <u>together</u>

5. _____ **terranean:** lying <u>beneath</u> the earth's surface.

B Circle the letter of the answer that correctly completes each sentence. Finding the prefix in each underlined word will help you.

1. At a <u>conference</u>, people work

   A. together.　　　　　**B.** under a boss.　　　　　**C.** against one another.

2. A king's <u>subjects</u> are the people who serve

   A. equally with the king.　　**B.** against the king.　　**C.** under the king.

3. When you <u>object</u> to a plan, you speak out

   A. for it.　　　　　**B.** against it.　　　　　**C.** under orders.

4. At a <u>concert</u>, band members are expected to play

   A. against one another.　　**B.** together.　　**C.** under the stage.

Vocabulary: Prefixes *con-*, *sub-*, and *ob-*

Read each definition. Then, write *con-*, *sub-*, or *ob-* on the line to form a word that fits the definition. The underlined words will help you.

1. _____ **normal:** <u>below</u> normal

2. _____ **current:** existing <u>together</u>, side by side

3. _____ **jection:** statement <u>against</u> an idea

4. _____ **forming:** going along <u>with</u> the rules

5. _____ **marine:** a ship that goes <u>under</u> the sea

B Circle the letter of the word that fits each definition. The underlined word in the definition will help you.

1. An event where people come <u>together</u> for meetings:

    A. objection   **B.** convention   **C.** subjection

2. Stubbornly going <u>against</u> what other people want to do:

    A. constant   **B.** subordinate   **C.** obstinate

3. A person who ranks <u>below</u> others:

    A. subordinate   **B.** confederate   **C.** obstacle

4. To bring all your thoughts <u>together</u> on one topic:

    A. concentrate   **B.** subjugate   **C.** obliterate

5. Something that <u>blocks</u> your way:

    A. convection   **B.** obstruction   **C.** subtraction

Grammar: Adjectives

Practice

An **adjective** describes a noun or a pronoun. Adjectives often answer the question "What kind?" or "How many?" The words *a, an,* and *the* are special adjectives called **articles.**

A Circle each adjective in the following sentences. Include articles.

1. Parents choose simple stories for young children.

2. A youngster likes easy tales and books with many illustrations.

3. The older child likes happy stories with funny plots.

4. On every visit Julius tells us a dramatic yarn or recites a sad poem.

5. He is a welcome visitor, and we love him.

6. Julius recited a delightful poem by Robert Service on a recent visit.

7. It told about the hard and adventurous life of miners in Canada.

8. We laughed at the humorous end of the long poem.

9. Robert Service wrote several poems about the frozen north.

10. The new library might have a complete collection of the poet's works.

B Complete each sentence with the article *a* or *an.*

11. _____ icicle formed on _____ sled.

12. _____ polar bear walked on _____ frozen lake.

13. _____ excellent guide led us through _____ storm.

14. We saw _____ warm fire at _____ distance.

15. _____ eager dog met us on _____ windy ridge.

16. It is _____ Alaskan husky, _____ ancient breed.

Grammar: Adjectives

Assess

A Circle the articles in each sentence.

1. A model railroad is a miniature imitation of an actual train.

2. The assembly of a railroad kit is a difficult task.

3. A model railroad is a pleasant hobby.

B Underline all the adjectives, including the articles, in the following paragraph.

The model railway has metal tracks and seventeen cars. The train includes a locomotive and a red caboose. It has a miniature station with an office. The train goes through a dark tunnel. A steel bridge and realistic trees complete the scene.

C Read the following sentences. Add an adjective to describe each underlined noun.

1. What fun to watch the _____ train run over the tracks!

2. Each of the _____ cars resembles an actual car.

3. _____ cars were bought ready-made at the hobby shop.

4. Others were assembled from _____ parts.

Grammar: Adverbs

An **adverb** describes a verb, an adjective, or another adverb. It answers the questions *How? When? Where?* or *To what extent?*

A A verb, adjective, or adverb is underlined in each sentence. Circle the adverb that describes it.

1. Vann eagerly <u>visited</u> the Rio Grande Valley.

2. He always <u>enjoys</u> his vacations in that sunny land.

3. The people of the Valley grow wonderfully <u>tasty</u> grapefruit.

4. Grapefruit grow extremely <u>well</u> in the Valley.

5. Many people <u>live</u> here in winter.

6. Vann <u>will</u> soon <u>arrive</u> at McAllen, the City of Palms.

7. They <u>celebrate</u> a yearly folk festival called the Border Fest.

8. Corpus Christi has a very <u>protected</u> harbor.

9. Barrier islands effectively <u>block</u> the high waves.

10. People can keep their boats very <u>safely</u>.

B An adverb is circled in each sentence. Draw an arrow from the adverb to the verb, adjective, or other adverb it describes.

1. Corpus Christi is a busy seaport (today).

2. Vann went (immediately) to Padre Island.

3. He (soon) saw Padre Island National Seashore.

4. The government protects this (extremely) beautiful area.

5. Scientists at Padre Island study nature (very) closely.

6. An (almost) perfect visit to the King Ranch concluded Vann's visit.

7. Richard King, the founder, (once) piloted riverboats.

Grammar: Adverbs

Assess

A Underline the adverb in each sentence.

1. The Wright brothers formerly owned a bicycle business in Ohio.

2. They later went to Kitty Hawk, North Carolina.

3. Wilbur and Orville Wright soon began work on a plane.

4. No existing engine was quite right for them.

5. They finally built their own engine.

6. Their first flights were very brief.

7. They had very little recognition for five years.

B An adverb in each sentence is underlined. Write the word the adverb modifies.

1. Writers sneered <u>scornfully</u> at the Wrights' first efforts. _____

2. The Wright brothers <u>quietly</u> continued their experiments. _____

3. They tested their wing models <u>quite</u> thoroughly. _____

4. In 1905 they designed a <u>much</u> better airplane. _____

5. The plane <u>easily</u> flew over twenty-four miles. _____

6. Newspapers <u>eagerly</u> reported on their future flights. _____

7. The Wright brothers <u>very</u> successfully turned their dreams of flight into reality. _____

Grammar: Degrees of Adjectives and Adverbs

Both **adjectives** and **adverbs** have three forms to show comparison. They are the **positive form,** the **comparative form,** and the **superlative form.** Notice the endings or words that are used in building each of these forms. Also note that *more* and *most* are used with adjectives that are long words and with all adverbs that end in *-ly.*

	Positive	**Comparative**	**Superlative**
Adjectives	big	bigger	biggest
	speedy	speedier	speediest
Adverbs	soon	sooner	soonest
	seriously	more seriously	most seriously

Some adjectives and adverbs do not follow the usual rules. Their comparative and superlative forms are made differently.

	Positive	**Comparative**	**Superlative**
Adjectives	good	better	best
	bad	worse	worst
Adverbs	well	better	best
	badly	worse	worst

Write the comparative and superlative forms of each adjective or adverb.

1. quickly _____

2. cold _____

3. tall _____

4. bright _____

5. grumpily _____

Grammar: Degrees of Adjectives and Adverbs

Assess

A Write the comparative and superlative forms of each adjective or adverb.

1. steadily _____

2. beautiful _____

3. tan _____

4. gracefully _____

5. carefully _____

7. spicy _____

8. pretty _____

9. sad _____

10. much _____

B Rewrite the following sentences, using the form of the adjective or adverb indicated in parentheses.

1. A king loved one of his daughters (much) of all. (superlative)

_____

2. The (good) pie would win the contest. (superlative)

_____

3. The judge needed to determine which runner ran (far) than the other. (comparative)

_____

4. Which vegetable do you like (much): potatoes or beans? (comparative)

_____

5. The (little) used bicycle had new tires. (superlative)

_____

Spelling: Tricky or Difficult Words

Practice

A **syllable** is a word part with a single vowel sound. Some words contain syllables that are not heard when the word is pronounced. Often, those words become tricky or difficult to spell.

A In these sentences, underline the correctly spelled word in each pair in parentheses.

1. The harvest this year was (abundent/abundant).

2. That was a very (careless/carless) thing to do.

3. Susan made a (brillient/brilliant) remark in class today.

4. The (waether/weather) will be very hot tomorrow.

5. That was a complete (surprise/suprise) to me.

6. Our new (principle/principal) is Mrs. Burke.

7. I (reccommend/recommend) that we go to the movies instead of a play.

8. I received excellent (guidance/guidence) from my parents.

9. She is (fourty/forty) years old today.

10. I am sorry to (disappoint/disapoint) you.

B Spell each misspelled word correctly on the line. If a word is already spelled correctly, write *C* on the line.

Example: tragidy ___tragedy_____

1. sophmore _____

2. concider _____

3. appresiate _____

4. consede _____

5. losing _____

6. excape _____

Name _____ Date _____

Spelling: Tricky or Difficult Words

A Underline the correctly spelled word in each group. Then, write the word on the line. Check your answers in a dictionary.

1. hwere   where   wer   _____

2. finialy   finly   finally   _____

3. friend   firend   freind   _____

4. ov   oof   of   _____

B Underline the correct word for each sentence. Then, write the word on the line.

1. _____ Did you go (their, there) on Thursday?

2. _____ (Where, Hwere) is the principal's office?

3. _____ I think the snow is (thrugh, through) for the night.

4. _____ Turn the radio (of, off)!

5. _____ Gabrielle just saw her (favorite, favrit) movie star.

6. _____ (They, Thay) were first in line.

C Complete each sentence with the correct word from the box.

they're   there   their

1. If I am not here, then I will be _____.

2. I will be happy to help them with _____ homework.

3. It is always fun when _____ visiting us.

© Pearson Education, Inc., publishing as Pearson Prentice Hall.   **Reading Kit 89**

Writing: Anecdote

Practice

An **anecdote** is a brief story about an interesting or amusing event. Anecdotes are written to entertain or to make a point. When you are writing an anecdote, remember that it needs to have a beginning, a middle, and an end. An anecdote will often include a problem that needs to be solved. Sometimes the characters in an anecdote will learn a lesson.

A Answer the following question.

1. Which topic would make the best basis for an anecdote?

   A. instructions for building a model airplane
   B. building a model airplane with my ninety-year-old grandfather
   C. how to raise bean sprouts
   D. writing a shopping list

B Read the following anecdote and then answer the questions about it.

On my seventh birthday my uncle, who was usually very stingy, took me out to dinner. He took me to an expensive restaurant, so I was surprised. I ordered a huge plate of prime rib, which made *him* surprised! I usually didn't eat much, but I loved prime rib. Then my uncle told the waiter he wasn't that hungry, he'd just have a small salad. I knew what he was thinking: He thought he would be able to save some money by not ordering dinner for himself and just helping himself to my leftovers. He could still tell everyone he had taken me out to a restaurant, but he would only have to pay for one dinner!

Well, the final surprise was that I ate every bit of that prime rib. My uncle was very hungry and disappointed that night.

1. Was there a lesson learned in this anecdote? If so, what was it?

   _____

   _____

2. Give at least two reasons why this story is an anecdote.

   _____

   _____

Name _____   Date _____

Writing: Anecdote

Assess

Choose one of the following topics or choose a topic of your own. Then, write an anecdote on the lines provided. The anecdote may be a true story or one you have made up. Remember to keep the story short. Include a beginning, a middle, and an end.

A Visit to the Dentist	My Baby Brother	My Puppy
A Trip to the Zoo	The Best Trip Ever	A Rainy Soccer Game
My First Ballet Class	An Old Car	The Bird That Talked

_____

_____

_____

_____

_____

_____

_____

_____

_____

_____

_____

_____

_____

_____

_____

Name _____ Date _____

Writing: Letter to the Editor

Practice

A **letter to the editor** states an opinion on an issue. It is written to be published in a magazine or newspaper. Its purpose is to persuade readers to share the writer's opinion or to take an action that the writer recommends.

A Following are several topics for a letter to the editor. Determine a position and list details that would support your position.

1. *Topic:* Should schools have a dress code?

   Position: _____

   Supporting details: _____

   _____

   _____

2. *Topic:* Should schools charge admission to athletic events?

   Position: _____

   Supporting details: _____

   _____

   _____

3. *Topic:* Should new parks be developed?

   Position: _____

   Supporting details: _____

   _____

   _____

B Using one of the positions in Exercise A, write a letter to the editor on a separate sheet of paper. Remember to use the correct form of a letter.

92 Reading Kit

© Pearson Education, Inc., publishing as Pearson Prentice Hall.

Writing: Letter to the Editor

Assess

A Following are several topics for a letter to the editor. Determine a position and list details that would support your position.

1. *Topic:* Should airports have a curfew on when aircraft can depart and land?

Position: _____

Supporting details: _____

_____

_____

2. *Topic:* Should fans be ejected from sporting events for their behavior?

Position: _____

Supporting details: _____

_____

_____

3. *Topic:* Should students be allowed to have cell phones in school?

Position: _____

Supporting details: _____

_____

_____

B Using one of the positions in Exercise A, write a letter to the editor on a separate sheet of paper. Remember to use the correct form of a letter.

Writing: Short Story

Practice

A **short story** is a brief work of fiction. It presents a sequence of events, or plot, and is generally told from a consistent point of view. The plot centers on a central conflict within a particular setting.

A Write **P** if the item describes a plot. Write **S** if it describes a setting.

1. _____ a tent in a wooded area

2. _____ the Fourth of July weekend

3. _____ late at night, with the stars shining

4. _____ a bear arrived

5. _____ The bear stole our food!

B Here is the first paragraph in a story. Read the paragraph and answer the questions.

Kari was looking in her bedroom closet for her new outfit. She threw shirts and pants all over the floor. Suddenly, her younger sister Debbie said, "I took your new outfit. Doesn't it look great on me?" "Maaaaaaaa!" Kari yelled. "Debbie took my new outfit!"

1. What is the setting? _____

2. What is the plot? _____

3. What is the conflict? _____

C Rewrite the following sentences from the first-person point of view.

1. Pat and Nina tied for third place.

_____

2. Chris is a great soccer player.

_____

3. Ahmed is learning to swim.

_____

Writing: Short Story

A Read the following passages and write your answer to each question.

I entered the room quietly, hoping that I would not wake the dog asleep in the corner.

1. What is the point of view in this passage? _____

Angela slid into her desk before the bell rang. This was the first day at her new school. She was a year younger than her classmates, most of whom were 15. That made her feel even more shy. Her shyness made her blush as other students filed past her desk, looking at her. She stared down at her desktop, her long blond hair falling forward over her face.

2. A. Write some key details about the character in this passage.

_____

_____

B. What is the conflict or problem faced by the character in this passage?

_____

I knew that somehow the time machine had gone out of control. I found myself in a dense forest of strange plants that appeared to be huge ferns. Little light penetrated the forest, and a thick fog covered the ground. Suddenly I felt the ground begin to tremble. At the same time, I heard an ear-splitting roar very near. It was the roar of an animal—a *very large* animal.

3. Underline the details of the setting described in this passage.

B Choose one of the passages from Exercise A. Add one or more characters to the story. Then, create a brief dialogue between the characters. Make sure the dialogue is related to the story and adds to the action.

_____

_____

_____

_____

_____

Reading Skill: Main Idea

Practice

The topic of a paragraph or other written selection is what the material is about. The central point that is made about the topic is called the **main idea.** It summarizes all of the supporting details. The supporting details give examples, explanations, or reasons.

When reading nonfiction, adjust your reading rate to recognize main ideas or key points.

Read the paragraph. Then, answer the questions that follow.

Today, after forty-five centuries of exposure to the hazards of time, the Great Pyramid rises to a height of 450 feet. At its base the pyramid measures about 756 feet in length along each of the four sides. The pyramid's bulk is enormous. It is made up of 2,300,000 blocks of stone, each averaging two-and-a-half tons in weight; the biggest blocks weigh fifteen tons. If every block were cut into cubes a foot high, wide, and deep, and these were placed side by side along the equator, they would reach two thirds of the way around the world. The area of the base of the Great Pyramid is so large that the cathedrals of Florence and Milan, as well as St. Peter's in Rome and St. Paul's in London, could all be placed together inside it, with room left for Westminster Abbey.

1. What is the main topic of this paragraph? (Circle one.)

   A. large buildings   **C.** the Great Pyramid
   B. stone blocks   **D.** cathedrals in Europe

The topic tells the subject of the material. Notice that all the facts and supporting details given about the Great Pyramid focus on its size.

2. Which of the following statements best expresses the central focus or main idea in this paragraph? (Circle one.)

   A. The Great Pyramid is enormous.
   B. The Great Pyramid is so large that it could hold the cathedrals of Florence and Milan, as well as St. Peter's in Rome and St. Paul's in London, with room left for Westminster Abbey.
   C. The world has many very large structures.
   D. The Great Pyramid is one of the Seven Wonders of the World.

3. Underline the sentence that states the main idea.

Reading Skill: Main Idea

Assess

A Read the selection. Then, answer the questions that follow.

The opal miners of Australia have learned that it is cooler to live underground than aboveground in the Coober-Pedy region. Almost all of the world's opals are mined in this desert region, but the harsh climate makes it a difficult place in which to live comfortably. So almost half of the 5200 people in Coober-Pedy live underground. These are not crude caves; they boast wall-to-wall carpeting, running water, and electricity. But best of all, these underground dwellers never have to worry about escaping from the heat. The temperature in these homes is around 72°F all year-round. That's not bad—particularly in an area where the normal summertime temperature ranges from 120°F to 140°F in the day. Even at night, the thermometer seldom goes below 100°F. The thick sandstone walls and roofs provide nature's own protection against the hot desert sun.

1. What is the main topic of this selection? (Circle one.)

    A. opals   **C.** houses in Australia

    B. opal miners   **D.** housing in Coober-Pedy

2. Which of the following sentences best states the main idea of this paragraph?

    A. The opal miners of Australia have learned that it is cooler to live underground than aboveground in the Coober-Pedy region.

    B. These are not crude caves; they boast wall-to-wall carpeting, running water, and electricity.

    C. So almost half of the 5200 people in Coober-Pedy live underground.

    D. Their homes are cut deep into sandstone mounds and go far beneath the surface of the earth.

B Read the passage and underline the direct statement of the main idea in the paragraph.

Not only does it seem that everybody is juggling these days, they seem to be tossing around just about anything you can imagine. Street performers, businesspeople, students, professional ice skaters who juggle as they glide—all can be found in increasing numbers practicing how to keep from one to five objects revolving in the air. As to what's up there swirling around, it varies from oranges and apples and juggling clubs to frosted cupcakes, scarves, knives, and even chairs.

Literary Analysis: Expository Essay

Practice

An **expository essay** is a short nonfiction work that explains, defines, or interprets ideas, events, or processes. A well-written essay is organized to present information in a clear, understandable manner.

A Read the following essay and determine the best organization to present the information. List the number of the sentences in correct order on the line following the essay.

(1) Colors of leaves can range from bright yellow to shocking orange to fiery red. (2) Fall is a season when nature produces a pageant of vibrant color. (3) All leaves contain a substance called chlorophyll, which is a green pigment present while the leaves are growing. (4) Just how do leaves change color? (5) The cooler temperatures of autumn cause the leaves to begin to stop producing chlorophyll in anticipation of days with less sunlight. (6) Chlorophyll reacts with sunlight to enable leaves to produce food or energy. (7) Once the chlorophyll dies, other pigments such as anthocyanins (reds) and carotenoids (yellows and oranges) become dominant.

_____

B Read the following sentences to determine which would fit in an expository essay. If the sentence is from an expository essay, write *E* on the line. If the sentence is not from an expository essay, write *N* on the line.

1. _____ Rollerblades are close relatives of roller skates.

2. _____ There was a princess who lived in a fairy kingdom far away.

3. _____ First assemble all of the ingredients listed in the recipe.

4. _____ Joel could not believe his good fortune in finding his lost puppy.

5. _____ Due to several factors, gasoline prices have continued to rise over the past decade.

Literary Analysis: Expository Essay

Assess

A Match the most effective method of organization from the list with each topic. Write your answer in the space provided.

Chronological organization
Comparison-and-contrast organization
Cause-and-effect organization
Problem-and-solution organization

1. a history of Civil War battles

_____

2. oil spills and wildlife

_____

3. similarities and differences in political events leading up to World War I and political events leading up to World War II

_____

4. illegal immigration and a simpler citizenship process

_____

B Identify which of the following titles would go with an expository essay. Then, if the title goes with an expository essay, list which type of organization would best present the information clearly and logically.

1. The Development of Hiking Trails in the Pacific Northwest

_____

2. My Favorite Summer Adventure

_____

3. The Differences Between Amateur and Professional Football

_____

4. A Holiday to Remember

_____

Literary Analysis: Reflective Essay

Practice

A **reflective essay** is a brief prose work that presents a writer's thoughts and feelings, or reflections, about an experience or idea. An author may write a reflective essay when these thoughts and feelings are especially strong.

A Read the following excerpt from a reflective essay. What does the author admire in her grandmother? Write your answer on the lines.

    I began a written correspondence with my grandmother when I was a young child. We did not live within visiting distance, and writing was a way for us to "visit" each week. Sunday was the day she would rest from her labors on the farm. Taking her dime store pad of paper and a pencil she had no doubt sharpened with a paring knife, she would share her week with me in written words. Perhaps she had worked on her tatting or a new quilt pattern. She might have spent a day weeding and hoeing the garden or washing and hanging laundry on the line to dry. Each week's letter captured her work and the details of her life. Through these letters I learned the value and satisfaction of hard work, patience, diligence in accomplishing what needed to be done, and self-reliance at being able to do something yourself.

_____

_____

_____

B Read each of the following sentences and determine which would fit in a reflective essay. If the sentence is from a reflective essay, write *R* on the line. If the sentence is not from a reflective essay, write *N* on the line.

1. _____ Geraniums are hardy, outdoor flowering plants that add color to any garden.

2. _____ My mother was a tall, willowy woman who cared for all creatures.

3. _____ A healthful diet includes at least five servings of fruits and vegetables each day.

4. _____ I was born in a bustling city but was raised in the country.

5. _____ The drugstore is located down the street and around the block.

Literary Analysis: Reflective Essay

Assess

A Read the selection. Then, answer the questions that follow.

The wild blackberry patch in our backyard is an untamed jungle of brambles and intertwined branches. Its thick tangle provides a refuge for mice and rabbits all year, while bees share the nectar of the blossoms in the late spring. In my mind the blackberry patch will forever be associated with my mother and her delicious cobbler. What a treat it is to eat blackberry cobbler fresh from the oven and to know that I picked the berries from our own patch.

1. What is the main purpose of this essay?

_____

2. What would be a likely title for this essay?

_____

B Read the selection. Then, answer the questions that follow.

Most students have an unforgettable teacher at some point during their education. Mrs. Horwitz was my third grade teacher at White Creek Elementary School. Her approach to teaching had evolved through many years of working with students. We began each day by singing songs as she accompanied us on the piano. She required all of her students to complete a list of weekly assignments and to turn them in on time. Every week we memorized a new poem and learned a new skill, ranging from knitting to playing Parcheesi. While I may have thought I was learning facts in third grade, I learned more. I discovered that starting the day with a song always puts one in a good mood. I also found out that time management can help you get through any list of tasks, whether they are weekly assignments or job responsibilities. Perhaps the greatest lesson Mrs. Horwitz taught was that learning is not always found in books but also in doing new things.

1. What is the main purpose of this essay?

_____

2. What would be a likely title for this essay?

_____

Literary Analysis: Biography and Autobiography

In an **autobiography,** a person tells his or her own story. In a **biography,** a writer will tell the story of another person's life. Both forms focus on actual events, although there are some differences. Because an autobiography is written from memory by the individual who witnessed the event, it is more personal and emotional. In contrast, a biography is more objective because it is based on research.

A Read the selection. Then, answer the question that follows.

I was born in 1931 during the Dust Bowl years of our country in a small town in Oklahoma. My earliest memories all seem to be steeped in shades of beige and dull brown. Whether this is because snapshots from the era were in sepia or because everything was covered in dust I'll never know. All I know is that I spent the first eight years of my life traveling from one small town to another. Finally, my family reached the west coast of California, and there was no where else to go.

Explain why this selection is either an autobiography or a biography.

_____

_____

_____

B Read the selection. Then, answer the question that follows.

Ernest Hemingway was born in Oak Park, Illinois, in 1899. While he is best known for his novels and winning the Pulitzer Prize in Literature in 1954, his first job was a writer for a newspaper in Kansas City, Kansas, at the age of 17. The first of many jobs and adventures for Hemingway, it was while working in a newspaper office that he developed his straightforward writing style. Longing for adventure, he joined an Italian volunteer ambulance corps during World War I and worked on the front lines.

Explain why this selection is either an autobiography or a biography.

_____

_____

_____

Literary Analysis: Biography and Autobiography

Assess

Read each selection. Then, answer the questions that follow.

1. Washington Irving (1783–1859) was the first American author to achieve fame in both Europe and America. While living in England as a young man, he read old German folk tales in search of subjects he could use for stories of his own. One tale strongly appealed to him. He changed the setting from Europe to America, made other changes, and thus created "Rip Van Winkle."

Is this selection a biography or an autobiography? Why?

_____

_____

2. I began to work alongside my father in his carpentry shop when I was twelve. My schooling had consisted of several years in a one-room log cabin for which my parents had "subscribed" me for a couple of sessions. School wasn't free and open to all when I was growing up; it was paid for by the parents of the students. I learned enough to be able to read furniture plans and do simple sums. What I didn't learn in school, I was able to learn as an apprentice to my father.

Is this selection a biography or an autobiography? Why?

_____

_____

3. Robert Service was a twentieth-century Canadian poet who grew up in Glasgow, Scotland. He moved to Canada at the age of twenty and was hired by a bank in 1905. When the bank transferred him to a branch in the Yukon, Service began to write lively poems about the trappers and prospectors he met there. These poems were an instant success.

Is this selection a biography or an autobiography? Why?

_____

_____

Vocabulary: Prefixes *ir-* and *in-*

Practice

A **prefix** is a word part that is added to the beginning of a base word. A prefix changes the meaning of a word.

The prefixes *ir-* and *in-* can both mean "without" or "not." Adding *ir-* to the base word *regular* makes *irregular,* which means "not regular." Adding *in-* to the base word *accurate* makes *inaccurate,* which means "not accurate."

A Choose the word from the box that best completes each sentence. Write the word in the blank.

incoherent	incompetent	indecisive	inexcusable
inflexible	irregular	irresistible	irresponsible

1. The beautiful ring was _____ to the buyer.

2. The _____ customer kept changing his mind about the purchase.

3. Other coaches gave their teams some time off, but the baseball coach was

_____ about practice.

4. The man was rushed to the hospital due to his _____ breathing.

5. In many families, being rude to a guest is completely _____.

6. Carlo was _____ when he forgot to lock the front door.

7. In the interview, the secretary appeared to have many good skills, but on

the job, he turned out to be _____.

8. No one could make sense out of what the man said. His words were

_____.

B Write a word you wrote for Part A that matches each meaning.

1. not competent _____   **3.** not coherent _____

2. not responsible _____   **4.** not flexible _____

Vocabulary: Prefixes *ir-* and *in-*

Assess

A Choose the word from the box that best completes each sentence. Write the word in the blank.

incoherent	incompetent	indecisive	insufferable
intangible	irregular	irreplaceable	irresponsible

1. Ralph was _____ about his plans for vacation as he could not decide whether to go to the beach or the mountains.

2. High temperatures made the long summer days _____.

3. The administrative assistant was proven _____ when she lost and misfiled hundreds of documents.

4. Not writing down homework assignments and forgetting to turn work in on time are characteristic of an _____ student.

5. The baby's _____ babble could not be understood.

6. Deliveries were _____ due to the disruption of the storm.

7. Family heirlooms passed down from one generation to the next are

_____.

8. The rewards of helping others are not always concrete but

_____.

B Write a sentence in which you use the following words correctly.

1. insensitive

_____

2. irreversible

_____

3. intolerable

_____

Grammar: Coordinating Conjunctions

Practice

A **conjunction** connects words or groups of words. **Coordinating conjunctions** connect words or groups of words that are similar: two or more verbs, two or more prepositional phrases, or even entire sentences.

Coordinating Conjunctions						
and	for	or	yet	but	nor	so

A Underline the conjunctions in the following sentences.

1. My brother and I share a room over the garage.

2. The movie about the Civil War was long but extremely interesting.

3. The vegetable garden needs to be weeded and hoed.

4. We could not decide whether to sell lemonade or iced tea at the fair booth.

5. The trail went through a dense forest and up a rugged hill.

6. Our magazine sale was very successful, for every school family bought a subscription.

B Fill in each blank with the appropriate conjunction.

1. He left after the game _____ went to the grocery store.

2. Phoebe could not decide whether she enjoyed knitting _____ sewing the most.

3. Neither the bedroom _____ the den has been cleaned.

4. The heavy snow all day canceled the debate _____, it was rescheduled for the following week.

5. The test was difficult _____ fair in its coverage of the material assigned.

6. Our teacher lists the assignments on the board _____ on the school Web site.

Grammar: Coordinating Conjunctions

Assess

A Circle the coordinating conjunctions in each of the following sentences. Then, underline the word or group of words connected by the conjunction.

1. Alex and Ethan live in the village.

2. I exercise before breakfast or before dinner.

3. We had carrots and peas with our meal.

4. I would like to bake a cake, but I am missing a few ingredients.

5. I will be late coming home from school, for I have to go the library.

6. You have a choice of vanilla, strawberry, or chocolate ice cream.

7. The weather report promised blue skies and no rain.

8. Ellen drew a picture of horses and llamas.

9. I forgot to get milk and sugar at the grocery store.

10. Cats and dogs do not always fight when living in the same house.

B Fill in each blank with the appropriate coordinating conjunction.

1. I have three brothers, four sisters, _____ two parents.

2. We get along well, _____ we do disagree about money.

3. Two of my brothers _____ three of my sisters have jobs.

4. I don't care much about money, _____ I am not careless with it.

5. I occasionally borrow money from a brother _____ sister.

6. I try to pay them back promptly _____ I know they need the money.

7. A barter system would end all our disagreeing, _____ I cannot convince the family of this.

8. No one except me finds my idea interesting _____ acceptable.

Grammar: Prepositions and Prepositional Phrases

Practice

A **preposition** is a word used with a noun or a pronoun to form a **prepositional phrase.** A prepositional phrase is a group of words that begins with a preposition and ends with a noun or pronoun.

Prepositions are words such as *in, under,* and *over.* In the following list of prepositions, notice that a preposition can consist of more than one word.

aboard	about	above	according to	across
after	against	along	among	around
at	before	behind	below	beneath
beside	besides	between	beyond	but
by	down	during	except	for
from	in	in addition to	inside	in spite of
instead of	into	like	near	of
off	on	onto	out	out of
outside	over	past	since	through
throughout	till	to	toward	under
underneath	until	up	with	within

A Underline the prepositional phrases in each sentence.

1. The actress with red hair held a book in her hand.

2. She stood in the very center of the huge stage.

3. She was auditioning for the director and the producer.

4. The stage manager sat inside the wings to the right.

5. Behind him stood various members of the cast.

B Write sentences using the following prepositional phrases.

1. before the play

_____

2. down the shadowy street

_____

Grammar: Prepositions and Prepositional Phrases

Assess

A Underline each preposition in the following sentences.

1. The chipmunk ran under the picnic table to eat the crumbs.

2. Our trip to the park was an annual event.

3. The cups and saucers are in the cabinet above the sink.

4. During the hurricane, we heard wind and rain lashing at the windows.

5. We always have a large dinner except when we have a game at night.

6. The school addition will be completed within the next few months.

7. The camp was across the lake from our cabin.

8. The cook prepared a special dessert to be served after the dinner.

B Circle the prepositional phrases in the following sentences.

1. Our car went over the river and through the woods on our trip.

2. I painted under the shelves when I painted the cabinets.

3. The cabin was beneath the large chestnut tree.

4. During the night the wind began to blow.

5. A set of drums was in the music room.

6. Eva lost her backpack on the class trip.

7. Charlie collected stamps and coins and put them in large binders.

8. A shadow appeared from behind the curtain.

C Write a sentence containing a prepositional phrase on each of the following lines.

1. _____

2. _____

Grammar: Conjunctions

Practice

Small, short sentences can lead to choppy, uneven writing. **Conjunctions** combine short sentences, creating a smoother writing style that is easier to read. Coordinating conjunctions, such as *and* or *but,* as well as subordinating conjunctions, such as *after* or *until,* enable writers to combine short sentences.

Read the following groups of sentences. Combine the sentences using conjunctions such as *and, but, or, although, because,* or *unless.* Write each new sentence on the lines provided.

1. Alex and his brother went to the grocery store. They forgot to take their shopping list. They came home.

_____

_____

2. You think soccer is fun. I don't. Chris doesn't.

_____

3. The mothers baked cookies. The fathers put up the decorations.

_____

4. Our country once had dense forests. Today many forests are gone.

_____

5. The store has canned peaches. The store has canned mixed fruit.

_____

6. We went to the beach on vacation. We could have gone to the mountains.

_____

7. I could not go to the football game. I was sick.

_____

8. Our team cannot go to the semifinals. They need to win the playoffs.

_____

Grammar: Conjunctions

Assess

A Read the following paragraph. Then, rewrite the paragraph by using conjunctions to combine sentences where needed.

Albert ran track. Elsa ran track. Both were members of the same school track team. Albert's favorite event was the 100-meter run. Elsa's was the long jump. Their team trained after school. They also trained on Saturdays. To warm up, Albert ran up and down the bleacher stairs by the track. Elsa did long leg stretches to warm up. As members of our school's winning track team, both Albert and Elsa had learned the discipline of hard work and practice.

_____

_____

_____

_____

_____

_____

_____

B Read the following sentences. Then, add the missing conjunctions.

1. Ramone did not win the art award, _____ he had expected to win.

2. We could go to the skating rink _____ to the ball field.

3. We could not go to the beach _____ the weather was cold _____ rainy.

4. Our team would not go to the playoffs _____ we did not win enough games.

5. We entered our dog in the pet show, _____ she did not win.

Writing: Problem-and-Solution Essay

A **problem-and-solution essay** identifies a problem and presents one or more solutions. It is an example of nonfiction writing. The author's purpose in a problem-and-solution essay is to inform and explain.

Prepare to write a brief essay about the amount of litter in the community park in your town. Use the following chart to help you list the problems and solutions. For each problem, be sure to identify a solution.

Community Park	Problems Faced	Solutions
Ball fields		
Playground		

1. Clearly state the problems on the following lines. Be sure you focus the statement to the audience.

_____

_____

2. How will you solve the problems step by step? List the steps on the following lines.

_____

_____

3. List examples to support each solution on the following lines.

_____

_____

4. What is the conclusion? Write it on the following line.

_____

Writing: Problem-and-Solution Essay

A Write a brief problem-and-solution essay about the importance of using public transportation to reduce pollution. Complete the following chart.

Problem Faced	Solutions

B Answer the following questions.

1. Write your statement of the problem.

_____

_____

2. How will you solve your problems step by step? List your steps on the following lines.

_____

_____

_____

3. List examples to support each solution on the following lines.

_____

_____

_____

4. Summarize the solution in a concluding statement. Write your conclusion on the following lines.

_____

_____

Writing: Outline

Practice

When you make an **outline,** you show the main ideas, key points, and supporting details in a written work. To write an outline, use an outline format:

- Use Roman numerals to identify each key point or main idea.
- Use capital letters to identify supporting details.

Read the following selection. Then, fill in the blanks to complete the outline.

Keeping a Journal

Keeping a journal is a very worthwhile thing to do. Not only do you keep a record of your day-to-day life, which will be fun to look back on in later years, but also journal writing is a great way to express your feelings.

It is easy to begin. Select a notebook or other blank book to use as a journal. Set a time for journal writing each day and try to stick to your routine. Choose a time that is convenient. Pick a time when you will be relaxed but not too tired. You will be surprised to see how quickly the pages add up, and how much your writing skills improve as you go!

Outline

[1] _____ Keeping a journal is worthwhile

    A. [2] _____

    [3] _____ fun to look back on

    [4] _____ helps express feelings

[5] _____ Beginning

    A. Select book to use

    [6] _____ [7] _____

Writing: Outline

Read the passage and then complete the following outline. Remember that you will list details that support the main ideas.

Alice Walker

The author Alice Walker was born in Eatonville, Georgia, in 1944. She was the youngest of eight children. Her parents, Tallulah Grand Walker and Willie Lee Walker, worked as sharecroppers. They worked long, hard hours but earned very little money. All the Walker children did their part by doing chores: They worked in the fields, helped with housework, and milked cows. Though the family did not have a lot of money, it was a strong family in many ways.

Alice Walker's career as a writer is rooted in a tradition of storytelling. Both of her parents were gifted storytellers, so she grew up hearing folk tales and family stories. With her mother's encouragement, Alice went to college. There her gift for writing blossomed, and she eventually became a popular and important writer. Her novel *The Color Purple* won the Pulitzer Prize and was also made into a successful motion picture.

Outline

[1] _____ Alice Walker's childhood

    A. [2] _____

    [3] _____ [4] _____

    C. [5] _____

    D. [6] _____

II. Alice Walker's [7] _____

    A. Rooted in storytelling

    B. [8] _____

    C. [9] _____

    D. [10] _____

Writing: How-to Essay

A **how-to essay** is a written, step-by-step explanation of how to do or make something. For example, how-to essays can explain how to repair a bicycle or care for a pet. How-to essays should feature the following elements:

- a narrow focused topic that can be fully explained in the essay
- a list of materials needed
- multistep directions explained in sequential order using transitional words
- appropriate technical terms relating to your topic
- error-free writing, including the use of conjunctions

Select a topic about which to write a how-to essay. Then, answer the following questions.

1. Write a topic sentence for your essay.

_____

_____

2. List and itemize the details for the topic. Have you included all of the steps and materials? What transitional words indicate the order of the steps?

_____

_____

3. Organize the details in sequential order. A chart can help organize the details.

List Steps	Itemize Materials

4. Write a concluding sentence that can be added to the end of your essay.

_____

_____

Writing: How-to Essay

Read the following how-to essay. Then, answer the questions and complete the activities.

A peanut butter and jelly sandwich can be a delicious lunch or a quick snack. It is easily made with two slices of bread, jelly or jam, and peanut butter. First, place both slices of bread on a plate. Next, spread peanut butter on the face of one of the slices of bread with a butter knife. Then, use a butter knife to spread jelly or jam on the face of the other slice of bread. Place both slices of bread together, making sure the peanut butter and the jam are face to face, and apply light pressure.

1. What does this essay instruct readers to do?

_____

2. What transitional words help readers follow the order of the steps? List at least three words.

_____

3. What materials are needed? What equipment is needed?

_____

_____

4. List the main steps in order that are needed to accomplish this task.

_____

_____

_____

5. The conclusion of this essay is weak. It simply ends with the final instruction. Write a strong concluding sentence that could be added to the end of this essay.

_____

_____

_____

Reading: Fact and Opinion

Practice

A **fact** is something that actually happened or that can be proved. An **opinion** is a person's belief or judgment and cannot be proved. Recognizing clue words, such as *I think*, that indicate an opinion and checking facts with reference sources are ways of judging information.

A Read the following sentences and put a check next to those you think are facts.

1. _____ Nantucket Island is a little south of Cape Cod.

2. _____ Nantucket Island is the best summer vacation spot.

3. _____ Nantucket Island was once a center for the whaling industry.

4. _____ Visitors will always be able to admire Nantucket Island's quaint homes and beautiful scenery.

5. _____ Herman Melville used Nantucket Island as the hometown for some of the characters in his novel *Moby Dick*.

B Read each statement. Then, write *F* next to each statement of fact and *O* next to each statement of opinion. If it is a fact, indicate what source you would use to verify it.

1. _____ David Kunst was the first person to walk around the world.

_____

2. _____ Aluminum is used in place of steel in different automobile parts.

_____

3. _____ There will always be more registered Democrats than Republicans in the United States.

_____

4. _____ Wool is the best material to use if you are going to make a sweater.

_____

5. _____ Golf was invented in Scotland and played by the royal family.

_____

Reading: Fact and Opinion

A   Read the paragraph. Then, answer the questions that follow.

Walt Disney will always be known for his cartoons and animated films. Several other artists who are less well known have also worked at the Disney studios. Frank Thomas and Ollie Johnston worked on many animated movies, including *Pinocchio*, *Snow White*, and *The Fox and the Hound*.

1. How could you check the facts found in the paragraph?

_____

2. Why is the first sentence an opinion?

_____

3. The second sentence has both fact and opinion. Write the part of the sentence that is fact.

_____

4. Is the third sentence a fact or an opinion? How do you know?

_____

B   Read each statement. Then, write *F* next to each statement of fact and *O* next to each statement of opinion.

1. _____ *Pinocchio* was produced in 1937.

2. _____ *Pinocchio* cost $2.8 million to make.

3. _____ One thousand people worked on the film, and the artists made 2.5 million drawings.

4. _____ Walt Disney was devoted to the quality of his films, and he did everything possible to improve them and make them the best.

5. _____ Disney built a zoo at his studio, and his artists studied the animals raised there.

6. _____ The main character in *Bambi* was a baby deer; the character was based on a real fawn raised at the zoo.

Reading: Check Facts

You can **check facts** by using reference sources. Sources include manuals, dictionaries, encyclopedias, reliable Web sites, or unbiased experts.

Resource	Characteristics
almanac	a collection of facts and statistics on climate, people, places, and so on that is updated yearly
atlas	a collection of maps
biographical dictionary	an alphabetical listing of famous or historically significant persons with identifying information
dictionary	an alphabetical listing of words with their pronunciation and definition
encyclopedia	an alphabetically organized collection of articles on a broad range of subjects
reliable Web sites	Internet pages and articles on an extremely wide variety of topics

Read each statement. Then, identify each one as a fact or an opinion. If the statement is a fact, indicate the best reference source for checking it.

1. The Incas and Aztecs had large cities and organized forms of government.

   Fact/Opinion: _____ **Resource:** _____

2. Tropical rainforests are lush, steamy, and rich in animals and plants.

   Fact/Opinion: _____ **Resource:** _____

3. Croatia, located on the Balkan peninsula, extends southward into the Mediterranean Sea.

   Fact/Opinion: _____ **Resource:** _____

4. The current exchange rate for Canadian dollars to U.S. dollars is $0.73 to 1.00.

   Fact/Opinion: _____ **Resource:** _____

Reading: Check Facts

Read each research problem. Determine the best, most reliable reference source and write it on the line provided. Also include why you selected that particular source.

1. Nuclear power is economical, although it is potentially dangerous. Where would you look for the most up-to-date information on the dangers of nuclear power?

_____

_____

2. Glacial ice in Alaska is receding due to the climate. Where would you go to determine how much glacial ice was lost last year?

_____

_____

3. A radio news report mentions the excessive drought plaguing Sudan. You are not sure where Sudan is located. Where would you look?

_____

_____

4. You are writing a report on James Watt, the inventor who built the first steam engine. You need to know the dates when he was born and died. Where would you look?

_____

_____

5. A homework assignment requires that you find the origin and definition of several words. Where will you look?

_____

_____

Literary Analysis: Persuasive Essay

Practice

A **persuasive essay** is a brief piece of writing in which an author aims to change readers' minds about a topic. The author may want readers to agree with his or her ideas, for example, that the school needs a new baseball field. The author may want to convince readers to take a certain action, for example, to eat less fat. When writing to convince readers of something, an author will use persuasive techniques, such as the following:

- **Appeals to authority:** The author uses opinions of experts and well-known people to back up his or her ideas.

Example: According to the Surgeon General, every American should get a yearly physical examination.

- **Appeals to emotion:** The author uses words that convey strong feelings.

Example: We will mourn the loss of natural beauty in our town if we foolishly allow the great oaks along Main Street to be heartlessly cut down.

- **Appeals to reason:** The author uses logical arguments backed by facts.

Example: The team has won six games this season.

For each selection, write the type of technique it uses. Then, underline the words that show that it uses this technique.

1. The student council is thrilled to ask all of our classmates to jump in to Spirit Week. We promise you that it will be without a doubt a week you will always remember!

Appeals to _____

2. Why will Spirit Week be so great? We have organized more special events this year than ever before, including a 4-H pig race. We have also included the traditional events: the Spirit Assembly on Tuesday and the dance on Friday. The poll we took shows that 80 percent of the students have enjoyed each of these events in past years.

Appeals to _____

3. In fact, Principal Norris said that this was the best Spirit Week schedule he has ever seen.

Appeals to _____

Name _____ Date _____

Literary Analysis: Persuasive Essay

Assess

Answer the questions by circling the letter of your choice.

1. What is the author's purpose when writing a persuasive essay?

   A. to inform
   B. to entertain
   C. to persuade
   D. to inspire

2. Which persuasive technique does this sentence use?

   Crime is down 40 percent in the city, making this the safest year on record, so we should reelect our mayor.

   A. appeal to emotion
   B. appeal to reason
   C. appeal to authority
   D. all of the above

3. Which persuasive technique does this sentence use?

   I was shivering with fright, and my heart was pounding after reading this terrifying tale, so unless you love to be frightened, do not read it!

   A. appeal to reason
   B. appeal to authority
   C. appeal to emotion
   D. appeal to logic

4. Which persuasive technique does this passage use?

   Students should be able to fill their physical education requirement by taking dance classes. Dance is physically as demanding as any sport, and studies show that young dancers are as fit as young athletes.

   A. appeal to style
   B. appeal to emotion
   C. appeal to authority
   D. appeal to reason

5. Imagine that a local animal shelter was about to be closed down due to a lack of money. The shelter was run by caring people and saved hundreds of animals' lives each year. You decide to write an article about the shelter, hoping to convince people to donate money to it. Write the opening sentence of that article on the lines provided. Use at least one persuasive technique.

   _____

   _____

   _____

Literary Analysis: Diction

A writer's **diction** is his or her word choice and can make writing seem difficult or easy, formal or informal. Diction also includes how sentences are put together. The writer's word choice and diction affect how you respond to a text. Depending on a writer's diction, a selection may be humorous or serious. Character traits can also be revealed through the writer's choice of diction.

A Read the selection. Then, answer the questions that follow.

> The birds were all quiet way up in the trees. It seems the air became all still, and silence wrapped itself all around. A big storm was brewin' off to the southwest, and the skies were fixin' to burst.
> Ma yelled, "You youngins' hurry up—quick, hide in the cellar."

1. Is the writer's choice of words formal or informal? How do you know?

_____

_____

2. Why might a writer have chosen to have a character describe an approaching storm in this way? What does the diction reveal about the character?

_____

_____

3. Rewrite the third sentence using a different style of diction from the writer's.

_____

_____

B Read each sentence, paying special attention to the diction. Then, mark each sentence with an *I* for informal diction and an *F* for formal diction.

1. _____ Rachel knew she had flunked the test before she handed it in.

2. _____ Maxine wore a new green velvet suit to the concert.

3. _____ Well, duh—she should have known he was pulling her leg.

Literary Analysis: Diction

Assess

A Rewrite each sentence to change it from formal to informal diction or informal to formal diction. Then, indicate whether you changed the sentence from formal to informal or informal to formal.

1. John said, "Stop! Who is there?"

_____

2. The taxi driver asked me where I would like to go.

_____

3. Colin trotted down the trail faster than a fox after a mouse.

_____

B Read the selection. Then, answer the questions that follow.

After a day of shining brilliantly in the cloudless sky of the Caribbean, the sun began to slip from the sky. Rays of lingering sunshine slowly advanced and then diminished across the white sandy beach. A gentle rosy glow began in the west along the horizon as the sun began its descent into night. Cool breezes blew across the hot sand as darkness overcame the dusk of day.

1. Was the writer's choice of words formal or informal? How do you know?

_____

_____

2. Why might a writer have chosen to describe the sunset in this way?

_____

_____

3. Rewrite the last sentence using a different style of diction from the writer's.

_____

_____

Literary Analysis: Humorous Essays

Practice

Humorous essays are works of nonfiction meant to amuse readers. Writers may use one or more comic techniques to create an entertaining work. Techniques include

- Presenting an illogical, inappropriate, or unusual situation
- Contrasting reality with characters' views
- Exaggerating the truth or exaggerating the feelings, ideas, and actions of the characters

Read the selection. Then, answer the questions that follow.

Chang dialed the phone and waited to hear "Hello" on the other end of the line. He couldn't wait to ask Marilyn to the dance. As soon as he heard the phone being answered, he quickly asked the question, "Will you go to the dance with me on Friday night at the school gym?"

There was a long pause and at long last he heard, "Why sure I'd like to go."

"Wa, what, what did you say?" asked Chang as he tried to remember what number he had called. Then he remembered the number and the voice. It was neither Marilyn nor her number but his grandmother's! Now he would be taking her to the dance!

1. What kind of situation does Chang find himself in?

_____

_____

2. Does the writer contrast reality with the character's views? How?

_____

_____

3. If the writer were to convey a serious message in this selection, what would it be?

_____

_____

4. Of the two characters in the selection, which was the most humorous? Why?

_____

_____

Literary Analysis: Humorous Essays

Assess

A Read each sentence. Then, decide which of the following responses best applies to each sentence. Write the letter of your choice on the line provided.

A. Presents an illogical, inappropriate, or unusual situation
B. Contrasts reality with characters' mistaken views
C. Exaggerates the truth or exaggerates the feelings, ideas, and actions of the characters

1. _____ Eric found himself knee-deep in ducks without a pond in sight.

2. _____ Uncle Rex was convinced that the lights in the night sky were those of alien beings, not planes landing at the airport.

3. _____ When Max jumped in, the swimming pool seemed to be filled with lime juice and coconuts.

4. _____ Greta was so moved by the opera that she felt she needed to sing the last note from the stage and not hum it in her seat.

5. _____ Gramps put on his helmet every time he went outside because if leaves fell, so could the sky.

B Fill in the blanks with words and phrases to create a humorous essay.

Jasmine and _____ went _____ and found a large

_____. What do we do with this _____ prize?

Fortunately, they _____ and _____ until

_____. Falling _____, I _____. Who

knew what would happen next? This event _____.

Vocabulary: Borrowed and Foreign Words

Practice

The English language includes many **borrowed and foreign words** from other languages. Study the examples in the following chart.

Word and Definition	Borrowed from
taco: tortilla filled with meat and vegetables	Spanish
canyon: long, narrow valley between high cliffs	Spanish
denim: sturdy cotton cloth used in jeans	French
garage: building in which to keep a car	French
piano: large musical instrument	Italian
balcony: platform outside an upper floor of a building	Italian
hurricane: violent storm that begins in tropical waters	American Indian languages
moccasins: soft leather shoes	American Indian languages

Choose a word from the chart to complete each sentence. Write the words on the lines.

1. We keep our car and our bikes in the _____.

2. My feet felt cozy in my new _____.

3. She learned to play the _____ when she was only six.

4. I have a blue _____ jacket that matches my jeans.

5. The _____ damaged many buildings along the coast.

6. I went to a Mexican restaurant and ordered a _____ for lunch.

7. The view from the _____ at our hotel was beautiful.

8. A river flowed through the _____ between the two mountains.

Vocabulary: Borrowed and Foreign Words

Assess

A Write the letter of the correct definition for each word.

1. _____ canyon   **A.** soft leather shoes

2. _____ garage   **B.** tortilla filled with meat and vegetables

3. _____ balcony   **C.** long, narrow valley

4. _____ moccasins   **D.** violent storm

5. _____ hurricane   **E.** sturdy cotton cloth

6. _____ piano   **F.** platform outside an upper floor

7. _____ denim   **G.** building in which to keep a car

8. _____ taco   **H.** large musical instrument

B Complete the paragraph by writing a word from Exercise A in each blank.

My uncle lives in a house located on a mountaintop. He keeps his truck in

a [1] _____ that he built himself. When I visited him, he was

wearing [2] _____ pants and had soft [3] _____

on his feet. He was playing jazz music on his [4] _____. For

lunch, he made me a [5] _____, and we sat on his

[6] _____, enjoying the view of the narrow

[7] _____ below us. As I ate, he was reading the newspaper.

He told me about a [8] _____ that had destroyed property
in Florida.

Grammar: Subjects and Predicates

Practice

Every sentence has two parts: the **subject** and the **predicate.** The **subject** describes whom or what the sentence is about. The **simple subject** is a noun or pronoun that states exactly whom or what the sentence is about.

The predicate is a verb that tells what the subject does, what is done to the subject, or what the condition of the subject is. The simple predicate is a verb or verb phrase that tells what the subject of the sentence does or is.

A   Use each of these subjects in a sentence with the predicates listed.

1. Subject: bird   Predicate: flew

_____

2. Subject: fluffy cat   Predicate: ran

_____

3. Subject: ball   Predicate: threw

_____

4. Subject: movie star   Predicate: signed

_____

5. Subject: cup   Predicate: broke

_____

B   Add the missing subject or predicate to create a complete sentence.

1. _____ was found in the old barn.

2. A black bear _____.

3. The football team _____.

4. _____ ran toward the goalie.

5. Large fishing boats _____.

Grammar: Subjects and Predicates

Assess

A Underline the simple subject once and the predicate twice.

1. The artist painted in her studio all day.

2. Alma ran to the grocery store for milk.

3. The aquarium was filled with tropical fish.

4. The ranger gave an informative presentation about the meadow.

5. The puppies barked when we arrived.

6. The notebook is on the hall table.

7. Raccoons are nocturnal animals.

8. A large turtle was in the middle of the road.

9. Our house is blue with green shutters.

10. Fred fed the hamsters and the fish before leaving the house.

B Use each of these subjects in a sentence with the predicates listed.

1. Subject: parks   Predicate: clean

_____

2. Subject: birthday   Predicate: surprised

_____

3. Subject: fox   Predicate: ran

_____

4. Subject: goat   Predicate: climbed

_____

Grammar: Compound Subjects and Predicates

Practice

A **compound subject** contains two or more subjects that share the same verb. A **compound predicate** contains two or more verbs that share the same subject. Compound subjects and compound predicates are joined by conjunctions such as *and* and *or*.

Compound subject: *Colin* and *Steve* ran the marathon yesterday.

Compound predicate: At the lake, we *swam* and *fished*.

A Read the following sentences. Then, underline the compound subjects.

1. Baseball and football are my favorite sports.

2. Hikers and mountain bikers often share the same trail.

3. The rain and wind caused flood damage.

4. Doors and windows need to be ordered for the house.

5. Trout and pike are in the lake.

6. Canoes and rowboats can be rented by the hour.

7. Sandstone and shale are found in our neighborhood.

8. Books and tapes are available at the library.

B Read the following sentences. Then, underline the compound predicates.

1. I went snowboarding and sprained my ankle this weekend.

2. The waves crested and broke against the rocks.

3. The ring glistened and glimmered in the sun.

4. The tourists stopped and watched the street performer.

5. Christopher wrote and directed the play.

6. The lettuce wilted and drooped on the counter.

7. The team scored two runs and won the game.

8. The students brought crayons but forgot paper.

Grammar: Compound Subjects and Predicates

Assess

A Read the following sentences and underline the compound subject or compound predicate in each. Indicate whether the sentence has a compound subject or compound predicate on the line.

1. Felix and Rex went to the circus in town.

_____

2. They saw many clowns and ate lots of popcorn.

_____

3. Lions and tigers are ferocious animals.

_____

4. The homeowner ordered new rugs and threw out her old rugs.

_____

5. I bought a new bicycle and rode it to school.

_____

6. I collected cans and brought them to the recycling center.

_____

7. Blackberries and raspberries grow by the house.

_____

B Complete each of the following sentences with either a compound subject or compound predicate.

1. _____ went to the holiday celebration.

2. Ethan enjoys _____

3. Our family vacation always includes _____.

4. _____ went to the store to get ingredients for cookies.

5. The movie was about _____.

Grammar: Adjective and Adverb Usage

Practice

Usage problems with **adjectives and adverbs** typically occur when these words are placed incorrectly in a sentence or are confused due to similar meanings. For example, the position of *only* in a sentence can affect the entire meaning of a sentence:

> *Only* he ate the vegetables. (Nobody else ate the vegetables.)

> He *only* ate the vegetables. (He did nothing else with the vegetables.)

> He ate *only* the vegetables. (He ate nothing else.)

These problems can be fixed by determining which word is being modified and the intended meaning of the sentence. Using a dictionary can also help determine meaning.

A Revise the sentences in which the underlined modifier is placed incorrectly. If the sentence is correct, write *correct* on the line.

1. I <u>only</u> ate a little bowl of ice cream.

_____

2. I <u>badly</u> played at the tennis tournament.

_____

3. I made <u>just</u> a huge birthday cake.

_____

4. She had <u>fewer</u> aches and pains after her game than in the past.

_____

B Write a sentence that correctly uses each modifier indicated.

1. less

_____

2. fewer

_____

3. only

_____

Grammar: Adjective and Adverb Usage

Assess

A Read each sentence. Correct the placement of the underlined modifiers by rewriting the sentences on the lines provided. If the sentence is correct, write *correct* on the line.

1. I wanted to play ball <u>badly</u>.

_____

2. Luis asked questions about the test <u>fewer</u> than Shelia.

_____

3. Do you <u>just</u> want to play a game or go fishing?

_____

4. Ryan was <u>bad</u> at climbing trees because he always fell.

_____

5. Samantha ate <u>less</u> at dinner than at lunch.

_____

B Write a sentence that correctly uses each modifier indicated.

1. only

_____

2. less

_____

3. fewer

_____

4. bad

_____

5. just

_____

Spelling: Tools for Checking Spelling

Practice

Most word-processing programs contain a **spell-check** feature. After you type a word incorrectly, the program will mark it. Here are a few things you should remember about spell-checking programs:

- They cannot tell you if you used the wrong homophone.

- They cannot tell you if you typed the wrong word by mistake—for example, *is* instead of *in*.

Use a **dictionary** for spelling by following these steps:

- **Check the first letter of a word.** If you wrote *rench* and it looks wrong, think of other spellings of that "r" sound.

- **Check the other letters.** Once you spell the first sound right, sound out the rest of the word.

A Underline the correctly spelled word in each group.

1. high   hie   hyeh   hy

2. drem   dreme   dreem   dream

3. wi   why   hwy   wy

4. sleap   slep   sleep   slepe

5. stay   sta   stae   stai

B If the underlined word is spelled correctly, write *OK* on the line. If the underlined word is not spelled correctly, write the correct spelling of the word on the line. Use a dictionary as needed.

1. There are <u>ninty</u> chairs in the classroom. _____

2. I did not know who to <u>beleve</u>. _____

3. My <u>height</u> has increased two inches this year. _____

4. The weatherman <u>siad</u> it would rain today. _____

5. Where <u>were</u> you after school today? _____

Spelling: Tools for Checking Spelling

Assess

A Determine if each word is spelled correctly. If the word is spelled correctly, write *OK* on the line. If the word is not spelled correctly, write the correct spelling of the word on the line. Use a dictionary as needed.

1. tomb _____

2. theef _____

3. couzin _____

4. Fryday _____

5. present _____

6. victum _____

7. batterys _____

8. drouned _____

9. receive _____

10. werld _____

B Read and edit the following paragraph. Find and cross out the seven misspelled words. Then, spell the words correctly on the lines after the paragraph.

This past Sunda, Laura went to the beech. She watched the childrin play in the sand. She saw many fishing bots in the ocean. She enjoyd swimming in the watter the best. Laura had a grate day.

1. _____

2. _____

3. _____

4. _____

5. _____

6. _____

7. _____

Writing: Persuasive Letter

Practice

A **persuasive letter** uses the techniques of persuasion to convince readers to believe or act in a certain way. Persuasive techniques include the following:

- appeals to authority, using opinions of experts or well-known people
- appeals to emotion, using words that convey strong feelings
- appeals to reason, using logical arguments backed by facts

Read the persuasive letter. Then, answer the questions and complete the activities that follow.

Dear Citizens,

To some of you, voting for elected officials may seem like a waste of time. After all, a ballot is just a piece of paper with boxes on it. But is it merely a piece of paper? To me, it is something much more—a chance to decide the future and a reflection of democracy.

Voting is a right for all citizens living in our country. This right is ensured by the Constitution and Bill of Rights. Yet, many citizens do not exercise this right. Corporations and public service groups spend large sums of money reminding citizens to vote. Although there is no financial profit in getting people to vote, money continues to be spent. Why?

Voting is your chance for your voice to be heard. We are part of a democracy, and it is our responsibility as members to vote. It is your opportunity to determine your future. An unused ballot is a silent voice forever.

A Fellow Citizen

1. Use the following chart to identify the persuasive points the writer made. Indicate which persuasive technique each point is an example of.

Points	Persuasive Techniques

2. Write a sentence that could be added to this letter that includes an appeal to emotion.

_____

_____

Writing: Persuasive Letter

Assess

Circle one of these topics for a persuasive letter. Then, answer the questions and complete the activities that follow.

Effectiveness of recycling

Healthy cafeteria food offerings

Charging admission to school sports events

Oil exploration in the sea

1. State your opinion on your topic.

_____

_____

2. Complete the following chart, listing your points and the persuasive techniques you will use.

Points	Persuasive Techniques

3. What language will you use to stir readers' emotions?

_____

_____

4. Write a conclusion to your persuasive letter.

_____

_____

_____

Writing: Adaptation

Practice

An **adaptation** is a retelling of a story in words that are appropriate for the readers. An adaptation reflects the needs and interests of an audience. For example, words and concepts are often simplified.

A Read the selection. Then, rewrite the passage to adapt it for a group of preschoolers.

Currently, more than 58 million dogs live as pets in our country. Domesticated, or pet, dogs are all members of *Canis familiaris*. This scientific name means "familiar dog." Cave paintings dating from over 5,000 years ago have been found showing humans and dogs together. Throughout history, dogs have helped people by being guide dogs, messengers, watch dogs, and companions. Today, there are hundreds of breeds of dogs that do many jobs, but the most important job of all is family pet!

_____

_____

_____

_____

_____

_____

_____

B Read each of the following sentences. Then, list reference sources that would be helpful in writing an adaptation.

1. We can reduce waste and conserve landfill space by developing recycling technology to make new products from old things.

_____

2. Herds of horses, descended from Spanish herds, once freely roamed the vast ranges of the American West.

_____

Writing: Adaptation

Assess

A   Read the selection. Then, write an adaptation on the lines that follow. Identify your audience and list it on the first line.

We would be traveling on an extended journey by ocean liner to begin a new life in America. How excited we were the day that Papa came home clutching the tickets to our adventure. We would be leaving from Southampton, England, on the maiden voyage of the *R.M.S. Titanic* in April 1912. Several days were spent anguishing what would go into the trunk that would accompany us. Each item that might go into the trunk was carefully considered because space was limited.

Audience: _____

_____

_____

_____

_____

_____

_____

B   Answer each of the following questions. Write the letter of your answer on the line.

1. _____ If you were adapting a scientific article from a journal so elementary students could understand the main ideas, which of the following sources would be helpful?

A. a dictionary, a college science book, and an almanac

B. an encyclopedia, a dictionary, and a health book

C. a reliable online source, a dictionary, and an encyclopedia

D. a manual, a directory, and a science book

2. _____ If you were adapting a fairy tale for very young children, where would you look to find synonyms?

A. a thesaurus

B. a literary guide

C. a directory

D. a rhyming dictionary

Writing: Comparison-and-Contrast Essay

Practice

A **comparison-and-contrast essay** describes the similarities and differences between two or more related subjects. A good comparison-and-contrast essay has the following features:

- a topic that includes two or more things that are neither nearly identical nor extremely different
- details that illustrate the similarities and details that illustrate the differences
- an organization that highlights the points of comparison

Read the passage. Then, complete the activity that follows.

Soccer and football are two popular sports. The two sports are similar in many ways. In both sports, two teams try to move a ball down the field to their opponent's goal. In both sports, players need to be able keep up a fast pace. Teamwork is important in both sports. A goal cannot be made without the help of the entire team.

While I like both sports, I prefer soccer over football. Soccer is nearly constant action. In football, there is a pause in action after each play. In football, plays usually end in large pileups of players. A spectator can easily lose sight of the ball. Although both are exciting sports, soccer is my favorite.

1. Circle the categories in which soccer and football are similar. Underline the categories in which soccer and football are different.

the goal of the game   the amount of action

the need for speed and stamina   teamwork

the ease in following the game

2. List two similarities between soccer and football. _____

_____

_____

3. List two differences between soccer and football. _____

_____

_____

Writing: Comparison-and-Contrast Essay

Assess

Choose one of the following topics or a topic of your own for a comparison-and-contrast essay. Then, complete the activities that follow.

dogs or cats as pets   the seasons of summer or winter
two action movies

1. List the topic and the categories that you will use to explain the similarities and differences. Choose categories that will help explain why you prefer one of the two items being compared.

_____

_____

_____

_____

2. Fill in the following chart with details for each category you have listed in the first item.

Category		

3. Write the opening paragraph of a comparison-and-contrast essay. Include what is being compared. Explain which of the two items you prefer. Then, write the second paragraph, comparing the two items using the first category.

_____

_____

_____

_____

Reading: Drawing Conclusions

Practice

A **conclusion** is a logical decision or opinion you reach by pulling together several facts or details. You can ask questions to identify important details to form conclusions. By connecting the details, you can draw conclusions.

A   Read this stanza from "The Village Blacksmith" by Henry Wadsworth Longfellow. Then, answer the questions that follow.

> Under a spreading chestnut tree
>   The village smithy stands;
> The smith, a mighty man is he,
>   With large and sinewy hands;
> And the muscles of his brawny arms
>   Are as strong as iron bands.

1. What details does the poet include and emphasize?

_____

_____

2. How are the details related?

_____

_____

3. What do the details mean altogether?

_____

_____

B   Read this haiku by Buson. Then, answer the questions that follow.

> Deep in a windless
> wood, not one leaf dares to move . . . .
> Something is afraid.

1. Circle the important details. What do the details suggest?

_____

2. What conclusion can you draw about the details and the poet's meaning?

Reading: Drawing Conclusions

Read the selection. Then, circle the letter that answers each question.

In the harbor between New York and New Jersey lies Ellis Island. Operating between 1892 and 1954, Ellis Island welcomed approximately 12 million steerage and third-class passengers arriving by ship to America. Passengers arriving in steerage and third class had often endured two weeks or more of seasickness in cramped, crowded conditions. Most had little in their home countries and had come to America in hopes of an opportunity to have a better life.

Upon arrival, passengers had to pass a medical examination before being allowed into America. Immigrants were required to walk up a long flight of stairs as doctors watched for signs of lameness and breathing problems. Immigrants also had their eyes, ears, noses, and throats checked for difficulties or sickness. Those who were sick were required to stay on Ellis Island until they were well. Those who failed to recover were sent back to their home countries.

1. Which conclusion can you make about one of the primary functions of Ellis Island?

   A. It was a place to dock the many ships arriving with immigrants.

   B. It provided a location to screen immigrants for medical problems.

   C. It was a location to provide much needed food and rest for the immigrants.

   D. It provided a place for sick immigrants to recover.

2. What can you conclude about the passengers arriving at Ellis Island?

   A. All were wealthy and could afford to travel.

   B. All were healthy because they had adequate food and space on the voyage.

   C. Most were poor and often sick on arrival.

   D. Many went back to their home countries.

3. What can you conclude about the doctors at Ellis Island?

   A. Doctors determined whether or not immigrants were allowed into the country.

   B. Doctors had well-equipped offices.

   C. Doctors were well educated.

   D. All doctors were immigrants.

Reading: Recognize Propaganda Techniques

Practice

Learning to recognize propaganda techniques and faulty reasoning is important so as to not draw false conclusions. **Propaganda** is information that is one-sided or misleading. **Faulty reasoning** is an argument that does not follow the rules of logic. An **advertisement** is a paid message intended to attract customers to buy products or services. The language and artwork in advertisements may contain hidden messages or other persuasive techniques. Here are some propaganda techniques:

- **Broad generalization:** Claims that cannot be proved, such as "It's out of this world!"

- **Hidden messages:** Pictures or words that convey an idea without stating it directly. For example, a picture of an Olympic runner, suggesting you'll be a winner if you wear a particular brand of shoes

- **Loaded language:** Words that appeal to our emotions, for example, "It's a miracle cream!"

- **Bandwagon appeals**: Implying everyone does it, as in "Millions use VitaVite daily."

- **Faulty reasoning:** Using unrelated or unconnected details as support. For example, more people have cats than dogs, so cats must be easier to care for.

Read the advertisement. Then, answer the questions that follow.

> Shiny, shiny Sparkle Bright,
> Leaves everyone's teeth so clean and white.
> A toothpaste that is out of sight,
> Get some at the store tonight.

1. Based on these lines, what conclusion can you draw about what the company that produces Sparkle Bright wants you to do?

_____

_____

2. List which propaganda techniques the advertisement uses. Be sure to use examples.

_____

_____

Reading: Recognize Propaganda Techniques

Assess

A Read each of the following advertising statements. Identify the propaganda technique from the box and write it on the line.

broad generalizations	hidden messages	loaded language
bandwagon appeals	faulty reasoning	

1. "It's the fountain of youth in a bottle."

_____

2. "Anyone who is anybody drives the new, luxurious Diamond."

_____

3. "Finally, an answer to all your everyday problems!"

_____

4. "More people have cable modems, so it must be the only way to communicate."

_____

5. "Wearing Tumble Togs will make you an Olympic gymnast."

_____

B Create your own advertisement for a product that contains a propaganda technique. Write your advertisement on the following lines.

_____

_____

_____

_____

_____

C List the propaganda technique you used.

_____

_____

Literary Analysis: Forms of Poetry

Practice

There are many different **forms of poetry**. A poet will follow different rules depending on the structure of the poem.

- A **lyric poem** expresses the poet's thoughts and feelings about a single image or idea in vivid, musical language.

- In a **concrete poem,** the poet arranges the letters and lines to create a visual image that suggests the poem's subject.

- **Haiku** is a traditional form of Japanese poetry that is often about nature. The first line always has five syllables, the second line has seven syllables, and the third line has five syllables.

Read this stanza from "The Tide Rises, the Tide Falls" by Henry Wadsworth Longfellow. Then, answer the following questions.

> The tide rises, the tide falls,
> The twilight darkens, the curlew calls;
> Along the sea sands damp and brown
> The traveler hastens toward the town,
> And the tide rises, the tide falls.

1. What type of poetic structure did the poet use? List several details that support your answer.

_____

_____

2. Select one of the images from the poem. Write a line that might be part of a haiku based on this image.

_____

_____

3. Using an image from the poem, decide what shape you would select if you were writing a concrete poem. Explain why you selected the image.

_____

_____

Literary Analysis: Forms of Poetry

Assess

Read each statement. Circle the letter of the choice that best completes each statement or answers the question.

1. A _____ expresses a poet's thoughts and feelings about a single image or idea in vivid, musical language.

   A. lyric poem   **C.** ballad poem
   B. concrete poem   **D.** haiku

2. The _____ is a traditional form of Japanese poetry that is often about nature.

   A. lyric poem   **C.** ballad poem
   B. concrete poem   **D.** haiku

3. A _____ has the letters and lines arranged to create a shape.

   A. lyric poem   **C.** ballad poem
   B. concrete poem   **D.** haiku

4. In a _____ the first line has five syllables, the second line has seven syllables, and the third line has five syllables.

   A. lyric poem   **C.** ballad poem
   B. concrete poem   **D.** haiku

5. A _____ uses a combination of rhythm and sound to produce musical language.

   A. lyric poem   **C.** ballad poem
   B. concrete poem   **D.** haiku

6. Which of the following lines is most likely from a haiku?

   A. When lilacs last in the   **C.** When the frost in on
       dooryard bloom'd   the pumpkin'
   B. Fall into water   **D.** I wandered as lonely as a cloud

Literary Analysis: Figurative Language

Practice

Figurative language is language that is not meant to be taken literally. Writers use figures of speech to express ideas in vivid and imaginative ways. Common figures of speech include the following:

- A **simile** compares two unlike things using a word such as *like* or *as*.
- A **metaphor** compares two unlike things by stating that one thing is another thing.
- In an **extended metaphor**, several related comparisons extend over a number of lines.
- **Personification** gives human characteristics to a nonhuman subject.
- A **symbol** is an object, person, animal, place, or image that represents something else.

A Read each line to determine which figure of speech has been used. Then, write the figure of speech on the line.

1. The wind howled like a wild goblin.

_____

2. The trees were raining tears of leaves.

_____

3. The eagle on the seal of the United States represents strength.

_____

B Write an example of figurative language on each of the following lines.

1. simile

_____

2. metaphor

_____

3. personification

_____

Literary Analysis: Figurative Language

Assess

A Read the following sentences. Then, write whether the sentence contains a simile or a metaphor.

1. He was as nervous as a long-tailed cat in a room full of rocking chairs.

_____

2. My bed is my magic carpet to dreamland.

_____

3. He ran the mile like a gazelle on the plains.

_____

4. The lessons of our lives are forged in the links of lasting memories.

_____

5. The dawning of a new day is like a blank page in a diary.

_____

B Read the following sentences. Then, write whether the sentence contains a personification or refers to a symbol.

1. The snow tickled my nose.

_____

2. An eagle with wings spread grasps arrows in its claws.

_____

3. The summer breeze kissed my face.

_____

4. A raven sits on a tombstone.

_____

5. The lawn mower coughed to life.

_____

Literary Analysis: Narrative Poetry

Practice

Narrative poetry combines elements of fiction and poetry to tell a story. It also

- includes characters, setting, plot, conflict, and point of view.
- uses sound devices such as rhythm and rhyme to create a musical quality.
- incorporates figurative language to create memorable images, or word pictures.

Narrative poetry is well suited to a wide range of stories. For example, narrative poems may be about bold heroes or wonderful deeds. Everyday stories about ordinary people can also be recounted in narrative poetry.

Read this stanza from "The Pied Piper of Hamelin" by Robert Browning. Then, answer the questions that follow.

> Hamelin Town's in Brunswick,
> By famous Hanover city;
> The river Weser, deep and wide,
> Washes its wall on the southern side;
> A pleasanter spot you never spied;
> But, when begins my ditty,
> Almost five hundred years ago,
> To see the townsfolk suffer so
> From vermin, was a pity.

1. What details describe the setting?

_____

_____

2. What conflict is presented?

_____

3. Create an example of figurative language that might appear in this stanza. Figurative language includes similes, metaphors, personification, and symbols.

_____

_____

Name _____ Date _____

Literary Analysis: Narrative Poetry

Assess

A Read the following questions. Circle the letter of the choice that best completes each statement.

1. Narrative poetry combines the elements of _____.

   A. short stories and nonfiction   **C.** short stories and poetry
   B. fiction and poetry   **D.** fiction and nonfiction

2. Sound devices such as _____ are used in narrative poetry.

   A. rhythm and language   **C.** rhyme and details
   B. music and language   **D.** rhythm and rhyme

3. Narrative poetry uses _____ language.

   A. formal   **C.** figurative
   B. conversational   **D.** romantic

4. Characters in narrative poems are _____.

   A. ordinary and common   **C.** historical
   B. larger than life   **D.** both A and B

5. All narrative poems _____.

   A. have a happy ending   **C.** use rhythm and rhyme
   B. have a character who speaks **D.** tell a story

B Read the following lines from "The Cremation of Sam McGee" by Robert Service. Then, answer the question.

> On a Christmas Day we were mushing our way
>   over the Dawson Trail.
> Talk of your cold! Through the parka's fold
>   it stabbed like a driven nail.

What elements of the narrative poem are in these lines?

_____

_____

Vocabulary: Roots *-fer-* and *trans-*

Knowing the meanings of word roots and prefixes can help you to figure out the meanings of many new words. Study these examples.

Root or Prefix	Meaning	Word Containing Root or Prefix	Meaning of Word
-fer-	"to bring" or "to carry"	ferry (*fer + ry*, an ending that means "something that does this")	a boat that carries people and often vehicles
trans-	"across" or "through"	transmit (*trans + mit*, a root that means "to send")	to send from one person to another across a distance

Write the meaning of each word. Use a dictionary to check your meanings. Then, write a sentence using each word.

1. *trans + atlantic* = **transatlantic**, which means _____.

_____

2. *trans + port* ("to carry") = **transport**, which means _____.

_____

3. *con* ("together") + *fer* = **confer**, which means _____.

_____

4. *of + fer* = **offer**, which means _____.

_____

5. *trans + fer* = **transfer**, which means _____.

_____

Vocabulary: Roots -*fer*- and *trans*-

Assess

Use the root meanings, as well as context clues, to figure out the meaning of each word in boldface type. Write your definitions on the lines provided.

1. The wicked elf **transformed** the prince into an ugly frog.

   _____

2. Can you **translate** this Greek poem into English for me?

   _____

3. Please **refer** to Chapter 2 to find the answers to your questions.

   _____

4. What **inference** can you make about the character, based on his words and actions?

   _____

5. When the Green Line bus arrives at the station, **transfer** to the Red Line bus.

   _____

Grammar: Infinitives and Infinitive Phrases

Practice

An **infinitive** is a verb form that acts as a noun, an adjective, or an adverb. An infinitive usually begins with the word *to.*

> Some cats like *to play.* (infinitive as a noun serving as the object of the verb *like*)
> *To learn* French is my goal. (infinitive as a noun serving as the subject of the sentence)
> Soccer is the game *to play.* (infinitive as an adjective modifying the noun *game*)
> Everyone waited *to hear.* (infinitive as an adverb modifying the verb *waited*)

An **infinitive phrase** is an infinitive plus its own modifiers or complements.

> Some cats like *to play all the time.* (phrase serving as object of the verb *like*)
> *To learn French in France* is my goal. (phrase serving as the subject of the sentence)
> Soccer is the game *to play in the spring.* (phrase modifying the noun *spring*)
> Everyone waited *to hear the news.* (phrase modifying the verb *waited*)

A Read the following sentences. Then, underline the infinitives and circle any infinitive phrases.

1. Rudolf wanted to play hockey this winter.

2. Beverly started to cook the peas and carrots.

3. To err is human, to forgive divine.

4. My dog likes to swim in the lake.

B Underline the infinitive phrase. Write on the line the part of speech the infinitive phrase serves.

1. Jerry likes to play golf everyday. _____

2. We went to listen to the opera. _____

3. I like to read stories to my brother. _____

Grammar: Infinitives and Infinitive Phrases

Assess

A Underline the infinitive or infinitive phrase in each of the following sentences.

1. Her goal, to write a novel, was never realized.

2. The purpose of the class was to teach conservation skills.

3. To achieve the highest grade, the students created a multimedia presentation.

4. Alex and Anna wanted to ride their bikes to the beach.

5. Felix began to paint the house last summer.

B Underline the infinitive or infinitive phrase in each of the following sentences. Write on the line the part of speech the infinitive phrase serves as.

1. All the campers wanted to swim in the lake. _____

2. The tailor made the dress to fit the princess. _____

3. The sound vibrations caused the table to shake. _____

4. Ethan was excited to fish in the lake. _____

5. The student artists began to paint watercolors. _____

C Use the following infinitives to write a complete sentence on each line.

1. to eat

_____

2. to run

_____

3. to jump

_____

Grammar: Appositives and Appositive Phrases

Practice

An **appositive** is a noun or pronoun that is placed after another noun or pronoun to identify, rename, or explain it. In the example, the appositive is underlined.

> Jeff, the <u>running back</u>, caught the ball and ran.

An **appositive phrase** is a noun or pronoun, along with any modifiers, that is placed after another noun or pronoun to identify, rename, or explain it.

> Maxine, <u>a kind and generous neighbor next door</u>, watched our house.

Appositives and appositive phrases are set off with commas or dashes.

A   Read the following sentences. Underline the appositive or appositive phrase in each sentence. Then, draw an arrow to the word each one modifies. The first one is done for you.

1. Servette, <u>who worked at the corner candy store</u>, always gave samples.

2. Bonnie, my cousin, lived on a farm.

3. The math teacher, Mr. Chang, was my homeroom teacher for the year.

4. Mark, the pitcher, threw many fast balls during the game.

5. The Garcias, our friends, invited us to the lake to go fishing.

6. Ms. Steffa, the school principal, canceled afterschool activities due to the weather.

7. Winnie the Pooh, a fictitious character, had many adventures with Christopher Robin.

8. Mollie and Max, golden retrievers, were the winners of the dog show.

9. My cat, Domino, likes to sleep with me.

10. The Racing Rocket, a new thriller roller coaster, is now open at the park.

Grammar: Appositives and Appositive Phrases

A In each sentence, underline the appositive or appositive phrase. Then, circle the noun that the appositive phrase identifies or explains.

1. Ernesto, my cousin, likes baseball and hockey.

2. A large black cloud, a sign of a thunderstorm, appeared in the sky.

3. William Shakespeare, a playwright and poet, wrote during the sixteenth and seventeenth centuries.

4. Only a few animals, mostly dogs and cats, were found.

5. Pete, my brother's friend, makes the best popcorn over a campfire.

B Use each phrase as an appositive phrase in a sentence. Correctly punctuate each sentence.

1. a treasure map

_____

2. a blanket of snow

_____

3. my best friend

_____

4. an inspiration to all soccer players

_____

5. prize-winning Arabian horses

_____

Grammar: Verbals

Practice

A **verbal** is any verb that is used in a sentence not as a verb but as another part of speech. **Participles** are one type of verbal. **Present participles** end in *-ing*. **Past participles** usually end in *-ed*. The **past participles** of some verbs are irregular, formed with endings other than *-ed*. A participial phrase consists of a present or past participle and its modifiers or complements. The entire phrase acts as an adjective, modifying a noun or pronoun.

Choppy: Albina mixed the dough. She added flour and salt.
Combined: Mixing the dough, Albina added flour and salt.

A Read the following sentences. Then, underline the single participle or participial phrase in each sentence.

1. Karen wore running shoes for the race.

2. Alicia modeled her dancing costume.

3. The bottled water was cold.

4. We arranged a walking tour of the museum.

5. The canned tuna will be on sale.

B Read the following sentences. Then, combine the choppy sentences into one sentence that uses a single participle or participial phrase. Write the sentence on the line.

1. The trophy glowed. It was won by our team.

_____

2. The snow melted. It made puddles in the street.

_____

3. The road was winding. It led to the park.

_____

4. The hikers were disoriented. They returned to the trail.

_____

Grammar: Verbals

Assess

A Read the following sentences. Then, underline the single participle or participial phrase in each sentence.

1. The determined campers put their tents up in the rain.

2. The grinning winners of the pie-eating contest sat down.

3. Swimmers, experienced and inexperienced, participated in the meet.

4. Frightened chipmunks ran across the lawn.

5. The picture of a laughing cow appears on cheese.

6. Exhausted children need to go to bed early.

B Read the following sentences. Then, underline the single participle or participial phrase. Write whether the participle is present or past on the line provided.

1. Satisfied, the shopper walked away with the lamp. _____

2. A banging sound came from under the hood. _____

3. The ground beef was used to make hamburgers. _____

4. Deep within the cave, we heard a fluttering sound. _____

5. Simplified instructions came with the mixer. _____

6. A muffled bark came from the covered basket. _____

7. Enthused, Billy began to rake the leaves. _____

8. Relieved, the mother hugged the lost child. _____

Name _____ Date _____

Poetry can take many different forms. Each form has a specific type of structure stemming from different rules.

- A **lyric poem** expresses the poet's thoughts and feelings about a single image or idea in vivid, musical language.

- In a **concrete poem,** the poet arranges the letters and lines to create a visual image that suggests the poem's subject.

- **Haiku** is a traditional form of Japanese poetry that is often about nature. The first line always has five syllables, the second line has seven syllables, and the third line has five syllables.

Select one of the forms of poetry to write. Then, complete the exercises.

1. In the following chart, list some details you might want to include in your poem. Be sure to consider the type of poem you selected.

Subject: _____

Vivid Descriptions	Action Words	Thoughts	Feelings

2. Review the characteristics of your poem's structure. Use these characteristics to write a draft of your poem.

_____

_____

_____

_____

3. Choose a creative title for your poem.

_____

Writing: Poem

A Select one of these poems type to write: lyric poem, concrete poem, or haiku. Then, complete the exercises that follow.

1. List the characteristics of the poem you choose.

_____

_____

_____

2. Using the following chart, list details that could be included in your poem.

Subject: _____

Vivid Descriptions	Action Words	Thoughts	Feelings

3. Write your poem on the following lines.

_____

_____

_____

_____

_____

_____

_____

_____

_____

Writing: Metaphor

Practice

A **metaphor** is a figure of speech in which one thing is spoken of as though it were something else. Unlike a simile, which compares two things using *like* or *as,* a metaphor implies a comparison between them. For example, in "She is the sunshine of my life," a person is metaphorically spoken of as if she were sunshine. An **extended metaphor** continues the comparison by adding more details of comparison. For example, "She is the sunshine of my life. Her presence gives light and warmth."

A Read each sentence. Write what thing is being compared to something. Then write to what that thing is being compared.

1. His angry words were a blast of cold air in her face. _____

2. The silence was a brick wall between us. _____

3. The upcoming test hung over my head, a black cloud that followed wherever

 I went. _____

4. The quiet lake was a shining mirror, reflecting the trees lining its shore and

 the puffy white clouds in sky. _____

5. The huge golden coin slowly sunk below the horizon, bringing on night.

 _____

6. Overhead, millions of tiny diamonds sparkled in the night sky.

 _____

7. His room was a peaceful island in the middle of a stormy sea. _____

8. The mist settled over the ground, a cold wet blanket that clung to the skin

 and chilled the bones. _____

B Choose two of the metaphors from exercise A. Create extended metaphors by writing one
 or two sentences with more details of the comparison.

_____

_____

_____

Writing: Metaphor

Assess

A Read the following poem. Then answer the questions that follow.

FOG
by Carl Sandburg

¹The fog comes
²on little cat feet.

³It sits looking
⁴over harbor and city
⁵on silent haunches
⁶and then moves on.

1. Explain the metaphor in lines 1–2 of this poem. _____

2. Explain the extended metaphor in lines 3–4. _____

3. What details in lines 5–6 continue the extended metaphor? _____

B Write an extended metaphor about one of the following items. Decide to what you will compare the item. You might use an object, an idea, or a living creature. Then, list several details or points of comparison and write the metaphor using vivid and descriptive language.

love	hope	beauty
a summer thunderstorm	friendship	a winter storm

1. Write the object, idea, or living creature to which you will compare the item.

_____

2. List several details or points of comparison. _____

_____

3. Write the extended metaphor using vivid and descriptive language.

_____

_____

_____

_____

Writing: Writing for Assessment

You take essay tests and standardized writing tests that evaluate your writing skills. **Writing for assessment** often depends on specific instructions. Time and space in which to write are often limited. Your essay should include the following elements:

- a position that address the writing prompt
- clear, concise writing
- evidence supporting the main points of the essay
- consistent organization
- error-free writing

Write an essay in response to the following prompt:

Choose two qualities that you believe all successful students should possess. Discuss these qualities as they relate to students.

1. What key words in the prompt identify the issue at hand?

_____

2. Gather details and list the key details for your essay.

_____

_____

3. Use the details to find a focus for your essay. Write a sentence that states your main thesis.

_____

4. Add details to strengthen your essay. What facts, examples, or descriptions can you add?

_____

_____

5. Write a concluding statement.

_____

Writing: Writing for Assessment

A Read the prompt and answer the questions that follow.

Your community has received a grant to improve the downtown area. Write a letter to the planning board detailing how you think the funds could best be spent. Explain why you feel this is the best use of the funds.

1. Write a sentence that would function as your opening statement.

_____

2. List several examples you would use to support your statement.

_____

_____

_____

3. Write a concluding statement.

_____

_____

B Read the prompt and answer the questions that follow.

Today, more visitors see America's national parks than ever before. But our national parks have problems: pollution, traffic, and overdue maintenance. Federal funding is not enough to pay for these problems. Write an essay in which you discuss whether (1) park entrance fees should be increased to help cover the shortfall or (2) more federal tax dollars should be spent.

1. Write a sentence that would function as your opening statement.

_____

2. List several examples you would use to support your statement.

_____

_____

_____

3. Write a concluding statement.

_____

Reading Skill: Paraphrase

Practice

To **paraphrase** means to restate something in your own words to make the meaning clear to yourself. Paraphrasing can often help you understand poetry, which sometimes contains difficult passages and ideas. Follow these steps:

- Look up unfamiliar words and replace them with words you know.
- Look for the main idea of the passage.
- Restate the line or passage using your own everyday words.
- Reread the passage to make sure that your version accurately restates it.

A   Read the lines from "This Moment Yearning and Thoughtful" by Walt Whitman. Then, answer the questions. Use your dictionary if you need help.

> This moment yearning and thoughtful sitting alone,
> It seems to me there are other men in other lands yearning
>   and thoughtful,
> It seems to me I can look over and behold them in Germany,
>   Italy, France, Spain,
> Or far, far away, in China, or in Russia or Japan, talking other
>   dialects,
> And it seems to me if I could know those men I should become
>   attached to them as I do to men in my own lands,
> O I know we should be brethren. . . .

1. What is the meaning of the word *yearning*?

_____

2. What is the meaning of the word *behold*?

_____

3. What is the meaning of the word *brethren*?

_____

4. What is the main idea of this passage?

_____

B   Write your own paraphrase of the lines from "This Moment Yearning and Thoughtful."

_____

_____

Reading Skill: Paraphrase

Assess

A Read the lines from "The Ecchoing Green" by William Blake. Then, answer the questions. Use your dictionary if you need help in answering any of the questions.

> The Sun does arise,
> And make happy the skies.
> The merry bells ring
> To welcome the Spring.
> The sky-lark and thrush,
> The birds of the bush,
> Sing louder around,
> To the bells' cheerful sound.
> While our sports shall be seen
> On the Ecchoing Green.
> Till the little ones weary
> No more can be merry.
> The sun does descend,
> And our sports have an end. . . .

1. The word *ecchoing* is most likely an old-fashioned spelling of which

present-day word? _____

2. A thrush is most likely what kind of animal? _____

3. What is the most likely meaning of the word *descend* as it is used

in the poem? _____

4. What is the likely meaning of "Green" in this poem?

_____

5. What is the main idea of this poem?

_____

B Write your own paraphrase of the lines from "The Ecchoing Green."

_____

_____

Literary Analysis: Sound Devices

Practice

Poets use different combinations and patterns of word sounds to create musical effects that appeal to the ear. Here are some of the most common **sound devices:**

- **Onomatopoeia** is the use of words whose sounds suggest their meaning.
  Example: boom, hiss
- **Alliteration** is the repetition of sounds at the beginning of words.
  Example: the sweet sounds of summer
- **Repetition** is the repeated use of words, phrases, or rhythms
  Example: As of some one gently rapping, rapping at my chamber door.
  "'Tis some visitor," I muttered, tapping at my chamber door. . . ."
- **Rhyme** is the repetition of sounds at the *ends* of words.
  Example: night/flight, rise/prize, real/feel

A In the space provided, identify the sound device or devices used in each sentence.

1. _____ O Cressid! O false Cressid! false, false, false!

2. _____ The moan of doves in . . . ancient oaks . . .

3. _____ Little Lamb who made thee?

4. _____ How sad and mad and bad it was!

B Read the lines from "The Raven" by Edgar Allan Poe. Then, circle the letter of the best answer for each question.

¹Deep into that darkness peering, long I stood there wondering, fearing,
²Doubting, dreaming dreams no mortal ever dared to dream before
³But the silence was unbroken, and the darkness gave no token,
⁴And the only word there spoken was the whispered word, "Lenore!"
⁵This I whispered, and an echo murmured back the word, "Lenore!"
⁶Merely this and nothing more.

1. Line 2 of the poem contains an example of which of the following?

   A. onomatopoeia   **C.** repetition
   B. alliteration   **D.** rhyme

2. Which of the following words in the poem is used as part of a pattern of repetition?

   A. doubting   **C.** Lenore
   B. silence   **D.** unbroken

Literary Analysis: Sound Devices

Assess

A In the space provided, identify the sound device or devices used in each sentence.

1. _____ Let the rain kiss you / Let the rain beat upon your head. . . .

2. _____ Seven nights they sleep / Among shadows deep. . . .

3. _____ Sweet sleep come to me. . . .

4. _____ Once again the bell clanged. . . .

B Read the lines from "The Raven" by Edgar Allan Poe. Then circle the letter fo the best answer for each question.

> [1]While I nodded, nearly napping, suddenly there came a tapping,
> [2]As of some one gently rapping, rapping at my chamber door.
> [3]"'Tis some visitor," I muttered, "tapping at my chamber door—
> [4]Only this, and nothing more." . . .
> [5]Let me see then, what [this] is, and this mystery explore—
> [6]Let my heart be still a moment and this mystery explore—
> [7]'Tis the wind and nothing more. . . .

1. Which of the words in this passage is the best example of onomatopoeia?

   A. tapping   **C.** wind
   B. door   **D.** moment

2. Two pairs of lines—lines 2 and 3 and lines 5 and 6—end with two-word phrases that are examples of which of the following?

   A. rhyme   **C.** alliteration
   B. repetition   **D.** onomatopoeia

3. The *last* words of which two lines do *not* rhyme with each other?

   A. 1 and 2   **C.** 5 and 6
   B. 2 and 3   **D.** 6 and 7

4. Which line contains an example of alliteration?

   A. 1   **C.** 5
   B. 3   **D.** 7

Literary Analysis: Rhythm and Rhyme

Practice

Rhythm and rhyme make poetry musical. **Rhythm** is a poem's pattern of stressed (´) and unstressed (˘) syllables. The stressed syllables receive more emphasis than the unstressed ones.

Meter is a poem's rhythmical pattern. It is measured in feet, or single units of stressed and unstressed syllables.

Rhyme is the repetition of sounds at the ends of words. In the following example, the words *sire* and *fire* create a rhyme.

> Half | in dreams | he saw | his sire
>
> With | his great | hands full | of fire.

A Mark the stressed (´) and unstressed (˘) syllables in the following lines. Then, show the meter by drawing a vertical rule after each foot.

1. I'm Nobody! Who are you?

2. She was a child and I was a child.

3. And I looked at it, and I thought a bit, and I looked at my frozen chum.

B Read this stanza from Edgar Allan Poe's "The Raven." Underline the rhyming words.

> Once upon a midnight dreary, while I pondered, weak and weary,
>
> Over many a quaint and curious volume of forgotten lore—
>
> While I nodded, nearly napping, suddenly there came a tapping,
>
> As of some one gently rapping, rapping at my chamber door—
>
> "'Tis some visitor," I muttered, "tapping at my chamber door—
>
> Only this and nothing more."

Literary Analysis: Rhythm and Rhyme

Assess

A Read this stanza from "Aftermath" by Henry Wadsworth Longfellow. Underline the rhyming words. Circle the words that are repeated.

When the summer fields are mown,

When the birds are fledged and flown,

    And the dry leaves strew the path;

With the falling of the snow,

With the cawing of the crow,

Once again the fields we mow

    And gather in the aftermath.

B Mark the stressed (') and unstressed (˘) syllables in the following lines. Then, show the meter by drawing a vertical rule after each foot.

1. It was many and many a year ago / In a kingdom by the sea

2. And this was the reason that, long ago / In this kingdom by the sea

C Complete the following sentences.

1. _____ is a poem's pattern of stressed (') and unstressed (˘) syllables.

2. A poem's rhythmical pattern is called _____.

3. _____ is the repetition of the sounds at the ends of lines.

4. Poetry is measured in _____.

Literary Analysis: Imagery

In poetry, an **image** is a word or phrase that appeals to one or more of the five senses. Writers use **imagery** to bring poetry to life with descriptions of how their subjects look, sound, feel, and smell.

A Read the following lines from "Miracles" by Walt Whitman. Then, answer the questions.

> Whether I walk the streets of Manhattan,
> Or dart my sight over the roofs of houses toward the sky,
> Or wade with naked feet along the beach just in the edge
>   Of the water,
> Or stand under the trees in the woods

1. Which image appeals to the sense of sight?

_____

2. Which image appeals to the sense of touch?

_____

3. Describe what you would feel if you were to "wade with naked feet along the beach just in the edge of the water."

_____

B Read the following lines. Write the sense to which the image appeals.

1. "sit at the dinner table"

_____

2. "watch honeybees busy around the hive of a summer forenoon"

_____

3. "animals feeding in the fields"

_____

4. "world is puddle-wonderful"

_____

5. "when the world is mud-luscious"

_____

Literary Analysis: Imagery

Assess

A Read the following lines from "Miracles" by Walt Whitman. Then, answer the questions.

> To me the sea is a continual miracle,
> The fishes that swim—the rocks—the motion of the
>   Waves—
> The ships with men in them,
> What stranger miracles are there/

1. What two images are contrasted in the second line?

_____

2. How do the two images function in the poem?

_____

3. What images appeal to the sense of sight?

_____

B Read the following lines. Write the sense or senses to which the image appeals.

1. "goat-footed balloon-man whistles"

_____

2. "look at strangers opposite me"

_____

3. "thin curve of the new moon"

_____

4. "from hopscotch and jump rope"

_____

5. "Betty and Isbel come dancing"

_____

6. "the sundown"

_____

Vocabulary: Synonyms

Practice

Synonyms are words with similar meanings. Examples include *declare* and *state.* Once you know the synonym for the base form of a word, you can apply your knowledge to use synonyms for other forms of the word. Study these examples:

Synonyms for Base Forms of Word	Synonyms for Other Forms of the Word
declare, state	declaring, stating declaration, statement

A Each word in Column A has a synonym in Column B. Find the synonym for each word. Write its letter on the line.

Column A

1. ____ significant

2. ____ intelligent

3. ____ conflict

4. ____ tiny

5. ____ bravery

6. ____ angry

7. ____ help

8. ____ doctor

Column B

A. courage

B. aid

C. miniature

D. important

E. problem

F. physician

G. mad

H. smart

B Each set of words is a pair of synonyms. These are the base forms of the words. Then, write another pair of synonyms, using other forms of the same words. Use this example as a guide.

Example: happy, glad <u>happiest, gladdest</u>

9. ask, inquire _____

10. hope, wish _____

11. sick, ill _____

12. common, usual _____

Vocabulary: Synonyms

A Each word in Column A has a synonym in Column B. Find the synonym for each word. Write its letter on the line.

Column A	Column B
1. ____ happiness	**A.** glow
2. ____ create	**B.** make
3. ____ nervous	**C.** huge
4. ____ shine	**D.** get
5. ____ calm	**E.** peaceful
6. ____ enormous	**F.** contentment
7. ____ try	**G.** attempt
8. ____ obtain	**H.** edgy

B Each set of words is a pair of synonyms. These are the base forms of the words. Then, write another pair of synonyms, using other forms of the same words. Use this example as a guide.

Example: common, usual _____uncommon, unusual_____

9. promise, vow _____

10. friendly, kind _____

11. slim, thin _____

12. box, crate _____

Grammar: Independent and Subordinate Clauses

Practice

A clause is a group of words with its own subject and verb. There are two types of clauses: independent clauses and subordinate clauses. An **independent clause** expresses a complete thought and can stand alone as a sentence. A **subordinate clause** (also called a **dependent clause**) has a subject and a verb, but it does not express a complete thought. Therefore, it cannot stand alone as a sentence.

Independent Clause	Subordinate Clause
S V He *arrived* this morning. 　　　　S　　　V The mosque *has* a golden dome.	S　　V **if** he *arrived* this morning 　　　　　　　S　　V **since** the mosque *has* a dome

A Read the following sentences. Then, underline the independent clause once and the dependent clause twice.

1. My book, which has many pictures, has little text.

2. That cat, which is mine, is an Abyssinian.

3. When cats prowl at night, their eyes adjust to the dark.

4. Although wild cats often hunt at night, they prefer dusk or dawn.

5. Whereas Angora cats have long hair, Siamese cats have short hair.

6. Cats, which vary in size, also have many different colorings.

7. Cats may shrill loudly when they are hungry.

8. Most lions in Africa live in national parks, where they are protected.

B Read the following sentence fragments. Complete each sentence by adding an independent clause or a subordinate clause.

1. The house has many windows _____.

2. Many people eat vegetables _____.

3. _____, although some prefer running.

Name _____ Date _____

Grammar: Independent and Subordinate Clauses

Assess

A Read the following sentences. Then, underline the independent clause once and the dependent clause twice.

1. Although she was in charge, she was not bossy.

2. Laura was in charge because she was an excellent camper.

3. Before we started, we checked our backpacks.

4. After we ate, we put out the fire.

5. We set up our tents when we arrived there.

6. Before an hour had passed, the stars came out.

7. Although breakfast was good, dinner was better.

8. Dan skis well, although he is slow.

9. If the sun shines, we will have a picnic.

10. Cats purr when they are happy.

B Complete each of the following statements.

1. A _____ is a group of words with its own subject and verb.

2. A dependent clause is another name for the _____ clause.

3. The two types of clauses are the _____ clause and the _____ clause.

4. The _____ clause expresses a complete thought and can stand alone as a sentence.

5. The _____ clause has a subject and a verb, but it does not express a complete thought.

Grammar: Sentence Structure

Practice

A **simple sentence** is one independent clause—a group of words that has a subject and a verb and can stand by itself as a complete thought.

Example: The dog chased the ball.

A **compound sentence** consists of two or more independent clauses linked by a word such as *and, but,* or *or.*

Example: Mr. Roberts was a teacher, <u>but</u> he also coached soccer.

A **complex sentence** contains one independent clause and one or more subordinate clauses—a group of words that has a subject and a verb but is not a complete thought.

Example: <u>Although he was a science teacher,</u> Mr. Roberts also taught math.

A   Read the following sentences. Identify each as either *simple, compound,* or *complex.* Write your answer on the line.

1. _____ Barry played football.

2. _____ Alicia lived in the city, and one of her cousins lived in the country.

3. _____ I am the student government president this year.

4. _____ Our tour guide showed us the house, and she demonstrated cooking on a cast iron stove.

5. _____ Although it was a holiday, Sheena worked on her science assignment.

B   Using the phrase provided, write a sentence. Label your sentences by writing *simple, compound,* or *complex* in parentheses after each one.

1. liked to write poetry

_____

2. Although he was

_____

Grammar: Sentence Structure

Assess

A Read the following sentences. Identify each as either *simple, compound,* or *complex.*
Write your answer on the line.

1. _____ The ducks and geese flew south.

2. _____ Some birds swam or hunted for grain.

3. _____ Although the tree squirrel is a wonderful acrobat, it
sometimes misses its mark.

4. _____ Mr. Gleason runs a pet store, and his two children
help him.

5. _____ The store is closed on Sundays, Mondays, and holidays.

6. _____ The cats are playmates, and both are good mouse
hunters.

7. _____ Tree squirrels, who are omnivores, can eat almost
anything.

8. _____ Many flocks of birds landed in a bird refuge.

B Using the phrase provided, write a sentence. Label your sentences by writing *simple,*
compound, or *complex* in parentheses after each one.

1. Although

_____

2. , but

_____

3. in the car

_____

4. and

_____

Grammar: Fragments and Run-On Sentences

Practice

A **fragment** is a group of words that does not express a complete thought. It is punctuated as if it is a sentence, but it is only a part of a sentence. Often it is missing a subject, a verb, or both. To correct a fragment, build a sentence that has a subject and a verb and that expresses a complete thought.

> **Fragment:** When I finished my homework.
> **Corrected:** It was nine o'clock when I finished my homework.

A **run-on sentence** is two or more complete thoughts that are not properly joined or separated. They may have no punctuation between them, or they may have the wrong punctuation. To correct a run-on sentence, use the proper punctuation and add a conjunction or a conjunctive adverb.

> **Run-on:** We raced to the dock, we rowed quickly.
> **Corrected:** We raced to the dock. We rowed quickly. (Use punctuation to indicate ideas.)
> **Corrected:** We raced to the dock, so we rowed quickly. (Use a comma and a coordinating conjunction.)

Read the following sentences. Then determine whether each is a fragment, run-on, or correct. Correct all fragments and run-on sentences in the space provided. Write *correct* if the sentence is correct.

1. Arrived early this morning.

_____

2. Luis felt energized after his workout.

_____

3. Because they had warned us not to.

_____

4. My sister has a horse she has been riding a long time his name is Ben.

_____

5. Emily received a new hat for her birthday.

_____

6. After his birthday meal.

Name _____ Date _____

Grammar: Fragments and Run-On Sentences

A On the line before each sentence, write F if it is a sentence fragment, R if it is a run-on sentence, or S if it is a complete, properly punctuated sentence.

1. ____ I always have applesauce, a sandwich, and a drink for lunch.

2. ____ Mike has a snare drum, he takes lessons on it.

3. ____ My sister, who knows carpentry. Built a chair.

4. ____ She built my brother a bookshelf for his room.

5. ____ Did you ever read about bees how amazing they are!

B Correct each of the following fragments and run-ons.

1. Working in Paris as a cook.

_____

2. For her next project at school.

_____

3. Work on the kitchen went fast. Once the cabinets arrived.

_____

4. They do not run well. For long distances.

_____

5. Mozart had severe hardships and disappointments his music is cheerful and vigorous.

_____

6. His father taught him carpentry he never attended a class.

_____

7. Kelly writes stories she does not write music.

_____

Spelling: Prefixes and Suffixes

Practice

A **prefix** is a syllable, group of syllables, or word joined to the *beginning* of another word to alter its meaning. Whenever you add a prefix to a word, do not change the spelling of the base word.

Example: un + able = unable   post + game = postgame

A **suffix** is a syllable or syllables added to the *end* of a word to alter its meaning. Unlike a prefix, a suffix sometimes does change the spelling of a word. Here are some guidelines:

- If the suffix is -*ness* or -*ly*, do *not* change the spelling of the base word.
  Example: rare + ly = rarely   late + ness = lateness

- Change the spelling of the base word when adding a suffix in the following cases:

  ✓ Drop the final *e* of the base word if the suffix begins with a vowel.
  Example: make + ing = making

  ✓ If the base word ends with a consonant followed by a *y*, change the *y* to *i* except when the suffix begins with *i*.
  Example: crazy + ness = craziness   bury + ed = buried

  ✓ If the suffix begins with a vowel, double the final consonant of the base word *if* the base word has only one syllable or the accent falls on the last syllable.
  Example: sit + ing = sitting

A Write the word box that is related to each of the following words. If the word has a prefix, underline the prefix. If the word has suffix, underline the suffix.

misspell	enlistment	unnecessary	occurred
happiness	reenlist	canceled	famous

1. spell _____   **2.** cancel _____

3. fame _____   **4.** necessary _____

B For each misspelled word, write the correct spelling in the space provided. If the spelling is correct, write *correct*.

1. renlist _____   **2.** unecessary _____

3. happiness _____   **4.** occurred _____

Name _____ Date _____

Spelling: Prefixes and Suffixes

A Add the indicated suffix to each word. Write the new word on the line.

1. suspense + ful _____

2. happy + ness _____

3. occur + ed _____

B Add the prefix to each word. Write the new word on the line.

1. post + dated _____

2. un + necessary _____

3. re + enlist _____

4. mis + spell _____

C Circle the letter of each sentence that contains no spelling mistakes.

1. A. Last night we saw a suspensful movie.
   B. I wrote my father a postedated check.
   C. I fanned myself with a piece of paper because it was so hot.

2. A. It is unecessary to fill out this form.
   B. Seeing my grandparents again gave me great happiness.
   C. The major said that he hoped I would renlist in the army.

3. A. The concert was cancelled because of poor ticket sales.
   B. He was embarrassed to see that he had mispelled his own name.
   C. The opposing team was penalized for unnecessary roughness.

© Pearson Education, Inc., publishing as Pearson Prentice Hall.

Writing: Poem

Alliteration is the repetition of sounds at the beginning of words. Poets use alliteration to create rhythm or a particular feeling in their poems. This sound device can reinforce meaning as well as contribute to the musical quality of a poem.

> Sally sells seashells by the seashore.
> Full fathom five thy father lies

Complete the activities on writing a poem.

1. Write a four line poem (it need not rhyme) in which you use alliteration. You may use one of the following subjects and the suggested consonant sound for alliteration, or you may choose another subject.

   The winter wind (w, as in wail, woosh, wild)
   A snake (s, as in *slither, slimy, silent*)
   A guitar (p, as in *pluck, play, pick*)
   The rain (d, as in *downpour, damp, decay*)

   _____

   _____

   _____

   _____

2. Why is this sound important to the poem?

   _____

3. Look at your poem again. Does it say what you want to say about the subject? List any changes you will make.

   _____

4. Look at each word to determine if any words need to be replaced to add more alliteration in the poem.

   _____

Writing: Poem

Assess

A Read the following questions. Circle the letter of the best answer.

1. Which of the following lines is an example of alliteration?

    A. Drearily down fell the drops of dew   **C.** Billy played on the boardwalk

    B. A baseball game was played   **D.** Green pastures were lush

2. Alliteration is used to create _____ in a poem.

    A. distortion   **C.** noise

    B. musical sound   **D.** balance

3. Poets use alliteration to create a particular _____ in the poem.

    A. feeling   **C.** character

    B. speaker   **D.** tone

B Write a four line poem (it need not rhyme) in which you use alliteration. Then, answer the questions that follow.

_____

_____

_____

_____

1. Why is sound important in your poem?

_____

2. Circle the words in your poem that show alliteration.

Writing: Paraphrase of a Poem

Practice

When you rewrite a poem in your own words, you are writing a **paraphrase of a poem.** To paraphrase poetry, follow these steps:

- Read each stanza of the original poem.

- Use a dictionary to define words you do not know. Replace these words with familiar synonyms.

- Restate the entire poem in your own language.

- Reread your paraphrase, making sure it has the same meaning as the original poem. Make revisions as necessary.

"The Walrus and the Carpenter"
by Lewis Carroll

The sun was shining on the sea,
Shining with all his might:
He did his very best to make
The billows smooth and bright—
And this was odd, because it was
The middle of the night.

The moon was shining sulkily,
Because she thought the sun
Had got no business to be there
After the day was done—
"It's very rude of him," she said,
"To come and spoil the fun!"

Here is an example of how one might paraphrase the first stanza of Lewis Carroll's poem "The Walrus and the Carpenter."

Paraphrase: The sun was shining. This made the sea waves bright. This was very strange because it was night, and the sun is not supposed to be shining.

Paraphrase the second stanza of Carroll's "The Walrus and the Carpenter."

_____

_____

_____

_____

_____

_____

_____

_____

188 Reading Kit

Writing: Paraphrase of a Poem

A Complete the following activities to paraphrase a stanza from Lewis Carroll's poem "The Walrus and the Carpenter." The walrus and the carpenter are speaking to a group of young oysters they have invited to come for a walk with them.

"The Walrus and the Carpenter"
by Lewis Carroll

"O Oysters," said the Carpenter,
"You've had a pleasant run!
Shall we be trotting home again?'
But answer came there none—
And this was scarcely odd, because
They'd eaten every one.

1. Circle any words you do not know. Use a dictionary or a thesaurus to write synonyms or short definitions for them.

_____

_____

2. Rewrite the stanza in your own words.

_____

_____

_____

_____

_____

3. Reread and revise your paraphrased stanza. Make sure your writing has the same meaning as Carroll's stanza. Write the final version of your paraphrased stanza. Make it as simple and easy to understand as possible.

_____

_____

_____

_____

_____

Writing: Persuasive Essay

Practice

When you use words to try to get others to think a certain way or to do something, you are using persuasion. A **persuasive essay** is a brief work in which a writer tries to convince readers to agree or disagree with a particular position. A persuasive essay should feature the following elements:

- a clear statement of your position on an issue that has more than one side

- evidence and reasons that support your position and persuade readers to agree

- statements that identify and address readers' possible arguments against your position

Read the following part of a student's persuasive essay. Then, answer the questions and complete the activities that follow.

I feel very strongly that homework for middle school students should take no longer than two hours a night. More than two hours of homework makes it very hard for students to do afterschool activities like sports or clubs. It also makes it almost impossible to spend time with their families.

1. What issue is addressed in this essay? _____

2. What is the writer's position? _____

3. What reasons does the writer give for his or her position on this issue?

_____

_____

4. What is one argument a reader might make against this position? How might the writer address this argument?

_____

_____

5. Write what you think should be the next two sentences in this essay.

_____

_____

_____

Name _____ Date _____

Writing: Persuasive Essay

Complete the following activities.

1. Write three issues that have more than one side. Write your position about each issue.

_____

_____

_____

2. Choose and circle one of the three issues from above. Write three facts or reasons why someone should agree with your opinion on this issue.

_____

_____

_____

3. Write two arguments someone might make against your position. Then, write your responses to these arguments.

Argument against your position: _____

_____

Your response: _____

_____

Argument against your position: _____

Your response: _____

_____

4. Write the first paragraph of your persuasive essay.

_____

_____

_____

_____

Reading: Setting a Purpose for Reading

Practice

When you **set a purpose for reading,** you decide on your reason for reading. You answer questions such as the following: What kind of material is this? Why would I be reading it? Should I read it quickly or slowly; lightly or carefully? Three reasons for reading are to

- be entertained; for example, reading your favorite magazine
- learn new information; for example, reading an instruction manual
- be inspired; for example, reading a religious book

To set a purpose, look at title, captions, and beginnings of passages to see what sort of reading you will be doing. Previewing can also help if you *already* have a purpose and are looking for texts to suit that purpose.

Answer these questions by circling the letter of your choice.

1. When you go to the library and take out a collection of short stories by your favorite author, your purpose for reading is to

   A. learn new information.   **C.** be entertained.
   B. be inspired.   **D.** gain understanding.

2. When you check a book's table of contents, quickly skim over passages, and look at captions, what are you most likely doing?

   A. previewing the text   **C.** wondering if you would like it
   B. speed reading   **D.** proofreading

3. If an article is titled "The Life Cycle of Mosquitoes," and you notice charts, photos, and scientific captions in it, what purpose for reading would you set?

   A. to be inspired   **C.** to gain a new skill
   B. to be entertained   **D.** to learn about a subject

4. If your purpose for reading a chapter of a history book is to learn new information, how will you read that chapter?

   A. I will skim it to get the most important ideas.
   B. I will read it slowly and carefully.
   C. I will read it at a comfortable pace, as I would read a novel.
   D. I will only look at the title, captions, and photos.

Reading: Setting a Purpose for Reading

Assess

Read this selection. Then, answer the questions that follow by circling the letter of your choice.

Some Facts About Owls

Owls are birds of prey that are usually active at night and rest during the day. There are over 130 species of owls in the world.

All owls have large heads and very large eyes. One interesting fact about owls' eyes is that they are immobile: They do not move in their eye sockets. An owl must turn its head to see things to the side of it or behind it.

Because their feathers are extremely thick, owls make almost no noise when they fly. Their stealth helps them to surprise their prey. They catch their prey with hooked claws and beaks. Many types of owls hunt mice and other rodents; others hunt reptiles or large insects.

1. What does the title suggest about this selection?

   A. The selection is a short story.

   B. The selection is factual.

   C. The selection will inspire the reader.

   D. The selection is about current events.

2. Based on the title and the first paragraph, which is the best purpose to set for reading this passage?

   A. to be entertained

   B. to learn how to do something

   C. to be informed about a topic

   D. to get help with a personal problem

3. How would you read this selection if you were writing a report on owls?

   A. slowly and carefully

   B. quickly

   C. at a comfortable rate

   D. I would preview it.

Reading: Adjust Reading Rate

Practice

Your **reading rate** is the speed at which you read. Your reading rate will vary depending on <u>what type of material</u> you are reading and what your <u>purpose for reading</u> is. Sometimes you need to read slowly and carefully to understand and remember information. Other times you may read quickly for enjoyment or to get a general idea of what is being said. When you read to be inspired, as when you read religious writings or poetry, you may reread parts that you particularly like.

Purpose for Reading	Suggestions for Reading Rate
To be entertained	Read at a comfortable rate; for some people this is a quick rate.
To learn or to gain understanding	Read slowly and carefully; sometimes you may stop and take notes.
To be inspired	Read at a comfortable rate, and reread parts that are meaningful to you.

Decide whether the following statements are true or false. Write T or F in the line provided and then explain your answer.

1. _____ You should read slowly and take notes when you read a sports magazine.

_____

2. _____ When you read your favorite poem, you should read quickly.

_____

3. _____ When studying for a test, it is best to read carefully and slowly.

_____

4. _____ When reading a fantasy novel, you should read at a comfortable rate.

_____

Reading: Adjust Reading Rate

Assess

Answer the following questions by circling the letter of your choice.

1. Which of these is best read slowly?

   A. the Sunday comics

   B. an instruction manual

   C. a science-fiction story

   D. an advertisement for a new shampoo

2. Which of the following factors is *most* important in helping you to decide your reading rate?

   A. the size of the type

   B. the number of pages

   C. the author's purpose in writing

   D. your purpose for reading

3. What reading rate would you set to read a novel by your favorite author?

   A. a slow reading rate, to catch every word

   B. a comfortable reading rate, to enjoy the book

   C. a quick rate to get to the end faster

   D. scanning the book to find the best parts

4. Which of these would you most likely read to be inspired?

   A. an article about a new band in a music magazine

   B. a chapter in a world history textbook

   C. a newspaper article about the high-school soccer team

   D. a book of poetry by young people

5. When are you most likely to stop and take notes while reading?

   A. when reading for enjoyment

   B. when reading to gain information

   C. when reading instructions

   D. when reading for inspiration

Literary Analysis: Dialogue

Practice

Dialogue is a conversation between characters. In a play or in fiction, characters reveal themselves through dialogue, or what they say. Dialogue also advances the action of the plot and develops the conflict.

Read the selection. Then, write the letter of the choice that best answers each question.

Emily and Kelly had just received terrible news: They would not be in the same class next year at school. "I do not even want to go to school anymore," Emily said, as she and Kelly walked home.

"Hang in there Emily," Kelly replied, "at least we will have lunch together every day." As the two girls walked, Kelly kept looking over at Emily's face.

"Why do you keep watching me?" Emily asked.

Kelly stopped and said, "I just want to make sure you are okay. I care about you." She started to laugh and added, "We could just stay at lunch all day."

Emily smiled back and replied, "No way—the food is terrible!"

1. _____ Which of these statements best describes dialogue in a literary work?

   A. a conversation between characters
   B. a portrait of a character
   C. the way a writer reveals the setting
   D. a struggle between opposing forces

2. _____ What does the dialogue in this selection reveal about Emily?

   A. She does not like Kelly.
   B. She is excited about school.
   C. She values Kelly's friendship.
   D. She enjoys school food.

3. _____ What does the dialogue in this selection reveal about Kelly?

   A. She cares about her friend.
   B. She is glad that they will be in separate classes.
   C. She does not like school food.
   D. She is not planning to return to school next year.

4. _____ Why is Emily's response, "No way—the food is terrible!" important?

   A. It shows that she will not return to school the following year.
   B. It shows that she feels better already since she is joking.
   C. It shows that she plans to go on a diet.
   D. It shows that Kelly likes cafeteria food.

Literary Analysis: Dialogue

Assess

Read the selections. Then, write the letter of the choice that best answers each question.

John: "Okay Pete, let us get on the field and win this game!"
Pete: "John, what if the other players will not let me have the ball?"
John: "What do you mean? This is a team sport, and that is how the
    game is played."
Pete: "No one passes the ball to me, even though I ask for it."
John: "Come on Pete, you are one of the best players on the team."
Pete: "Thanks John!"
John: "No problem. Now let us *all* go out and win this game together!"

1. ____ Which of these statements best describes the relationship between Pete
and John?

   A. strangers   **C.** opposing competitors
   B. friends and teammates   **D.** jealous rivals

2. ____ What pair of words best describes Pete in this scene?

   A. sneaky and mean   **C.** sleepy and bored
   B. worried and thankful   **D.** supportive and excited

Sam: "Mom! I thought you were going to the grocery store! We're out of
    everything!"
Mom: "I have not had time yet. I just got home from work and took my
    coat off."
Sam: "Well, I am hungry! What are we going to do about dinner? Can you
    still go to the store tonight?"
Mom: "Sure, Sam. Let me just sit down for a minute, and then I will go."

3. ____ Which of the following statements best describes the dialogue of this
scene?

   A. A tired mother and a hungry child discuss dinner plans.
   B. An excited mother and a tired child discuss dinner plans.
   C. A sad mother and a bored child discuss dinner plans.
   D. A funny mother and a smart child discuss dinner plans.

4. ____ What can you tell about the mother from this scene?

   A. She stays at home all day.   **C.** She is tired from work.
   B. She does not care about Sam.   **D.** She is hungry, too.

Literary Analysis: Stage Directions

Practice

In a play, it is important to read the **stage directions,** as well as the dialogue. Stage directions are words in a script that describe the set, characters, movement, lighting, and sound effects. This information helps make the characters and action clearer to the reader.

[The sun is setting on the farm. Two older men can be seen talking as they leave for their trucks. A soft, gentle voice is heard from within the stable, soothing the horses. A bell rings in the house.]

These stage directions offer the following information about the story:

Characters on Stage	Movement of Characters	Description of Lighting	Description of Sound	Other Special Effects
• 2 older men • person in the barn	• men walking • person tending to horses	• sunset	• person soothing horses	• bell rings

Read the selection. Then, write the letter of the choice that best answers each question.

[It was foggy and dark outside. Children could be heard in the distance giggling and screaming. It was Halloween night, and excitement filled the cool, misty air. A little boy and his father shuffled up the driveway with flashlights. As they approached the house, the boy grabbed his father's hand.]

1. ____ What is the purpose of the stage directions?

   A. to hide events from the other characters
   B. to reveal additional information
   C. to provide the central message in a play
   D. to show conversations among characters

2. ____ What information is revealed through this selection?

   A. the boy's costume description   **C.** a description of Halloween night
   B. the most popular candy   **D.** words between the father and the boy

3. To whom might these stage directions be of most use?

   A. the reader of the play   **C.** the audience
   B. the play's promoter   **D.** the author of the play

Literary Analysis: Stage Directions

Assess

A Read the selection. Then, fill in the chart with at least one example for each column.

[An older man walks alongside the train tracks with his camera. The sun is shining, causing him to wipe the sweat from his forehead with his handkerchief. He stops for a moment to hear the birds chirping and the squirrels scurrying around. Suddenly he jumps back, startled, and drops his camera. The train whistle screeches in the distance. White, puffy smoke can be seen through the treetops. The man stumbles to get his camera and dusts if off. The train sounds get louder, and the man steadies his camera for the shot.]

Characters on Stage	Movement of Characters	Description of Lighting	Description of Sound	Other Special Effects

B Read the selection. Then, answer the questions that follow.

[A single, white house sits on the hill. The morning sun lights the front porch, and a little dog is seen sleeping in his bed in the corner. Inside, lights are on in the rooms upstairs, and children's voices are calling back and forth to one another. A car races up the driveway, and the horn honks several times. The dog stirs, hops up, and barks. The front door to the house swings open wide, banging the house, and the children burst out of the door, struggling to be the first to the car. As the car door opens, a man gets out, his hands stacked with brightly wrapped packages and a bunch of balloons.]

1. In one or two sentences, explain what you think is happening in this scene. Then, provide three details to support your response.

_____

_____

_____

A. *Support Detail:* _____

B. *Support Detail:* _____

C. *Support Detail:* _____

Literary Analysis: Comparing Characters

Practice

In a literary work, there are characters that take part in the action of the story. When you **compare characters,** you look at their similarities and differences to tell them apart from each other. The different things that the characters do and say reveal their personalities.

A Several character traits are listed in the box. Write the word that best describes each character next to the description of the character's actions.

funny	smart	generous	daring	brave	sneaky

1. _____ Mark shared all of his birthday candy with his little sister.

2. _____ Trying not to be discovered, Sarah hid behind her mother's closet door.

3. _____ Telling jokes was Sue's favorite thing to do with her friends.

4. _____ Jennifer did not get scared when she was lost in the woods.

5. _____ Brett received an A+ on every math test, even the final exam.

6. _____ At the fair, Pat went on every roller coaster four times.

B Use these words to compare the characters who describe themselves in sentences.

shy	serious	calm	friendly	excited

1. _____ "People do not understand my joy sometimes and ask me to settle down."

2. _____ "I love reading a book when it is raining outside."

3. _____ "It is important to look at people when they speak to you."

4. _____ "When I do not know people in class, I stay away from them."

5. _____ "I look forward to meeting the kids in my new school."

Literary Analysis: Comparing Characters

Read the following passage. Then, fill in the chart.

Chris and Taylor have been neighbors for years. During the summer, they enjoy biking on the trails in town. Chris always has to remind Taylor to wear his helmet or else Taylor forgets. Every time that happens, Chris makes a joke about it and says that because he is older, it is his duty to remember. He adds that having red hair and freckles helps his memory.

One afternoon Taylor suggested that they ride their bikes into town for lunch at the diner. Because Taylor had been saving his money, he offered to pay for the meal. When Chris asked how he earned the money, Taylor replied, "I mow the lawn and take out the trash." Suddenly Chris seemed upset. His face turned bright red, and he quickly pedaled home.

The next day, Taylor was playing basketball in his driveway when Chris rode up on his bike. Taylor wiped the sweat from his sunburned face and slicked back his brown hair. He smiled at Chris, who smiled back and said, "I'm sorry for getting angry yesterday." He explained that he got mad because he helps watch his younger sister and feeds the family dog but does not get paid.

The two friends shook hands and happily played basketball for the rest of the afternoon. Chris made his usual jokes about things, and Taylor kept forgetting the score of the game— things were back to normal.

	Chris	**Taylor**
1. Compare how the characters look (name two details).	A.	B.
2. List a different personality trait for each character.	A.	B.
3. Compare the characters' actions (list two).	A.	B.
4. List something that the characters have in common.	A.	B.

Vocabulary: Suffixes -*ment* and -*tion*

Practice

A **suffix** is a syllable, or group of syllables, added to the end of a base word. The suffix changes the meaning and often the part of speech of the base word. Study these examples.

Base Word	Suffix	Meaning of Suffix	New Word
encourage (verb)	-*ment*	"the act or quality of"	encouragement (noun, meaning "the act of encouraging")
react (verb)	-*tion*	"the act, quality, or result of"	reaction (noun, meaning "the act, or result, of reacting")

Each sentence contains a verb in boldface print. Form a noun by adding the suffix shown. Then, use the new word in a sentence that shows its meaning.

add -*tion* **1.** The teacher will **instruct** us about suffixes.

New Word: _____ **Sentence:** _____

_____

add -*ment* **2.** Let us put up the tents and **encamp** by the stream.

New Word: _____ **Sentence:** _____

_____

add -*tion* **3.** I hope my dog's barking does not **distract** you from your work.

New Word: _____ **Sentence:** _____

_____

add -*ment* **4.** We have worked hard to **establish** the rules of our club.

New Word: _____ **Sentence:** _____

_____

Name _____ Date _____

Vocabulary: Suffixes -ment and -tion

Each question contains a verb in boldface print. Form a noun by adding the suffix shown. Write the new word on the line. Then, use the new word in a sentence that answers the question.

add -tion **1.** How do you plan to **illustrate** your book cover?

New Word: _____ **Sentence:** _____

_____

add -ment **2.** What did Captain Whiskers **state** in his message?

New Word: _____ **Sentence:** _____

_____

add -ment **3.** What magic spell did the tooth fairy use to **enchant** the dentists?

New Word: _____ **Sentence:** _____

_____

add -ment **4.** Why did Captain Warshaw **argue** with Professor Thompson?

New Word: _____ **Sentence:** _____

_____

add -tion **5.** Should we rest now so that we can easily **digest** that big lunch?

New Word: _____ **Sentence:** _____

_____

add -ment **6.** Did Captain Warshaw and Professor Thompson finally **agree**?

New Word: _____ **Sentence:** _____

_____

add -tion **7.** What shall we do after we **complete** this worksheet?

New Word: _____ **Sentence:** _____

© Pearson Education, Inc., publishing as Pearson Prentice Hall.

Grammar: Interjections

Practice

An **interjection** is a part of speech that expresses a feeling or an emotion, such as pain or excitement. Some common interjections are *wow*, *oh*, *aw*, *darn*, *ouch*, *gee*, *uh*, *tsk*, *huh*, *whew*, *well*, *oops*, *hey*, *boy*, *ugh*, *yuck*, *yikes*, and *hmm*. An interjection may be set off with a comma or an exclamation point.

> **Example:** Ouch! The dog bit me.
> Wow, she can run fast!

A Write an appropriate interjection from the list for the feeling shown in parentheses.

1. _____ (pain)! That really hurts.

2. _____ (joy)! That was a good book.

3. _____ (disgust)! Those cookies taste horrible.

4. _____ (fear)! I almost got run over.

5. _____ (hesitation), I am not sure of the answer.

6. _____ (surprise), you are really here!

7. _____ (relief)! They are finally gone.

B Fill in each blank with an appropriate interjection. Use commas or exclamation marks as punctuation.

1. _____ We lost again.

2. _____ I am so happy you are here for a visit.

3. _____ I just hammered my thumb.

4. _____ That was a close call.

5. _____ There is not enough snow to sled.

6. _____ I wish I had not eaten that.

7. _____ I can not wait all day.

Name _____ Date _____

Grammar: Interjections

A Add an interjection to help express emotion in each sentence.

1. _____ That pianist plays well.

2. _____ This milk tastes spoiled.

3. _____ Ralph, you almost ran into that wall.

4. _____ Where are you going?

5. _____ I dropped it.

6. _____ I sure am tired.

7. _____ I wonder where I put the keys.

B Write a sentence to go with each interjection given.

1. Yuck _____

_____

2. Hey _____

_____

3. Wow _____

_____

4. Hmm _____

_____

5. Oops _____

_____

6. Whew _____

_____

7. Boy _____

_____

© Pearson Education, Inc., publishing as Pearson Prentice Hall.   **Reading Kit 205**

Grammar: Double Negatives

Practice

Negative words, such as *nothing* and *not*, are used to deny or to say *no*. There should be only one negative word in a sentence. A **double negative** is the incorrect use of two or more negative words in a sentence.

> **Example:** We did *not* find *nothing.*
> We *never* go *nowhere.*

A   Underline the word in parentheses that is correct in each sentence.

1. I did not notice (any, no) telephone booth.

2. Jaime would not do (nothing, anything) wrong.

3. These grapes do not have (no, any) seeds.

4. Do not sign (nothing, anything) until you have read it.

5. I did not have (any, no) change to make a phone call.

6. He does not trust (anybody, nobody).

7. I have not (no, any) money to spend on junk food.

B   Rewrite each sentence to correct the double negatives.

1. The poor man does not have no shoes.

_____

2. We are not going nowhere this summer.

_____

3. Why will you not have nothing to do with him?

_____

4. Joan never reads nothing but books about horses.

_____

Grammar: Double Negatives

Assess

A   Underline the word in parentheses that completes each sentence correctly.

1. Our group (will, will not) never be able to finish on time.

2. I have not (ever, never) been to Japan.

3. We (could, could not) see nothing from where we sat.

4. She will not lend me (none, any) of her books.

5. Nobody had heard (anything, nothing) about the speech.

6. I (do, do not) want to see anything on television this evening.

7. I can not (ever, never) remember his name.

B   Rewrite each sentence in two different ways.

      Examples: I haven't never been to Cape Cod.

                 I have never been to Cape Cod.

                 I haven't ever been to Cape Cod.

1. Don't do nothing until you receive further instructions.

_____

_____

2. There isn't no one on our team who plays as well as James.

_____

_____

3. Bill can't find none of his original drafts of the story.

_____

_____

4. They won't allow no one in until 7:45 P.M.

_____

_____

Grammar: Word Usage

Practice

When you choose the wrong word in your writing, you can confuse readers or lead them to question the care you take with your work. The sets of words presented here are frequently confused:

accept, a verb that means "to take what is offered" or "to agree"

except, a preposition that means "leaving out" or "other than"

> **Example:** *Verb:* She walked up to *accept* her award.
> *Preposition:* Everyone except Joe went to the movie.

affect, a verb that means "to influence" or "to cause a change in"

effect, usually a noun, meaning "result"

> **Example:** *Verb:* A lack of sleep can *affect* your schoolwork.
> *Noun:* What is the *effect* of too much sleep?

A Underline the word in parentheses that completes each sentence correctly.

1. What is the worst (affect, effect) of a hurricane?

2. Please, (accept, except) this gift from all of us.

3. Nobody (accept, except) you would think of that.

4. The pouring rain will (affect, effect) our picnic plans.

5. The teacher will not (accept, except) late homework.

6. Our warnings had no (affect, effect) on his actions.

7. Everything is ready (accept, except) the dessert.

B Fill in the blank correctly with *accept, except, affect,* or *effect.*

1. Your test scores will _____ your grade.

2. A sandstorm will _____ the paint on your car.

3. Nobody showed up for the party _____ my sister.

4. In an essay, discuss the _____ of sunlight on plants.

5. George will _____ the award for the absent movie star.

Grammar: Word Usage

A   Underline the word in parentheses that completes each sentence correctly.

1. We were happy to (accept, except) your invitation.

2. What (affect, effect) will the new rules have on us?

3. Chemicals used on land can also (affect, effect) water and air.

4. Everyone (accept, except) Cinderella left for the ball.

5. Will the teacher (accept, except) your answer?

6. The (affects, effects) of the medicine will wear off soon.

7. All students, (accept, except) the band, please report to the office.

B   Rewrite each sentence using the word in italics correctly. If it has been used correctly, write *correct*.

1. The main *effect* of the experiment was a lot of smoke.

_____

2. Nothing *accept* snow will keep us from coming to your party.

_____

3. You must learn to *accept* the fact that you are very intelligent.

_____

4. The traffic jam will *effect* the whole city.

_____

5. Will you *except* this invitation to sing at my party?

_____

Writing: Friendly Letter

Practice

A **friendly letter** is much less formal than a business letter. It is a letter to a friend, a family member, or anyone with whom the writer wants to communicate in a personal, friendly way. Most friendly letters are made up of five parts:

- *Heading:* your address and date
- *Salutation or greeting:* **Dear** plus the person's name
- *Body:* the main part of the letter that contains the basic message
- *Closing:* **Sincerely** or **Yours truly** followed by a comma
- *Signature:* your name

A Match the greetings in the left column with the closings in the right column. Write the letter of the answer on the line.

1. ____ Dear Uncle Jack,   **A.** Your pal,

2. ____ Dear Mrs. Stanton,   **B.** Your loving niece,

3. ____ Hi Sam,   **C.** Sincerely yours,

B Write a short letter to a friend or relative.

_____

_____

_____

_____

_____

_____

_____

_____

_____

Name _____   Date _____

Writing: Friendly Letter

A   Write the letter of the correct answer on each line.

1. ____ If you were writing a letter to your best friend in another city to ask her to come visit you, what tone would you be most likely to use?

   A. informal   **C.** businesslike
   B. formal   **D.** angry

2. ____ For question 1, what type of letter would you be writing?

   A. business   **C.** letter to the editor
   B. thank-you   **D.** friendly

3. The salutation is another word for the ____.

   A. closing   **C.** greeting
   B. inside address   **D.** signature

4. One difference between a business letter and a friendly letter is that a business letter includes ____.

   A. an informal greeting   **C.** that day's date
   B. an informal closing   **D.** an inside address

B   Write a short letter to an adult who is not a relative.

_____

_____

_____

_____

_____

_____

_____

_____

_____

Writing: Tribute

Practice

A **tribute** is something that is said or given as an expression of gratitude, respect, and admiration. There might be a tribute printed in the yearbook to a favorite teacher who is retiring that year, for example, naming the many contributions that the teacher made to the school and to the lives of his or her students.

Use the following to help you prepare your tribute.

1. Name someone who has done something nice for you in the past. _____

_____

2. What did this person do to help you? _____

_____

3. List three adjectives that describe this person. _____

4. Why do you think that this person is worthy of a tribute? _____

_____

_____

_____

Writing: Tribute

Read the following paragraph. Then, pretend you are Mary and write a tribute to your best friend Olivia.

Olivia and Mary met in a ballet class when they were in the fifth grade. The day they met was Mary's first time in a ballet class, and she was having trouble keeping up with the rest of the group. As Mary struggled to keep up, Olivia offered to help her with the steps. Over the next few years, the girls became great friends. They practiced every day after school and became better and better at dancing. Then, in eighth grade, Mary was chosen to be the lead dancer in the school's performance of *The Nutcracker*. It was Olivia's help on that first day of class that kept Mary interested in ballet and helped her become the graceful ballerina that she is today.

_____

_____

_____

_____

_____

_____

_____

_____

_____

_____

_____

_____

_____

_____

_____

_____

Writing: Multimedia Report

Practice

A **multimedia report** includes video, photos, slides, maps, music or audio, written material. Multimedia reports use sight and sound in creative ways to hold the audience's attention. In choosing a topic for a multimedia report, consider whether you will be able to find information in both print and nonprint sources. Also, make sure that your topic is focused and not too broad. In preparing your multimedia report, keep your audience and purpose in mind.

Answer the following questions.

1. Which of these topics would be the best choice for a multimedia report? Circle the letter of your choice. Then, briefly explain your reason for choosing it.

   A. Types of Whales   **C.** Fractions
   B. The History of the World   **D.** Local Train Schedules

   _____

2. Imagine that you are preparing a multimedia report about how chocolate is made. You have found a photo of a toddler eating a chocolate bar and decide to use it in your introduction. Write a brief caption for this photo.

   _____

   _____

3. For a multimedia report about guitars, you might want to include some audio materials to give examples of how guitars sound. Which of the following activities would be *least* helpful?

   A. looking in the library's CD collection   **C.** asking a music teacher for advice
   B. researching music on the Internet   **D.** reading the local newspaper

4. Imagine that this is your multimedia assignment: Prepare a lesson on the color red for a preschool class. List some of your ideas for what to include in this presentation.

   _____

   _____

   _____

Writing: Multimedia Report

Assess

Of the topics listed, pick the one that interests you the most and describe a multimedia report that you would prepare for your class. Tell what media—both print and nonprint—you would use, and how you think your audience will respond.

Dolphins   A Dancer's Life

The Space Shuttle   History of Skateboards

1. Topic for my multimedia report: _____

2. Print media I would use: _____

_____

3. Nonprint media I would use: _____

_____

_____

4. How I think my audience will respond: _____

_____

5. Write a two-sentence introduction for your multimedia report.

_____

_____

_____

Reading: Summarize

Practice

To **summarize** means to tell briefly in your own words the main ideas of a piece of writing. When you summarize, you can condense your ideas or those of the writer into precise statements and omit unimportant details.

 Read the paragraph. Then, answer the questions that follow by circling the correct letter.

Gina was so excited when her mother finally agreed to take her to the local bookstore after school. The latest book by Thomas Rand was being released, and Gina could not wait to read it. Gina's friend, Sheila, had bought her a copy of Thomas Rand's first book for her birthday, and Gina has been reading his books ever since. After she purchases Thomas Rand's latest book, Gina plans on spending the weekend reading it from cover to cover.

1. Who is the paragraph mainly about?

   A. the author Thomas Rand
   B. Gina
   C. Gina's friend Sheila
   D. Gina's mother

2. What is Gina looking forward to doing after school?

   A. going for a hike with her friend Sheila
   B. visiting her grandmother
   C. going to the local bookstore
   D. washing her bike

3. Which of the following is the best summary?

   A. Gina gets excited about getting out of school because she gets to go for a ride in her mother's new car.
   B. Thomas Rand is an excellent author, and it is no surprise that he is Gina's favorite author.
   C. Gina looks forward to the weekends so that she can clean up her room.
   D. Gina loves to read, and Thomas Rand is her favorite author.

Reading: Summarize

Read the paragraph. Then, answer the questions that follow.

The Willow Grove botanical garden is famous for having a rare breed of purple rose bushes. These purple roses are so rare that the gardeners are not allowed to cut flowers from them. However, the Willow Grove botanical garden does have many other beautifully colored roses—every color of the rainbow, in fact, from shades of white and ivory to pale oranges and golds to deepest reds. From these varieties the gardeners are allowed to cut freely, and they often donate rose bouquets to local hospitals. The purple roses also help the hospital, though. Each year, the Willow Grove botanical garden donates one small purple rose bush to the hospital's fundraising auction.

1. What is the main idea of this paragraph? _____

_____

_____

2. List two details that provide more information about the main idea.

_____

_____

3. How would you summarize this paragraph?

_____

_____

Reading: Close Reading for Applications

Practice

Applications are the forms that you need to fill out for purposes such as getting a library card or a driver's license. You may also need to fill out an application to get a job.

To make sure you fill out an application properly, you must give the application a close reading. A **close reading** involves reading *every* word.

- Read each direction on the form.

- Fill out every section. Do not leave a section blank unless it is clearly marked *Optional, For Employer's Use,* or with some other indication that you should not or need not fill it out.

- Be sure to read the *fine print,* or material printed in small letters.

Read the following portion of an application. Then, answer the questions that follow.

Dee-Lish-Us Whole Foods—Job Application

1. Name (last name first): _____
2. Social Security # _____
3. Address (include zip code): _____
4. Phone Number (include area code): _____
5. Date of Birth (month/day/year): _____
6. Position for which you are applying (circle):   manager   waiter   head waiter
7. Days available for work (circle): S M T W T F S
8. Names and phone numbers of two references: _____

_____
If you are applying for work as a manager, please list all restaurants where you have worked on the lines below.

1. How should Rita Ann Smith write her name on line 1?

A. Rita Ann Smith   **B.** Smith, Rita Ann

2. Which of the following would fit the format suggested for item 4?

A. 31 July 1991   **B.** July 31, 1991   **C.** 7/91   **D.** 31/7/91

3. Who must list all of the restaurants where he or she has worked?

A. all applicants   **C.** applicants for a job as manager
B. applicants for a job as busboy   **D.** applicants for a job as waiter

Reading: Close Reading for Applications

Assess

Read the following portion of an application. Then, answer the questions that follow.

Baker's Flats Charity Art Fair—Volunteer Application

1. Name (last name first): _____

2. Date of Birth (month/day/year): _____

3. Social Security # _____

4. Phone Number (include area code): _____

5. Address (include zip code): _____

6. Post for which you would like to volunteer (circle):

   booth building   refreshments stand   ticket booth   security   parking

   Due to insurance requirements, no one under the age of 18 is allowed to work on construction, as security, or as a parking lot attendant.

7. The fair will be held on the third weekend of each of the months of June, July, and August. Please circle all days that you would be available to work:

   June 18   June 19   July 16   July 17   August 20   August 21

   Reserved for Clerical Use: _____

1. How should Donald Felix write his name on line 1?

   A. Donald Felix, printed in black ink   **C.** Felix, Donald, in black script
   B. Donald Felix, printed in blue ink   **D.** Felix, Donald, printed in black ink

2. Donald is going with his family to Arizona for the month of July. Which date should he NOT circle?

   A. June 18   **B.** June 19   **C.** July 16   **D.** August 21

3. What should Donald write on the last blank line?

   A. his name   **C.** the parking spaces he needs to reserve
   B. the date he wants to volunteer   **D.** nothing

4. Donald is 14. For which post can he volunteer?

   A. ticket booth   **B.** booth building   **C.** security   **D.** parking

Literary Analysis: Character's Motives

Practice

A **character's motives** are the reasons for his or her actions. Motives are usually related to what a character wants, needs, or feels. For example, the desire to win might motivate an athlete to practice daily.

A Several powerful motives are anger, fear, and hope. Write the motive that best describes each of the character's actions.

1. _____ Mrs. Marshall walked to the train station for the third morning in a row. All day, she watched passengers come and go as she sat knitting on a nearby bench. Her son promised he would be coming home soon. She wanted to be the first to greet him.

2. _____ Briana slammed down the phone without saying good bye. When it rang a few minutes later, she ignored it. She abruptly turned up her music to drown out the ringing.

3. _____ Alex thought he heard a noise outside. He turned down the television and cautiously parted the curtains. He peered anxiously into the darkness. Then, he walked to the front door and locked it.

B Circle the letter of the word that best answers the question. Then, explain your choice.

1. A small sign caught Vicki's attention. It said "Volunteers Needed" and showed a picture of a sad-looking dog at a local animal shelter. Teary-eyed, Vicki scribbled her name and phone number on one of the sign-up lines. What motivates Vicki to help at the shelter?

   A. jealousy   **B.** compassion   **C.** hope   **D.** fear

   _____

   _____

2. Members of the science club have been working for months to design a bridge for an upcoming competition. Every time they think they have it figured out, something goes wrong. Still, they refuse to give up. What motivates the science club members?

   A. frustration   **B.** fear   **C.** determination   **D.** kindness

   _____

   _____

Literary Analysis: Character's Motives

Read the passage. Then, circle the letter that best answers the questions that follow.

Tyra felt fast and strong. She easily sprinted up the last hill of the course. Today was the final cross-country meet of the season. After this, the championship races would begin. All season Tyra had fought hard to maintain her place as the seventh member of the varsity team. It had not been easy. A sophomore runner, she had fierce competition from Caley, a freshman, and Danielle, a senior. They always started out strong, but Tyra usually overtook them both at the end of the race. She knew her place on varsity was secure.

In addition to being the final meet, it was also senior day. It was the last time seniors would run in a home meet as part of the team. As Tyra rounded the final curve in the trail, she saw Caley up ahead. She sprinted past her. Two hundred feet before the finish line, she was on Danielle's heels. Tyra could hear her breathing hard. She knew Danielle had worked just as hard as she had this season. It would mean a lot to her to finish seventh today. Tyra crossed the finish line a fraction behind her.

1. A character's motives are best defined as _____.
   A. his or her personality traits
   B. the main theme of the story
   C. the reasons for his or her actions
   D. the problems that he or she encounters

2. Tyra has been running hard all season because _____.
   A. she does not like Caley and Danielle
   B. she wants to be on the varsity team
   C. she wants to be the best runner on the team
   D. she will graduate this year

3. Tyra slows down her pace in the end because _____.
   A. she wants Danielle to finish before her
   B. she's not very competitive
   C. she feels tired
   D. she wants Caley to catch up

4. The word that best describes Tyra's motive for doing so is _____.
   A. kindness
   B. fatigue
   C. pity
   D. guilt

Literary Analysis: Comparing Dramatic Speeches

Practice

Dramatic speeches are performed by actors in a drama or play. They can be spoken by a single character or be part of a larger scene between two or more characters. Either way, these speeches move the action of the story forward and help define the conflict. There are two main types of dramatic speeches:

- Monologues are long, uninterrupted speeches that are spoken by a single character. They reveal the private thoughts and feelings of the character.

- Dialogues are conversations between or among characters. They reveal characters' traits, develop conflict, and move the plot along.

A Read each dramatic speech. Then, answer the questions that follow.

Speech 1: We have worked really hard this year to create a sense of team spirit in debate club. We have looked at the issues from all angles. We have helped one another fine-tune our arguments. We have prepared and practiced. I just know all our hard work will pay off.

Speech 2: **Miles:** I hear you think we have a weak team this year. Why is that?
Emily: Frankly, Miles, it is because of you. You are the weakest debater on the team.
Miles: What do you mean? I work just as hard as you do!
Emily: Really? Then why have you missed so many meetings? And why are you never prepared when you do show up?

1. How do you know that Speech 1 is a monologue?

A. It is a conversation between characters.

B. It moves the action of the story forward

C. Only one character is speaking.

D. The speaker is outside the action.

B Give examples from the speeches that show the character traits listed in the chart.

Character Trait	Character	Speech	Example
optimistic			
unreliable			
honest			

Literary Analysis: Comparing Dramatic Speeches

Assess

Read the speeches. Then, fill in the chart.

Speech 1: **Chrissy:** Mrs. Healy is such a busybody.

Jamal: Why do you think so?

Chrissy: She is so nosy. She is always asking people where they are going or what they are doing. She should mind her own business.

Jamal: I think she is just being friendly.

Speech 2: **Janet:** There are a few people in our neighborhood that some might call nosy, and I can see their point. Some prefer to keep their business to themselves and not have to answer to anyone. Others, however, find comfort in a friendly, inquisitive neighbor. They feel someone is paying attention, who is interested in their well-being, even looking out for them. Being gone most of the day, I certainly appreciate having neighbors who know when something out of the ordinary is happening. I know they will alert the authorities to suspicious activities, and that gives me peace of mind.

	Speech 1	**Speech 2**
Type of speech		
Main characters		
Description of characters		
How I learned about characters		

Vocabulary: Suffixes -*ize* and -*yze*

Practice

A **suffix** is a letter, syllable, or group of syllables added to the end of a base word. The suffix contributes to the meaning of the new word and often changes its function. The suffixes -*ize* and -*yze* mean "to make." Of the two suffixes, -*ize* is commonly used in English, but -*yze* is quite rare. Study these examples of how they change the meanings and functions of base words.

Base Word	Suffix	Meaning of Suffix	New Word
summary (noun)	-ize	"to make"	summarize (verb, meaning "to make a summary")
analysis (noun)	-yze	"to make"	analyze (verb, meaning "to make an analysis")

Each sentence contains a word in boldface print. Form a verb by adding the suffix shown. Write the new word on the line. Then, use the new word in a sentence that shows its meaning.

add -**ize** 1. I have a strange **theory** about the solar system.

New Word: _____ **Sentence:** _____

_____

add -**yze** 2. The horse suffered a temporary **paralysis** after the accident.

New Word: _____ **Sentence:** _____

_____

add -**ize** 3. Are these wildflowers **familiar** to you?

New Word: _____ **Sentence:** _____

_____

add -**ize** 4. What exercises can I do to build up my **energy**?

New Word: _____ **Sentence:** _____

_____

Vocabulary: Suffixes *-ize* and *-yze*

Each question contains a word in boldface print. Form a verb by adding the suffix shown. Write the new word on the line. Then, use the new word in a sentence that answers the question.

add **-ize** 1. How would you describe the main **character** of that story?

New Word: _____ Sentence: _____

_____

add **-yze** 2. Do you agree with Bob's **analysis** of that poem?

New Word: _____ Sentence: _____

_____

add **-ize** 3. How would you change that French recipe so that you could easily find all the ingredients in an **American** supermarket?

New Word: _____ Sentence: _____

_____

add **-ize** 4. Do you ever have problems storing poems and songs in your **memory**?

New Word: _____ Sentence: _____

_____

add **-ize** 5. Into what **category** would you place such strange animals as hippos?

New Word: _____ Sentence: _____

_____

add **-ize** 6. Did you ask the factory to place your **initial** on your new briefcase?

New Word: _____ Sentence: _____

_____

Grammar: Sentence Functions and Endmarks

Practice

Sentences are classified into four categories based on their function.

Category	Function	Endmark	Example
Declarative	to make statements	.	Our cat chased a squirrel.
Interrogative	to ask questions	?	Where are you going?
Imperative	to give commands	. or !	Put your books away. Do not touch that stove!
Exclamatory	To call out or exclaim	!	That is a great idea!

A   Add the appropriate punctuation mark for each sentence.

1. What are you doing this afternoon

2. I'm cleaning my room and vacuuming the rug

3. How long will it take you

4. It's really a mess this time

5. Well, hurry up

6. It may take me all afternoon

B   On each line, write D for declarative, I for interrogative, E for exclamatory, or Im for imperative. Then, add a punctuation mark to the end of each sentence.

1. _____ Is that a bear over there in the park

2. _____ That is a black bear beyond the evergreens

3. _____ Oh, how friendly he looks

4. _____ Do not go near him or you may be sorry

5. _____ He may not be so friendly up close

6. _____ Please take a picture of him for our album

Name _____ Date _____

Grammar: Sentence Functions and Endmarks

Assess

A Add the appropriate punctuation mark for each sentence.

1. I wanted you to go to the movies with me

2. I would like to, but I can not finish doing my chores in time

3. Let me come over and help you

4. I can not ask you to do that

5. I will come right over on my bike

6. Do you mean it

7. Of course I do

8. I will see you soon

B On each line, write D for declarative, I for interrogative, E for exclamatory, or Im for imperative. Then, add a punctuation mark to the end of each sentence.

1.____ How does the homing pigeon find its way home

2.____ I read an interesting magazine article about pigeons

3.____ Read this article if you want to learn about them

4.____ Did you know that pigeons can see special light rays

5.____ These light rays are invisible to humans

6.____ Pigeons use their vision to find the sun's position

7.____ How remarkable that pigeons can do this

8.____ Imagine the world from a pigeon's-eye view

9.____ How different it must look

© Pearson Education, Inc., publishing as Pearson Prentice Hall.

Reading Kit **227**

Grammar: Subject-Verb Agreement

Practice

To fix **subject-verb agreement with compound subjects,** identify whether the subjects joined by *and, or,* or *nor* are singular or plural. Then, use one of the following methods.

- If the subjects joined are plural, use a plural verb.
- If the subjects are singular and joined by *and,* use a plural verb.
- If the subjects are singular and joined by *or* or *nor,* use a singular verb.

   Example: A swimming lesson **or** a tennis lesson **is** good exercise.

- If the singular and plural subjects are joined by *or* or *nor,* the verb agrees with the closer subject.

   Example: Concert tickets **or** a fancy dinner **is** a great gift.
   Neither the roast **nor** the potatoes **are** cooking.

Circle the correct singular or plural form of the verb in parentheses.

1. Two dogs and a cat (lives, live) in that house.

2. They (is, are) always playing together.

3. Neither the dogs nor the cat (likes, like) strangers.

4. Mr. Terry and one dog (takes, take) long walks.

5. Either Mr. Terry or his housekeeper (feeds, feed) the animals.

6. Neither the cat nor the dogs (strays, stray) from home.

7. Both cats and dogs (is, are) easy to care for.

8. Juan and his sisters (wants, want) to put on a pet show.

9. Neither his parents nor the neighbors (objects, object).

10. Both Cindy and Maria (has, have) agreed to help.

11. Two boxers and a cat (is, are) entered already.

12. Either the twins or Jamie (has, have) entered a snake.

13. Either a blue ribbon or some treats (is, are) to be first prize.

14. I (know, knows) it will be a good pet show.

Grammar: Subject-Verb Agreement

Assess

A Circle the correct singular or plural form of the verb in parentheses.

1. The cherry tree and the maple tree (has, have) been cut down.

2. The road to the right or the one straight ahead (leads, lead) home.

3. Soldiers or police officers (was, were) blocking the roadways.

4. Carol and her sister (is, are) hiking in Argentina.

5. The Thomases or the Millers (is, are) taking us in their car.

6. They and the Barbers (lives, live) across the street from the library.

7. The girls and boys (takes, take) turns collecting the classroom assignments.

8. Neither the cake nor the ice cream (has, have) been served yet.

9. A pencil or a pen (is, are) necessary to take the test.

10. Both Joe and Michael (is, are) interested in fishing.

B Circle the correct singular or plural form of the verb in parentheses.

1. Either Dad or Mom (picks, pick) us up after school.

2. An apple or a pear (tastes, taste) good with cheese.

3. Billy or his sister (cooks, cook) dinner every night.

4. Every suit and jacket in the store (is, are) on sale.

5. Neither the book nor the magazine (has, have) the information.

6. Neither Rachel nor her sisters (is, are) able to come to the party.

7. The house next door and one around the corner (is, are) painted yellow.

8. Both Sarah and Eileen (drives, drive) to the mountains on weekends.

9. Either Karen or the boys (takes, take) the dog for a walk every day.

10. The leaves and the grass trimmings (has, have) to be raked today.

Spelling: Plurals

Follow these guidelines for spelling the plurals of most nouns:

- Add *s* to the noun. This is the regular way to form plurals of nouns.
  Example: cat/cats   boat/boats   stair/stairs
- Add *es* to nouns that end in *s, sh, ch,* or *x.*
  Example: pass/passes   dash/dashes   beach/beaches   fox/foxes
- If a noun ends in a *y* that follows a consonant, form the plural by changing the *y* to *i* and adding *es.*
  Example: party/parties   sky/skies   memory/memories
- If a noun ends in a *y* that follows a vowel, then simply add an *s.*
  Example: day/days   monkey/monkeys.
- For some words ending in *f,* just add *s.*
  Example: chef/chefs   whiff/whiffs
- For other words that end in *f,* change the *f* to *v* and add *es.*
  Example: half/halves   leaf/leaves
- If a noun ends in an *o* that follows a vowel, then add *s.*
  Example: duo/duos   trio/trios
- If, however, the final *o* follows a consonant, add *es.*
  Example: cargo/cargoes   tomato/tomatoes

Note these irregular plurals and exceptions:

- Some nouns have the same spelling in both the singular and plural.
  Example: fish/fish
- Some nouns have irregular plurals.
  Example: foot/feet   woman/women   child/children

A Write the singular form of each plural word.

1. knives _____

3. boxes _____

2. countries _____

4. disks _____

B State the rule that applies to spelling each plural word.

1. envelopes _____

4. potatoes _____

2. patios _____

5. countries _____

3. classes _____

6. sheep _____

Spelling: Plurals

Write the letter of the sentence in which the italicized word is spelled correctly.

1. _____

   A. Our class has put on several *plaies*.

   B. Shakespeare wrote many great *playes*.

   C. My favorite *plays* are comedies.

   D. No *playz* are complete without scenery.

2. _____

   A. We visited a farm that had lots of *sheep*.

   B. At the petting zoo, we were able to pet the *sheeps*.

   C. *Sheepes* are a source of wool.

   D. *Sheepess* do not make good house pets.

3. _____

   A. Every cook needs a set of *knifes*.

   B. *Knifs* are useful for a variety of tasks.

   C. Some *knivs* are especially designed for camping.

   D. Careless people can hurt themselves when using *knives*.

4. _____

   A. *Potatose* are the basis for many dishes.

   B. *Potatoes* can be used in stews.

   C. My favorite dish is mashed *potatos*.

   D. My sister prefers French fried *potatoze*.

5. _____

   A. Some day I hope to visit several overseas *countrees*.

   B. Pedro can name all the *countreez* that belong to the United Nations.

   C. Canada and Mexico are two *countries* that border the United States.

   D. I think that the people of all *countres* have basically the same hopes and dreams.

6. _____

   A. Math is one of my favorite *classez*.

   B. I wish all my *classies* were in the afternoon.

   C. Some of our *classes* do not require homework.

   D. Most *classese* encourage student participation.

Writing: Report

A **report** is a written description of a situation or event. It can be done by one person who carefully examines a particular subject. It can also be done by a group of people. When you choose the subject of your report, remember to include details about what you know, what you have observed, what you learned, what others think about the situation or event, and what changes you would recommend given what you have observed and learned.

Answer the following questions.

1. Which of these reports could you write by yourself? Circle the letter of your choice. Then, briefly explain your reason for choosing it.

   A. Your aunt's birthday party next month
   B. The short stories of Walter Dean Myers
   C. Lunchtime at the school cafeteria
   D. How you get to school each morning

   _____

   _____

2. For the report you have chosen, list the details you plan to include.

   _____

   _____

   _____

   _____

   _____

Writing: Report

Your teacher has asked you to write a report on how you get your homework done each night. She also asked you to recommend any changes you might make to increase your efficiency.

1. List at least five details about how you do your homework each night. In addition to time spent and location, include information about whether your style varies depending on the subject, extracurricular activities, or responsibilities at home.

_____

_____

_____

_____

_____

2. For your report, put the details you have listed in the order they would appear in your report. Explain your reasons.

_____

_____

_____

_____

3. Explain why you think your style of doing homework is worth recommending. If you think it needs improvement, explain what you would recommend to achieve better results.

_____

_____

_____

_____

Writing: Cause-and-Effect Essay

A **cause-and-effect essay** is expository writing that explains why something happens or what happens as a result of something else. A cause-and-effect essay might focus on causes, such as why the days get shorter in the fall, or on effects, such as what will happen if you do not wear sunscreen.

Choose one of the causes or effects listed as a topic for your cause-and-effect essay. Then, with your choice in mind, answer the questions that follow.

Cause Choices	Effect Choices
Not Washing Your Hands	A Sunburn
Not Brushing Your Teeth Every Day	A Stomachache

1. What topic did you choose? _____

2. If you chose a cause as your topic, what are some of the effects that might happen as a result of this cause? If you chose an effect, what are some causes that might have led to this effect?

_____

_____

3. Where might you gather more information about your topic?

_____

_____

4. What do you think your audience can learn from reading your cause-and-effect essay?

_____

_____

Writing: Cause-and-Effect Essay

Use the following graphic organizer to help you organize the first four paragraphs of your cause-and-effect essay.

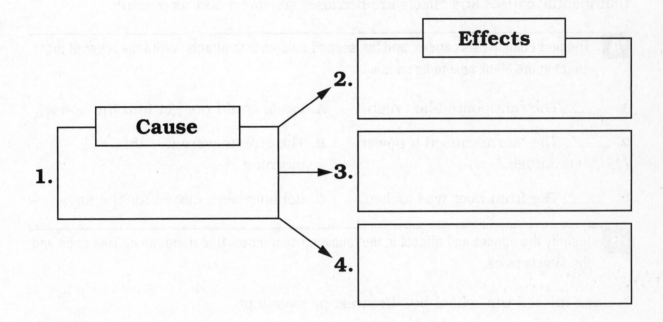

5. What do you want your audience to learn from reading your cause-and-effect essay?

_____

_____

Reading: Cause and Effect

Practice

A **cause** is an event, action, or feeling that produces a result. That result is called an **effect.** If you do not see the cause-and-effect relationship in a passage, **reread to look for connections** among the words and sentences. Some words that identify causes and effects are *because*, *so*, *since*, and *as a result.*

A The first column lists causes, and the second column lists effects. Write the letter of the effect in the blank next to its cause.

1. _____ The rain poured last night.   **A.** Paula could not get into the house.

2. _____ The storm caused a power   **B.** The streets were wet this
   outage.   morning.

3. _____ The front door was locked.   **C.** Schools were closed for the day.

B Identify the causes and effects in the following sentences. Underline the causes once and the effects twice.

1. Jack missed the school bus because he overslept.

2. Traffic was terrible, so we were two hours late getting home.

3. Rachel felt unhappy because she was unable to find a summer job.

4. Ice covered the road, so traffic moved slowly.

5. Kathy could not ride her bike because it had a flat tire.

C Read the paragraph. Then, list two causes and their effects in the chart.

   I told my brother that it was foolish to drive over the speed limit. He did it anyway because he liked to show off. But I think he learned his lesson last Saturday. First, he hit a pothole too fast and damaged his car. Then, he got a speeding ticket. Mom said he had to pay the fine and could not drive the car for a month. I do not think he will be speeding again.

Causes	Effects

Reading: Cause and Effect

A Identify the causes and effects in the following sentences. Underline the causes once and the effects twice.

1. Because of the rain, our basement flooded.

2. Jake broke his leg; therefore, he could not play in the game and had to use crutches to walk.

3. As a result of last night's power outage, we ate a cold dinner by candlelight.

4. Jane forgot to put the top on the grasshopper's box; consequently, the insect escaped.

5. Since it has not rained in several days and because it has been cold, the new seedlings have died.

6. Joe's dad left his car's headlights on last night; so the car did not start this morning.

7. The farmland meant everything to the Hutchinsons because it had been in the family for generations.

8. Rosemary overslept this morning and as a result, she did not have time to eat breakfast and was late for work.

B Complete each sentence.

1. Our air conditioner is broken; as a result, _____

_____.

2. If transportation were cheaper, _____

_____.

3. _____ consequently, I could not complete my homework.

4. I fell and twisted my ankle because of _____

_____.

5. _____ therefore, I am not going to the party.

Reading: Skim and Scan

When you need to locate specific information in a text that you have already read, **skim** and **scan** instead of rereading every word. Skimming is glancing through a written work to get a general idea of what it is about. Scanning is reading quickly while looking for keywords or ideas. Textbooks are easy to scan through; their pictures, captions, charts, photos, and headings always show keywords and ideas.

Decide if the following statements are true or false. Write T or F on the line before each statement. If the statement is false, give a correct version of the statement on the second line.

1. ____ I would read every word of the table of contents in a textbook to find the chapter I needed.

_____

2. ____ I would not skim headings to see what topics were covered in a chapter.

_____

3. ____ Photo captions and graph labels are not worth scanning.

_____

4. ____ I would scan paragraphs for key words and phrases related to the question I am trying to answer.

_____

5. ____ I might skim a glossary if I was looking for a particular vocabulary word.

_____

6. ____ If I was looking for a key idea in a textbook, I would only look at chapter titles, not headings within the chapter.

_____

7. ____ Maps and pictures are always important to the text and can quickly give main facts and ideas to a reader who is skimming and scanning.

_____

Reading: Skim and Scan

■ **Read the following paragraph and complete the activity.**

   Mr. Danson gave his history class an open book quiz on Chapter Three of their American History textbook. The class was allowed to use their textbooks to answer these questions:

Open Book Quiz
American History, Mr. Danson

1. Explain what "taxation without representation" means.
2. List the thirteen colonies.
3. Define what a lobsterback is.

Explain what you would do to find the answers. Remember to look for maps, photo captions, and key phrases.

_____

_____

_____

_____

_____

_____

_____

_____

_____

_____

_____

_____

_____

Literary Analysis: Myth

Since time began, people have tried to understand the world around them. Ancient peoples created **myths**—stories that explain natural occurrences and express beliefs about right and wrong.

Every culture has its own collection of myths, or *mythology*. In many of these myths, gods and goddesses have human traits, while human heroes possess superhuman traits. Myths explore universal themes and explain the world in human terms.

Read the selection. Then, circle the letter that best answers each question.

The Abenaki people enjoyed a good life with many gifts from the Creator. One gift was the maple tree with its thick sweet sap. The people appreciated this gift, but a few abused it. They drank so much sweet sap that they grew fat and lazy. They neglected their homes and their duties. The Creator became angry and sent Gluskabe to teach the people a lesson. He told him to take a bucket and fill the trees with water. Soon the sap that flowed was thin and no longer sweet. The people begged for the return of their thick sap, but Gluskabe refused. He told them that from now on they could collect the sap only once a year. Then, they would have to make fires to heat the sap and boil out the water. All this would take much time and effort. To this day, that is how maple syrup is made.

1. What superhuman powers does Gluskabe have?

   A. He can fly into space.   **C.** He can lift anything.
   B. He can pour water into every tree.   **D.** He can speak all languages.

2. What lesson does this myth teach?

   A. Humans should love the earth.   **C.** People should not be lazy.
   B. People should eat sweets.   **D.** People can do what they want.

3. What natural occurrence does this myth explain?

   A. why rain falls on maple trees   **C.** why leaves change colors
   B. why maple sap is thin   **D.** why maple sap is sweet

Literary Analysis: Myth

Read the passage. Then, circle the letter that best answers each question or write your answers on the lines.

Phaëthon is the son of the god Apollo and the mortal woman Clymene. He often brags about his father, who drives the sun's golden chariot across the sky each day. When another boy accuses him of making false claims, Phaëthon visits his father to ask for proof.

Apollo promises to give Phaëthon anything he wants. When Phaëthon asks to guide the sun's chariot across the sky, Apollo warns him that he does not have the skills to handle such a difficult task. However, Phaëthon proudly insists. Shortly after Phaëthon sets out, he loses control and the chariot swerves too close to Earth. The heat of the sun scorches the earth until Zeus finally hurls a thunderbolt at Phaëthon, sending him crashing to the ground.

1. Who are the humans in this myth?

A. Phaëthon and Apollo

B. Apollo and Zeus

C. Apollo and Clymene

D. Clymene and Phaëthon

2. What natural event does this myth explain?

A. a lunar eclipse

B. thunder and lightning

C. the rising and setting of the sun

D. the movement of clouds in the sky

3. Who are the gods and/or goddesses in this myth? How do you know?

_____

_____

_____

4. What lesson does this myth teach?

_____

_____

Literary Analysis: Legend

Practice

A **legend** is a traditional story about the past. Every culture has its own legends. Before legends were written down, they were passed on orally. Legends are based on facts that have grown into fiction in the many retellings over generations. Most legends include these elements:

- a human who is larger than life
- fantastic elements
- roots or basis in historical facts
- details that reflect the culture that created the story

Decide which elements of legends are shown in each of the following and write your answer on the line. The first one is done for you. There may be more than one answer.

1. Geromino, a brave Apache warrior, led his people in a fierce resistance against the U.S. army. When soldiers murdered his wife and children, Geromino vowed to kill as many enemies as possible.

   Element(s) of legend: based on historical fact

2. Guided by visions, he led successful raids against enemy armies and evaded capture for years at a time.

   Element(s) of legend: _____

3. It is said Geromino could walk without leaving footprints and hold off the dawn so that his people would be safe.

   Element(s) of legend: _____

Literary Analysis: Legend

Assess

Read the legend. Then, circle the letter that best answers each question.

Johnny Appleseed dreamed of a land blossoming with apple trees, a land where no one would ever have to be hungry again. For nearly fifty years he roamed the country, collecting and planting seeds. He traveled simply, carrying only what he needed to survive and going barefoot most of the time. His feet became so gnarled and tough that once, when a rattlesnake tried to bite him, its fangs could not go through his foot.

Johnny made friends with everyone he met: settlers, Native Americans, even wild animals. It is said that once he went into a dark cave for shelter. There he found a hibernating bear and her cubs, but he curled up anyway and slept peacefully through the night. Johnny spread his apple trees far and wide. Today, many of his trees continue to grow.

1. The legend is *most likely* based on which of these facts?

   A. Settlers often welcomed strangers into their homes.
   B. Apple trees can be found all across the country.
   C. John Chapman was a nurseryman who planted apple orchards.
   D. The best time to plant apple trees is in the spring.

2. What does this legend suggest about the culture that created it?

   A. It was a culture that loved apples.
   B. It was a culture in which people did not trust strangers.
   C. It was a culture that went everywhere on foot.
   D. It was a culture that encouraged people to pursue their dreams.

3. What elements of fantasy does this story contain?

   A. The trees Johnny planted continue to grow today.
   B. Johnny's bare feet grow tough and gnarled.
   C. Johnny befriends everyone he meets.
   D. Rattlesnakes and bears do not harm Johnny, even when they attack.

4. What makes Johnny Appleseed a "larger than life" hero?

   A. He spends his whole life planting trees.
   B. He carries only what he needs to survive.
   C. He is helped by friendly Native Americans and settlers.
   D. He loves apples.

Literary Analysis: Epic Conventions

Practice

An **epic** is a story or long poem about the adventures of a larger-than-life hero. The hero's parents are often gods or members of royal families. Epic tales usually focus on the hero's bravery, strength, and success in battle or adventure. In addition to telling the story of a hero, an epic is also a portrait of the culture that produced it. The following epic conventions are traditional characteristics of this form of literature:

- a dangerous journey, or quest, that the hero must take
- gods or powerful characters who help the hero
- a broad setting that covers several nations or even the universe
- a serious, formal style

Read the selection. Then, write the letter of the choice that best answers the question.

All of the townspeople loved Julius, the fierce and mighty prince. In those days, the ancient city of Ridgeland was attacked frequently. The Peppers, who lived in the nearby wooded forest, wanted to steal all the gold and riches from the people of Ridgeland. Every time the Peppers charged the city, Julius rallied his friends to fight back. Under the leadership of the prince, the Ridgelanders always won.

Although Prince Julius never lost a battle in his homeland, his adventures at sea won him the most fame. One time the fearless prince battled a sea monster that was charging the ship! Julius aimed his spear in just the right spot, defeating the animal and saving the lives of his entire crew. Many years later, once he became King of Ridgeland, he died at sea while trying to save another boat in distress.

1. _____ Which part of the epic of Julius involves dangerous journeys?

   A. the love that the townspeople have for him
   B. when he becomes king
   C. the fact that he is fierce and mighty
   D. his adventures at sea

2. _____ What can you conclude about the culture that produced the epic of Julius, based on the details within it?

   A. It is a culture that exists today.
   B. It was a culture that admired courage and loyalty.
   C. It was a culture with no conflict.
   D. It was a culture with little knowledge of the sea and sailing.

Literary Analysis: Epic Conventions

Assess

A Read the selection. Then, circle the letter of the choice that best answers the question.

Rushing through the field, King Massy and his men charged the giant snake that kept attacking their homeland. At one point, they forced it underground. Believing it was gone, the men asked King Massy if they could begin their long journey home. The king agreed but declared that he would stay and fight. He insisted on chasing the huge serpent across the world, for however long it took, until he caught it.

The men admired the king for his loyalty and bravery and decided to stay and help him. They continued to chase the snake over land and sea for seven years. Finally, they trapped their enemy in a shallow hole. King Massy approached the hissing snake and cut it in half with his sword. After their victory, they began their long trip back home. Because King Massy fought so bravely for his people, the gods helped him and his men return home safely and swiftly.

1. What is King Massy's role in this story?

   A. He is the antagonist.
   B. He is someone who learns a lesson.
   C. He is the hero.
   D. He is a supernatural hero.

2. Which of the following is the best example of the gods' involvement?

   A. the snake getting trapped in the hole
   B. the men staying to help King Massy
   C. the men returning home quickly and in good health
   D. King Massy cutting the snake in half

B Read each paragraph and decide if it is an epic convention. Then, write *yes* or *no* on the line and explain your response.

1. _____ Peter left his home to fight the fire-breathing dragon. He traveled across three countries and many rivers to find his enemy. Finally he battled the dragon and won.

   _____

2. _____ The men were laughing and joking about their day at sea. One of them caught a large fish and planned to feed his entire family with it.

   _____

Vocabulary: Denotation and Connotation

A word's **denotation** is its strict, literal meaning. In other words, it is the word's dictionary definition. Every word has a denotation, and some words also have a **connotation**. A connotation is made up of positive or negative feelings that are often associated with the word. Words that have neither positive or negative connotations are said to be neutral. Study these examples. Each word has the same denotation but very different connotations.

Word	Denotation	Connotation
thrifty	tending to save money	positive
stingy	tending to save money	negative
economical	tending to save money	none; this is a neutral word.

Each sentence contains a word in boldface print. On the line following the sentence, write the word's denotation. Think about the word. Does it have any positive or negative connotations? Write *positive, negative,* or *neutral* to show its connotation.

1. The dress was a **bargain.**

Denotation: _____

Connotation: _____

2. The dress was **inexpensive.**

Denotation: _____

Connotation: _____

3. The dress was **cheap.**

Denotation: _____

Connotation: _____

Vocabulary: Denotation and Connotation

Each sentence contains a word in boldface print. On the line following the sentence, write the word's denotation. Think about the word. Does it have any positive or negative connotations? Write *positive, negative,* or *neutral* to show its connotation.

1. There was a **rainstorm** this morning.

Denotation: _____

Connotation: _____

2. There was a **downpour** this morning.

Denotation: _____

Connotation: _____

3. There was a **shower** this morning.

Denotation: _____

Connotation: _____

4. The dog was **scrawny.**

Denotation: _____

Connotation: _____

5. The dog was **slender.**

Denotation: _____

Connotation: _____

6. The dog was **thin.**

Denotation: _____

Connotation: _____

Grammar: Colon

Practice

A **colon** looks like two periods, one above the other (:). Colons can be used to introduce lists of items.

A Insert colons where they are needed in the following sentences.

1. My favorite sports are the following baseball, basketball, soccer, and tennis.

2. Four states border Mexico California, Arizona, New Mexico, and Texas.

3. The box had the following rocks, marbles, shoes, and rope.

4. Add these things to your list bread, eggs, milk, and flour.

5. This is what I have to do on Sunday clean my room, baby-sit for my brother, and finish my homework.

6. Sam is afraid of these jungle animals tigers, leopards, and snakes.

B Supply an appropriate list to complete each of these sentences. Insert colons and commas where they are needed.

1. I am taking the following subjects this year _____.

2. You need these supplies for a picnic _____.

3. We have seen the following birds this summer _____.

4. Marie traveled to three cities _____.

C Insert colons where they are needed in the following sentences. Not every sentence needs a colon.

1. We have studied the following kinds of punctuation marks commas, colons, and apostrophes.

2. Susan's favorite colors are blue, red, and green.

3. We have two excellent players this year Tom and Mike.

4. The three items we bought were a pencil, a pen, and an eraser.

Grammar: Colon

Insert colons where they are needed in the following sentences.

1. Four team sports are popular in U.S. schools basketball, baseball, football, and soccer.

2. The day after Thanksgiving is a holiday in these states Florida, Maine, Minnesota, Nebraska, and Washington.

3. The basic unit consists of three rooms a living room, bedroom, and kitchen.

4. Maryanne chose three different poets to study Dickinson, Frost, and Sandburg.

5. In this wallet are my life's savings six dollar bills, eight quarters, and two nickels.

6. Their birthdays were all in the summer June 27, July 11, and August 9.

7. The salad contains three ingredients lettuce, tomatoes, and mushrooms.

8. My father always grows a variety of vegetables carrots, squash, tomatoes, and cucumbers.

9. Campers need the following items a sleeping bag, a tent, warm clothing, and sturdy shoes.

10. We have the following trees on our property maple, elm, and oak.

11. Bees do things such as the following sing, sting, and fly away.

12. I have two favorite seasons spring and fall.

13. We have practice on the following days May 18, May 20, and May 21.

14. I had to choose a book about one of these topics the Civil War, the Industrial Revolution, or immigration.

15. The first three U.S. presidents were the following George Washington, John Adams, and Thomas Jefferson.

16. I met the following people at the party Gary, Patty, and James.

17. The following roads will be closed by today Dover, Webster, and Bell.

Grammar: Commas

A **comma** signals a brief pause. Commas can be used between items in a series, after an introductory phrase or clause, or before a conjunction joining independent clauses.

A Add commas where they are needed between the items in the series.

1. Jan Dot Steve and Corey are coming to the party.

2. I have called the guests bought the food and warned the neighbors.

3. I think this will be a loud enjoyable and exciting party.

4. Can you bring plates napkins and cups?

5. Sarah walked ran and even rode a bike to get here.

B Add commas where they are needed after each introductory phrase or clause.

1. After we eat we will do the dishes.

2. With very little money she left home to spend a day in the city.

3. After he finished school he went to visit his father at work.

4. To win the state championship the team practiced day and night.

5. Whenever you are ready we can leave.

C Add commas where they are needed between the independent clauses.

1. You were away having a good time and I was here bored and lonely.

2. Mars is closer but Jupiter appears brighter.

3. The hours ticked away but the phone never rang.

4. I enjoy watching football but I like baseball better.

5. It was a superbly written book and I could not put it down.

Grammar: Commas

A Add commas where they are needed. Not every sentence needs a comma. Write *correct* for any sentence that does not need a comma.

1. _____ Jerry tried out for the lead but Tom got the part.

2. _____ Sandy ran up the block across the park and around the school.

3. _____ The storm caused great damage and washed away several bridges.

4. _____ Last Saturday was windy cold and rainy.

5. _____ I stopped by to pick you up but you had already left.

6. _____ We arrived early and stayed late.

7. _____ My shoes are not under my bed in the closet or under the couch.

8. _____ If it does not rain tomorrow the roads will be jammed.

9. _____ Jackie and Katie will be roommates next year.

10. _____ Firs spruces and pines are evergreen trees.

B Write each pair of sentences as a compound sentence, using the conjunction in parentheses. Place a comma where it is needed.

1. Spring came. The birds flew north. (and)

_____

2. I can hand in a written report on spiders. I can give an oral report. (or)

_____

3. They had been working very hard. They did not seem especially tired. (but)

_____

4. Usually we study in the morning. We go swimming in the afternoon. (and)

_____

Grammar: Revising Incorrect Use of Commas

Practice

A **comma** is a punctuation mark used to indicate a brief pause. Apply the following rules to use commas correctly.

- Commas separate two adjectives in a series, not the adjective from the noun.
- Commas do not separate parts of a compound subject.
- Commas separate clauses that include both a subject and its verb, not parts of a compound verb.

A Add commas where they are needed. Not every sentence needs a comma.

1. The campers were hot and tired for they had been hiking all day.

2. The doctor examined the patient carefully but she did not say a word.

3. Kevin is not very heavy but is the best football player on the team.

4. An Arabian stallion is a fast beautiful horse.

5. The long dark pathway led to a grim ruined house.

6. Jack hit a line drive and dashed for first base.

7. Elephants are lazy friendly and good natured.

8. Everyone wondered who had been in the house what he had wanted and where he had gone.

9. Cathy likes tennis and golf but does not like softball.

10. We had eaten everything in the refrigerator but we were still hungry.

B In the following paragraph, some commas are incorrectly used and others are missing. Cross out the commas that do not belong and add commas where they are missing.

Val was almost ready to give up but she finally, spotted a light in the distance. She had been lost, in the woods for hours, yet she had kept moving. The day had started out beautifully and it had seemed like a good idea to go for a hike. Valerie was a person, who always tried to plan ahead. She had put some provisions in a backpack for she wanted to be prepared for a hike of several hours. She had not counted on being out, for so long. Since she used up her supplies hours ago now she was hungry, and thirsty. The distant light was a signal that all would be well and Valerie hurried toward it.

Grammar: Revising Incorrect Use of Commas

Assess

A Add commas where they are needed. Not every sentence needs a comma.

1. Bike riding brisk walking and swimming are good forms of exercise.

2. The victims of the hurricane were stunned for they had lost everything.

3. Crabs and lobsters are both shellfish.

4. The quiet obedient dog is a pleasure to be around.

5. The pilot boarded the plane checked her instruments and prepared for takeoff.

6. The tornado took a heavy toll in lives and property.

7. Susan wanted to explore the cave but her parents had forbidden it.

8. He and his wife skied in the Alps and enjoyed it very much.

9. We had lessons in swimming canoeing and archery.

10. The radio announcer warned of the storm but no one paid any attention.

B Add commas where they are needed. Not every sentence needs a comma.

1. Mowing a lawn on such a hot hazy humid day was no fun.

2. Sandy folded the clean laundry and I placed it in a basket.

3. The teacher repeated the directions but I was still confused.

4. We found seaweed in the water on the sand and under the rocks.

5. The writer opened her book and started to read one of her stories to the audience.

6. The doctor recommended plenty of liquids extra rest and a light diet.

7. You can use this free ticket for yourself or you can give it to a friend.

8. Several tired hikers straggled back to camp.

9. Dad has several old valuable stamps in his collection.

10. I eat balanced meals take vitamins and get enough sleep.

Writing: Myth

Practice

Myths began as ways to explain natural occurrences, like bolts of lightning or the changing shape of the moon, which early people could not understand. When preparing to write a short myth of your own, start by thinking of a natural phenomenon that you would like to write a creative explanation for. The natural phenomenon will be the *problem* in the myth, and your explanation for it will be the *solution.* Your myth will have characters and action in it. Try to keep the story simple by using few characters.

A   Circle the letter that best answers each question.

1. Which of the following describes a natural occurrence a myth might explain?

   A. why glass is clear   **C.** why birds fly south
   B. why fire engines are red   **D.** why airplanes have landing gear

2. Which of the following actions would best describe a character as <u>brave</u>?

   A. helping a lost dog   **C.** donating money to a worthy cause
   B. running a marathon   **D.** leading the way into a dark cave

3. Which physical detail would best create an image of a <u>timid</u> character?

   A. small and hunched   **C.** sharply dressed
   B. sparkling eyes   **D.** tall and muscular

4. What types of details would you want to include in your myth?

   A. scientific explanations   **C.** weather data
   B. character descriptions   **D.** measurements

B   Begin your myth by completing the following.

1. Select a topic for your myth and write it on the line.

_____

_____

2. Think of two characters you would like to include in your myth. You may use supernatural beings as well as human characters.

_____ and _____

3. Think of two words to describe each character. _____

_____   _____   _____   _____

Writing: Myth

Read the passage. Then, answer the questions that follow.

Rascal stood before the evening fire, his eyes blazing with mischief. "Come," he called to the villagers. "Gather round. Look at what I have to show you." Luna was the first to arrive. The moon trailed close on her heels, lighting the way for the people, who quickly followed. They formed a circle around the cool, dancing flames.

1. Underline the main characters in the passage. In the following chart, list a trait that describes each character.

Character	Trait

2. What additional details might you add to give the impression that Rascal cares about his appearance? _____

_____

3. What details might you add to the passage if you want to show that Rascal has supernatural powers? _____

_____

4. Based on details in the passage, what problem might you introduce to help you plan the action? _____

_____

5. Circle one or more details in the passage that suggest a natural phenomenon that might be explained by developing this myth. Then, identify the phenomenon and write one or two lines summarizing a creative explanation you might give for its occurrence._____

_____

_____

Writing: Description

A **descriptive paragraph** creates a vivid image of a person, place, or thing.

A Choose one of the following places or think of another place that is special to you. List six or seven details that describe this place on a separate sheet of paper. Include details that appeal to at least three senses. Some of the details should also reflect your feelings about the place.

1. A room in a house

2. A landscape through which you have traveled by plane, car, train, or boat

3. A place associated with a holiday

4. An imaginary place you would like to visit

5. The inside of a closet

B Complete the following activities on a separate sheet of paper as preparation for writing a descriptive paragraph. Use the place you chose in Exercise A.

1. Classify the details so that you will be able to present them in a clear and organized way.

2. Add appropriate adjectives and adverbs to your details.

3. Write down your feelings about this place. Try to reflect these feelings with vivid adverbs and adjectives.

4. Write two possible topic sentences that could be supported by your details.

5. Decide on a spatial order for your description. For example, will you order your details from near to far, outside to inside, or left to right?

C Write your descriptive paragraph on the following lines.

_____

_____

_____

_____

Writing: Description

A Sort these sensory descriptions into the correct categories in the following chart.

1. clear water
2. roaring engine
3. smooth stones
4. soggy bread
5. colorful shirt

6. loud voice
7. blinding light
8. sour lemon
9. chilling wind
10. chocotate ice cream

Sight	Sound	Taste	Touch

B Write a descriptive paragraph of a person you know. Use as many sensory descriptions as you can. Consider such things as the person's appearance, personality, manner of speaking and dressing, and so forth. Make your details as specific as possible.

_____
_____
_____
_____
_____
_____
_____
_____
_____

Writing: Business Letter

Practice

A **business letter** is a brief but formal letter written with a specific purpose. People write business letters to ask for information, to provide information, to express an opinion, or to complain. The format of a business letter includes:

- Heading: your address and the date
- Inside address: the address where the letter will be sent
- Greeting: *Dear* plus the person's name and title, followed by a colon, for example, *Dear Mrs. Smith:* (You may use *Dear Sir:* or *Dear Madam:* or *To Whom It May Concern:* if you do not have an exact name for your recipient.)
- Body of the letter: state your reason for writing and make your points.
- Closing: *Sincerely* or *Respectfully*, followed by a comma
- Signature: your full name and your signature above it

It is important to support your points with details and to use a polite tone in your letter.

Answer these questions about business letters.

1. You are going to write a business letter to your school principal, Dr. Robert Brown. Which is the correct greeting to use in your letter?

   A. Dear Bob,
   B. Dear Dr. Brown:
   C. Principal Robert Brown:
   D. Dear Sir:

2. If you were writing to Dr. Brown to request new lunch menu choices, which would be the most appropriate sentence to include in your letter?

   A. I think the lunches are disgusting.
   B. Everybody says the same thing: we are sick of soggy French fries!
   C. Since the beginning of the year, the lunch menu has been the same each week.
   D. I doubt you have been to the cafeteria lately.

   Why is this sentence appropriate? _____

3. What would be the best closing for the letter to Dr. Robert Brown?

   A. Thanks,
   B. Your friend,
   C. Sincerely,
   D. Write back soon!

Name _____ Date _____

Imagine that you bought a pair of sneakers from a company called First Sports Shoes. The shoes were expensive, but the sole ripped away after only two weeks of use. You decide to write a letter of complaint to the president of the company. You find the address of the company online.

A letter has been started below. Complete it by filling in the numbered items. First, fill in the blank greeting. Then, complete the body of the letter, stating your position. Finally, include a proper closing and signature.

April 28, 2006

President
First Sports Shoe Co., Inc.
1111 First Avenue
Anywhere, NH 00000

Dear [1] _____

I am writing to say that [2] _____

_____

_____

I hope that you will [3] _____

_____.

I think this would be fair because [4] _____

_____.

Thank you for your attention to this matter.

[5] _____

[6] _____

[7] _____

Reading: Compare and Contrast

Practice

A **comparison** tells how two or more things are alike. A **contrast** tells how two or more things are different. To help you compare and contrast stories, ask questions such as the following:

- What does this event bring to mind?

- Does this character make me think of someone I know or have read about?

Read the following passage and answer the questions.

Cousin Christine went to bed every night with the fear that a burglar was going to break into her house. To prevent this from happening, she always piled her money, jewelry, and other valuables in a neat stack just outside her bedroom, with a note reading: Please take it and do not bother me, as this is all I have.

Cousin Sophie was also afraid of burglars, but she approached this situation with a stronger spirit. She was sure that burglars had been getting into her house as well, but found they hadn't taken anything. She claimed that she scared them off before anything was taken, by throwing shoes down the hallway. When she went to bed, she piled all the shoes there were about the house, where she could get at them quickly.

1. How was Cousin Christine like Cousin Sophie?

_____

_____

2. How was Cousin Christine different from Cousin Sophie?

_____

_____

Reading: Compare and Contrast

A For each pair of items below, write a sentence that compares the items and a sentence that contrasts them on the lines provided.

1. aquarium, zoo

_____

_____

_____

2. encyclopedia, dictionary

_____

_____

_____

3. television, radio

_____

_____

_____

B Choose one of the following pairs of items to compare and contrast. List at least six similarities and/or differences between the two items. Use the lines provided.

snakes and birds	hockey and soccer
pencils and pens	photographers and painters
movies and TV shows	singers and dancers

_____

_____

_____

_____

_____

_____

Literary Analysis: Cultural Context

Practice

Cultural context refers to the background, customs, and beliefs of a particular society, as reflected in its folk tales, myths, stories, art, and other creations. People put their own world into the stories they tell and the art they create. This is true in our world today, just as it was true at any time or in any place. Knowing the cultural context of anything you read will help you appreciate and understand it.

Read the following portion of a letter written by an Englishman living in London in 1778, when the American colonies were fighting for their independence from England. Then, answer the questions that follow about the selection's cultural context.

I had expected to sail to the colony of Virginia in America next year to visit my brother. It is a difficult trip at any time. But now the ridiculous "war of independence" has made the voyage impossible. I do not understand why the American colonies wish to separate from us. They are Englishmen, as we are. Our armies protect them from their enemies. The taxes we charge them are payment for that protection. I wonder how my brother can bear to live among such people. Surely he cannot have taken up their cause.

1. _____ What seems to be the most important element in this letter's cultural context?

   A. the monarchy of George III   **C.** the American Revolution
   B. the price of tea and other   **D.** the Virginia colony's governor
   goods in 1778

2. _____ Who are "such people" (referred to in the next-to-last sentence)?

   A. Englishmen   **C.** rebellious colonists
   B. Virginians   **D.** the writer's brother

3. _____ Which quality seems most important in the letter's cultural context?

   A. loyalty   **B.** fairness   **C.** imaginativeness **D.** kindness

4. What does the writer's comment in the opening sentences about the trip from London to Virginia tell you about travel during his time?

   _____

   _____

   _____

   _____

Literary Analysis: Cultural Context

Read the following portion of a fictional journal and then answer the questions that follow.

The most difficult part of life on this backward planet—the thing I miss the most from ours—is the fact that the people here cannot fly. They do fly, of course, but only in very large, very noisy vehicles they call "airplanes." (These are similar to our flyers of a thousand years ago.) Unlike us, they have not discovered how to make their own bodies lighter than air. And as long as I am living here, I must pretend to be one of *them*. It will be difficult.

1. _____ What conclusion can you draw about the cultural context of this fictional journal?

   A. The journal's author comes from a planet more advanced than Earth.
   B. The journal is written by someone from present-day Earth living on another planet.
   C. Technology on Earth is superior to that of the author's home.
   D. The journal's author enjoys living on Earth because it is so similar to her home.

2. _____ When author says she must "pretend to be one of *them*," she means

   A. animals on this planet.   C. people living on Earth.
   B. people from her home.   D. aliens who can fly on their own.

3. _____ The cultural context of the journal cannot be earlier than the twentieth century because of the reference to

   A. "a thousand years ago."   C. making "bodies lighter than air."
   B. "very large . . . vehicles   D. "observing these creatures."
      called 'airplanes.'"

4. How is the journal author's cultural context different from our own?

   _____

   _____

   _____

   _____

   _____

Literary Analysis: Folk Tale

Practice

A **folk tale** is a story that is composed orally and then passed from person to person by word of mouth. Folk tales often teach a lesson about life. They show the world in simple terms, with a clear separation between good and evil. Many folk tales from different cultures have similar kinds of characters, plots, and themes.

Read the following summary of a folk tale. Then, answer the questions and complete the activities that follow.

Two quarreling brothers were lost in the woods. Each blamed the other for their problems. They grew hungry and came upon a house made out of food: fruit, bread, cheese, even meat. As they fought over some cheddar, a giant came out of the house and grabbed the elder brother. Later, the younger one peeked through a window and saw his brother in a cage near a huge tub of boiling water. The young man wept, for he knew the giant planned to cook his brother. The older brother saw him and waved. He pointed to the giant sleeping nearby and signaled for his brother to climb in. The younger brother freed the elder one, and together they killed the giant. Then they found their way home and never quarreled again.

1. _____ Which lesson about life does this folk tale teach?

   A. Do not take what is not yours.   **C.** People should cooperate, not fight.
   B. Giants can be dangerous.   **D.** Take extra food when you go to
                                                the woods.

2. _____ Which idea about good and evil does this folk tale portray?

   A. Good and evil are not very   **C.** Killing the giant is both good
   different.   and evil.
   B. You can be good and then   **D.** Good can overcome evil.
   become evil.

3. _____ Which fairy tale does this folk tale most resemble?

   A. "Hansel and Gretel"   **C.** "Cinderella"
   B. "Sleeping Beauty"   **D.** "Goldilocks and the Three Bears"

4. In what way does the folk tale about the brothers resemble this fairy tale—

   in its plot, characters, or theme? _____

   _____

   _____

Literary Analysis: Folk Tale

Assess

Read the following summary of a folk tale. Then, answer the questions.

A king had three daughters, all born on the same day but all very different from one another. One was strong; one was beautiful; one was gentle. When it came time to decide who should inherit the throne, the king asked each princess a question: "What do you want most in life?" The strong princess said, "Great wealth, for then I can buy anything I want." The beautiful princess said, "Great power, because I will be able to make others do what I want." The gentle princess said, "I want others to be as happy as I am." The king decided to make the gentle daughter his heir, for she would be the best queen.

1. _____ Which statement describes why the king chose the third daughter?

   A. The first two princesses thought only of themselves, but the third thought of others.
   B. A happy person is likely to be a good leader.
   C. It did not matter which princess he selected, so he chose the one who spoke last.
   D. The strong princess and the beautiful princess didn't seem to want to be queen.

2. _____ What lesson about leadership does this folk tale teach?

   A. Being royal does not guarantee that someone is a good leader.
   B. The best leader puts the happiness of others above his or her own.
   C. Money and power are useful for getting other people to do things for you.
   D. Gentle people are always better leaders than beautiful or strong people are.

3. _____ Which of these qualities does the folk tale show as the highest good?

   A. love   **C.** wisdom
   B. obedience   **D.** selflessness

4. _____ Which best explains why the king has *three* children in this folk tale?

   A. Two daughters would not be enough, while four would be too many.
   B. The kingdom cannot be divided easily among three queens, so the king has to choose.
   C. The pattern of "threes" is common in many folk tales and fairy tales.
   D. There are only three possible qualities for a leader to have.

Literary Analysis: Tone

Practice

The **tone** of a literary work is the writer's attitude toward his or her subject and characters. The tone can often be described by a single adjective, such as *formal, playful,* or *respectful.* Factors that contribute to the tone include word choice, details, sentence structure, rhythm, and rhyme.

Tone	Example
Matter-of-fact, informative	Jack ate three helpings because he was very hungry.
Surprised	I can't believe how hungry Jack was! At dinner, he ate three helpings.

A Write the word that best describes the tone of each sentence. Then, underline the words or phrases that contribute to the tone.

> angry   depressed   dreamy   humorous   informative

1. _____ Today on the island, we will have cloud cover and some rain.

2. _____ What Hey, look! More rain. Forget the sun block; let's go for a slosh on the beach!

3. _____ Another day of clouds and rain, and gloom settled over the island.

4. _____ We sat close together, watching the mist over the lake and listening to the light patter of rain on the sides of the tent.

5. _____ What, more rain? I *thought* you said the weather would be great!

B What is the tone of this passage from Yoshiko Uchida's "Letter from a Concentration Camp"? Underline four words or phrases that convey this tone.

> Here I am sitting on an army cot in a smelly old horse stall, where Mama, Bud, and I have to live for who knows how long. It's pouring rain, the wind's blowing in through all the cracks, and Mama looks like she wants to cry. I guess she misses Papa. Or maybe what got her down was that long, muddy walk along the racetrack to get to the mess hall for supper.

Tone: _____

Name _____ Date _____

Literary Analysis: Tone

Assess

A For each item, write the letter of the word from the following list that most closely describes the tone. One word may be used more than once.

A. dreamy   **C.** aggressive   **E.** scary
B. irritated   **D.** matter-of-fact   **F.** excited

1. _____ The policeman scowled as he interrogated Mei for hours about the crime.

2. _____ The policeman asked Mei what she knew about the crime.

3. _____ The boat bobbed gently as the light breeze blew over the still water.

4. _____ The breeze wasn't strong enough for us to sail back to shore, so there we sat, stuck in the middle of the lake.

5. _____ Wow! With a top speed of seventy miles per hour, that boat can almost fly!

6. _____ As the hurricane threatened, the winds' blasts caused angry fifty-foot waves to crash over the small houses near the seashore.

7. _____ The hurricane winds were incredible! They whipped the water in the bay into awesome fifty-foot waves!

B Write one or two words to describe the tone of each sentence.

1. _____ The blare of horns and screaming sirens shattered Kit's peace of mind.

2. _____ The crowds! The noise! The electricity in the air! What a great city!

3. _____ The crowds and noises made no impression on Elle as she trudged home.

4. _____ The dark shadows cast on the narrow streets by the tall buildings gave Max a chill.

© Pearson Education, Inc., publishing as Pearson Prentice Hall.

Reading Kit **267**

Vocabulary: Idioms

Practice

An **idiom** is an expression that people commonly use. It is not meant to be understood literally. For example, if someone gave you "a piece of her mind," she would **not** be giving you a slice of her brain! Instead, she would be giving you a strong opinion. Study these two sentences. One contains an idiom, and one contains the same thought expressed literally.

> Sentence with Idiom: I was **on pins and needles,** waiting for my turn to sing.
>
> Sentence without Idiom: I was nervous, waiting for my turn to sing.

Each sentence contains an idiom in boldface type. On the line provided, rewrite the sentence, expressing the same thought in literal language.

1. Let me give you a few **great tips** about how to do well on tests.

_____

2. After school, I like to **hang out** with my friends.

_____

3. I think that story is **full of baloney.**

_____

4. I was **dog-tired** after the game.

_____

5. Some people enjoyed the new television show, but I thought it was **garbage.**

_____

6. Guess who I **ran into** today.

_____

Vocabulary: Idioms

Each sentence contains an idiom in boldface type. On the line provided, rewrite the sentence, expressing the same thought in literal language.

1. **What's the matter** with Mr. Smith?

   _____

2. Solving that problem was **a piece of cake.**

   _____

3. Spectators sometimes have to **duck** so they won't get hit by a baseball during the game.

   _____

4. Let me **put all my issues on the table** and then let's discuss them.

   _____

5. His rude answer made me **blow my top.**

   _____

6. Could you loan me **a few bucks**?

   _____

7. **What's on your mind?**

   _____

8. Are you serious, or are you just **pulling my leg**?

   _____

9. **Have a blast** on your vacation.

   _____

10. Can you keep my secret, or will you **let the cat out of the bag**?

   _____

Name _____ Date _____

Grammar: Capitalization

Practice

Capital letters signal the beginning of a sentence or quotation and identify proper nouns and adjectives. Proper nouns include the names of people, geographical locations, specific events and time periods, organizations, languages, and religions. Proper adjectives are derived from proper nouns, as in *Greece/Greek* and *Spain/Spanish*.

A Underline the words that should be capitalized in each of the following.

1. my sister is interested in a radio career.

2. my dad said, "you could be a sports announcer."

3. my brother attends syracuse university.

4. olga assured us we were eating real german cooking.

5. "let's go to the beach," kate said.

6. aunt dora teaches at jefferson high school.

7. mayor bailey met with governor frey to discuss the bus strike.

B Underline the words that should be capitalized in each of the following.

1. sarah's mom said, "would you like some lemonade?"

2. my dog knows several tricks.

3. on her return from africa, rita had a number of stories to tell.

4. officer patricia cabot was awarded a medal for bravery.

5. when harriet answered the phone, she said, "what a shame!"

6. my uncle chris has traveled all over the united states.

7. mom told jackie, "i've been waiting for you."

Grammar: Capitalization

A Underline the words that should be capitalized in each of the following sentences.

1. when will i see you again?

2. the envelope was addressed to cathy jordan.

3. my brother will enter the university of wisconsin in september.

4. "she was out of school thursday and friday," mr. stevens commented.

5. in high school, i will study either spanish or italian.

6. the mohave desert is in california.

B Rewrite the following, inserting capitals where necessary.

1. we waited for the inspector. the atmosphere was tense. soon the inspector arrived.

_____

2. he said, "the case is over. we have found the thief."

_____

3. "it's not me," harry said.

_____

4. "relax, harry," the inspector said, "because you're innocent."

_____

5. the inspector had a note. everyone listened eagerly.

_____

6. "dear sir," he read. "max stole the jewels. He buried them in the yard. sincerely yours, Pat the Rat."

_____

7. "impossible!" Kay cried. "my dog is a good dog and is not a thief."

_____

Grammar: Abbreviations

An **abbreviation** is a shortened form of a word or phrase, such as *Dr.* for *Doctor* or *Rd.* for *Road.* Most abbreviations end with a period and are useful when taking notes or writing lists.

A Write each group of words correctly. Use capital letters and periods.

1. mr charles cunningham _____

2. 197 maple ave _____

3. dr frances thompson _____

4. thurs, sept 13 _____

5. 6:45 pm, wed, may 9 _____

6. d h lawrence _____

7. mon, 7:30 am _____

8. st. louis, mo _____

9. mr james s watson, sr _____

10. providence, r i _____

B Match each abbreviation with its long form.

1. _____ pint	**A.** Mar	6. _____ Reverend	**F.** pt.
2. _____ Junior	**B.** cm	7. _____ centimeter	**G.** Jr.
3. _____ inch	**C.** Gov.	8. _____ Governor	**H.** rd.
4. _____ March	**D.** oz.	9. _____ ounce	**I.** Rev.
5. _____ road	**E.** Prof.	10. _____ Professor	**J.** in.

Grammar: Abbreviations

Assess

A Write each message. Make the abbreviations and initials correct.

1. thurs, oct 15, 7:30 pm: babysit for mrs morris

_____

2. soccer practice: mon through fri, 9 am to 1 pm

_____

3. Girl Scout meeting: orchard st, wed, 8:00 pm

_____

4. 5:00 pm: appointment with dr hollings

_____

5. band rehearsal: tues, 9:30 am

_____

B Write the abbreviation for each of the underlined words.

1. _____ Robert Stevens, <u>Junior</u>, is the new school principal.

2. _____ The Historical Society sponsored a 5 <u>kilometer</u> race.

3. _____ We had to make a left turn onto Grand <u>Boulevard</u>.

4. _____ Karen is originally from Baltimore, <u>Maryland</u>.

5. _____ Jack is six <u>feet</u> tall.

Grammar: Correct Use of Pronoun Case

Practice

Many pronouns change form according to usage. *Case* is the relationship between a pronoun's form and its use. Personal pronouns in the **nominative case** may be the subject of a verb or a predicate nominative—a noun or pronoun that renames the subject. Pronouns in the nominative case include *I, you, he, she, it, we, you,* and *they.*

Personal pronouns in the **objective case** have three uses: as a direct object, as an indirect object, and as the object of a preposition. Pronouns in the objective case include *me, you, him, her, it, us, you,* and *them.* Notice that you and it are the same in both cases.

Circle the correct pronoun.

1. Jill and (I, me) are in the same history class.

2. Our teacher gave an assignment to (she, her)—a report on peasant life in the Middle Ages.

3. Toni and (they, them) are studying medieval home life.

4. (He, Him) and Manuel are researching knighthood.

5. Out teacher gave Jill and (I, me) a good grade.

6. She congratulated Toni and (they, them) for their report.

7. It was (they, them) who made the posters.

8. The judges awarded (she, her) a blue ribbon.

9. As usual, the first one to finish was (he, him).

10. Carla and (I, me) were born on the same day.

11. Can you come to the game with Sheila and (I, me)?

12. It must have taken (he, him) an hour to finish.

13. Mrs. Reilly gave the job to (she, her).

14. Who was sitting beside you and (he, him)?

15. Next week Pete and (me, I) are going away.

Grammar: Correct Use of Pronoun Case

Assess

A Circle the correct pronoun.

1. Rachel and (I, me) practiced giving our reports many times.

2. It was (I, me) who was nervous, not Rachel.

3. It was (she, her) who introduced the report.

4. The only two speakers today are Rachel and (I, me).

5. First, (she, her) will speak about the life of Daniel Defoe.

6. (I, Me) will also say something about Defoe.

7. About (he, him) we know very little.

8. (We, Us) know, however, that Defoe was a novelist, a journalist, and a secret agent.

9. It was (he, him) that Queen Anne threw in prison in 1702.

10. To Rachel and (I, me) *Robinson Crusoe* is his best novel.

B Circle the correct pronoun.

1. (She, Her) and Kristin left for Florida last night.

2. The last guests to arrive were Jamie and (her, she).

3. It will upset either (they, them) or Kathy very much.

4. My aunt brought gifts for my brother and (I, me).

5. On Sunday Dad and (I, me) are driving to Oceanside.

6. During the night, mosquitoes kept Danny and (I, me) from sleep.

Spelling: Unstressed Syllables

Practice

A **syllable** is a part of a word that has a single vowel sound. The syllables in some words are not always pronounced clearly. Sometimes people leave them out altogether—not just when they are pronouncing the word, but also when they are trying to spell it.

For example, the word *sophomore* has three syllables—SOPH[1]-O[2]-MORE[3]—but it is often pronounced as though the middle syllable—the middle *o*—is not there. So people often pronounce only two of the syllables—SOPH[1]-MORE[2]—and they often misspell it that way, too: *sophmore.*

The best way to avoid this problem is to look up each word in the dictionary. Notice how the word is broken into syllables. Say each syllable aloud—even the unstressed ones—and count the number of syllables. That way you will be less likely to leave out a syllable when you spell the word.

different	temperature	extraordinary	laboratory
practically	average	restaurant	

A In the blank space next to each word below, write the number of syllables it contains. (You may consult a dictionary if you wish.)

1. average _____

2. temperature _____

3. practically _____

4. family _____

5. different _____

B Underline the four misspelled words in the paragraph. Give the correct spelling for each in the lines that follow.

   The food they served us in that restraunt was awful. It tasted like it came from a labratory. Our whole famly agreed that we would never go back there. This was extrordinary, because we hardly ever agree on anything.

1. _____   **3.** _____

2. _____   **4.** _____

Name _____ Date _____

Spelling: Unstressed Syllables

Assess

A Choose the sentence in which the underlined word is spelled correctly.

1. _____ **A.** The color of your eyes looks <u>diffrent</u> at night.
   B. A scientist often works in a <u>labratory</u>.
   C. The <u>temperature</u> outside usually goes down at night.
   D. Every <u>famly</u> in our school helped out with the junior play.

2. _____ **A.** The magician's tricks were <u>extraordinary</u>.
   B. That pitcher <u>practicly</u> won the game all by himself.
   C. We all had a wonderful time at the <u>fambly</u> reunion.
   D. The doctor said that my height is about <u>avrege</u> for my age.

3. _____ **A.** After we had driven for four hours, any <u>restaurant</u> looked good to me.
   B. I thought the movie was just <u>avridge</u>.
   C. I liked the movie because it was <u>differint</u> from most others I had seen.
   D. Some day I would like to work in a <u>labritory</u>.

4. _____ **A.** The <u>temprachur</u> is always mild in San Diego.
   B. Our whole <u>family</u> took part in the tennis tournament.
   C. The menu at the new <u>restrant</u> featured all my favorite dishes.
   D. The ballet dancer made a leap that showed <u>extrordinary</u> skill.

B Choose the letter of the correctly spelled word.

1. She was so fast that she had _____ won the race before it started.

   A. practicly   **C.** practically
   B. pratickly   **D.** prackticaly

2. All the judges agreed that it was an _____ dive.

   A. extrodinary   **C.** extraordinary
   B. extradinary   **D.** ekstrordinary

3. It was hard for us to adjust after we moved to a _____ climate.

   A. difrent   **C.** differant
   B. diffrent   **D.** different

4. Our _____ speed on the cross-country drive was 55 mph.

   A. average   **C.** avrage
   B. avridge   **D.** averidge

© Pearson Education, Inc., publishing as Pearson Prentice Hall.

Reading Kit **277**

Writing: Plot Summary

Practice

A **summary** is a brief statement of the main ideas of an article or the major events of a story. When you write a review of a novel, a short story, or a film, you use the skill of summarizing. Follow these guidelines.

Guidelines for Summarizing

1. After you read something, ask yourself, "What is this about?"
2. Find the main idea. If this idea is not directly stated, you must infer it.
3. Begin your summary with a topic sentence that states the main idea. Add sentences that supply supporting details.
4. Avoid unnecessary details.
5. To summarize lists of things or actions, find a category that covers what is on the list. For example, do not say a character coughed, sneezed, felt dizzy, had the chills, and felt weak. Instead, say the character had the flu.

Read the following summary of "Cinderella" and answer the questions that follow.

This is the story of patience and virtue being rewarded. The kind and sweet-tempered Cinderella was constantly mistreated by her stepmother and stepsisters. When she was forbidden to accompany her stepsisters to a magnificent ball, she wept. Suddenly a fairy godmother appeared, dressed her in splendid clothes, and transported her to the ball in a magic coach. The unknown beauty dazzled everyone, including a prince. She quickly departed just before midnight, leaving a glass slipper in her haste. In the following weeks, the love-struck prince searched everywhere for the beautiful woman whose foot would fit the slipper. Finally, he found Cinderella and made her his princess.

1. What is the main idea stated in the topic sentence?

_____

2. Identify a detail that supports the main idea.

_____

3. Has any unnecessary information been provided?

_____

Writing: Plot Summary

A Choose the best answer to each of the following questions. Write the letter of the answer in the blank.

1. ____ A good summary is always

   A. much shorter than the original.
   B. about the same length as the original.
   C. slightly longer than the original.
   D. approximately three to five words.

2. ____ A summary of a passage includes

   A. only the main idea.
   B. at least two ideas.
   C. the main idea and the most important details.
   D. all of the passage's details.

3. ____ In a summary, you use

   A. quotations from the passage.
   B. your own words.
   C. only the passage's main idea.
   D. the title of the passage.

B Write a summary paragraph about a short story you have read. Use the following checklist to decide whether your summary accurately and briefly reflects the content of the story.

Summary Paragraph Revision Checklist

- Have I included a topic sentence that states the main idea?
- Have I added the details that support the main idea?
- Have I avoided unnecessary details?
- Have I used one or two words to cover lists of things or actions?

_____

_____

_____

_____

Writing: Review

A **review** is a response to a work of literature that gives readers an impression of a work, encouraging them either to read it or avoid reading it. A review should include the following:

- a strong, interesting focus on an aspect of the work
- a clear organization that groups related details
- supporting details for each main idea
- a summary of important features of the work
- a judgment about the value of a work

Choose a story that you have read recently to which you had a strong positive or negative response. Use the following table to make some notes about its four major elements: plot, character, setting, and theme (a question or comment about life). Think about which of the four elements is most important to the story and what the effect is of that element. Write the story's title on the line below.

_____

Plot	Character	Setting	Theme

1. Reflect on the part of the story you enjoyed most or responded to most strongly. Summarize your response to the story on the lines below. Make sure you include the basic reason for your response.

_____

_____

2. On the lines below, list details that support your response to the story.

_____

_____

_____

Writing: Review

Choose a poem that you have enjoyed reading. Use the following table to make some notes about its literary elements. Think about which of these elements is most important to the poem, and what the effect of the element is. Write the poem's title on the line below.

_____

Rhyme Scheme	Rhythm	Figurative Language	Theme

1. Reflect on the part of the poem you enjoyed most or responded to most strongly. Summarize your response to the poem on the lines below. Make sure you include the basic reason for your response.

_____

_____

2. On the lines below, list the details that support your response to the poem.

_____

_____

_____

3. Explain one way that writing this review helped you understand or appreciate the poem you chose more completely.

_____

_____

Writing: Research Report

Practice

A **research report** analyzes information gathered from reference materials, observations, interviews, or other sources to present a clear and accurate picture of a topic or to answer a question.

A Narrow each topic to one that could be covered in a research report of six to eight paragraphs.

1. South America

_____

2. Great Inventors

_____

3. Jungle Animals

_____

4. Weather

_____

5. Athletics

_____

B Choose five of the following topics. On your own paper, write three good questions to use in researching each of the selected topics.

1. Martin Luther King, Jr.   **6.** Marie Curie

2. The Civil War   **7.** Education in China

3. Life in a Mexican Village   **8.** African Art

4. Japanese Poetry   **9.** Death Valley

5. Ocean Tides   **10.** Careers in Law Enforcement

Writing: Research Report

Assess

Reference sources such as dictionaries, encyclopedias, atlases, almanacs, and *The Readers' Guide to Periodical Literature* are located in a reference section of a library.

A Answer the questions below.

1. Which reference source would you consult if you wanted to know who was the winner of the Rose Bowl in 1983?

_____

2. Which reference source would include an article on spacecraft?

_____

3. Which reference source would you consult if you wanted to find a map of Alaska?

_____

4. Which reference source would help you find a magazine article that was published last year?

_____

B Underline the reference source in parentheses that would be best to consult for the following information.

1. a map of Alberta, Canada (atlas, encyclopedia)

2. information about the history of motion pictures
(encyclopedia, nonprint media)

3. a 1959 magazine article on Hawaii becoming a state (atlas, *Readers' Guide*)

4. a film of the first walk on the moon (encyclopedia, nonprint media)

5. the author who wrote, "Neither a borrower, nor a lender be"
(book of quotations, encyclopedia)

6. The final standings of the East Division American League in 1986
(*Readers' Guide*, almanac)

Everyday Reading Strategies

Predictogram Relating Words

About the Strategy

Predictograms ask students to use what they know about words and phrases from a selection to make predictions about its content and structure. Prediction activities involve students in the text, engage their attention, and give them a stake in the outcome of a story.

A sample predictogram is provided using the story "Seventh Grade."

Predictogram Relating Words

(Title) _Seventh Grade_ **2**

Look at the words below. Draw lines between any items you think might be connected. Explain your connection on the line you draw. You might choose several connections with some words and none with others.

1 embarrassed

rosebushes of shame

a new year, new experiences

confusing, like the inside of a watch

Victor
(the main character)

bouquets of love

bluff

3

Victor is trying to impress someone.

impress

with greater conviction

A relating words predictogram works well with any fictional piece in which the words, phrases, and quotations selected can show associations between characters and concepts.

Step **1**
Choose nine words, phrases, or quotations from the selection that will help students predict what a story will be about.

Step **2**
Encourage students to use the title as they make their predictions.

Step **3**
Remind students to think about what they already know about the words and phrases.

Skills and Strategies: _predict outcomes, activate prior knowledge, draw conclusions_

Idea Exchange

Keep in Mind
• Choose appropriate words, phrases, quotations, and topical cues, such as titles or key words, to help students make associations.
• Model one prediction before individuals begin.
• Be sure students return to their predictograms after reading to confirm their predictions.

All Together Now
You might use the relating words predictogram to begin a class discussion. Students could state their predictions rather than writing them down.

Predictogram Relating Words

(Title) _____

Look at the words below. Draw lines between any items you think might be connected.
Explain your connection on the line you draw. You might choose several connections
with some words and none with others.

Predictogram Literary Features

About the Strategy

Predictograms ask students to use what they know about words and phrases from a selection to make predictions about its content and structure. Prediction activities involve students in the text, engage their attention, and give them a stake in the outcome of a story.

The following model is based on "All Summer in a Day."

A literary features predictogram works well with any fictional piece in which the words or phrases selected can help students identify specific features of a story.

Predictogram Literary Features

(Title) __All Summer in a Day__ ❷

Look at the selection title above and this list of words and phrases to write sentences that predict who and what this story might be about.

❶

teacher	silence was so immense	jungle
solemn and pale	remembered a warmness	Margot
muffled cries	turning their faces up	Venus
9 years old	rocket men and women	a closet
then looked away	raining for seven years	soon
It's stopping.	very frail	running

Characters: _____

_____

Setting: _____

_____ ❸

Problem: _____

_____

Events: _____

_____

_____

Outcome: _____

_____

Mystery Words or Phrases: _____

Step ❶

Choose five to ten words or phrases from the selection that will help students predict what the story will be about.

Step ❷

Encourage students to use the title as they make their predictions.

Step ❸

Remind students to think about what they already know about the words and phrases.

Skills and Strategies: *predict outcomes, activate prior knowledge, draw conclusions*

Idea Exchange

Keep in Mind
• Choose appropriate words, phrases, and topical cues, such as titles or key words, to help students make associations.
• Model one prediction before individuals begin.
• Be sure students return to their predictograms after reading to confirm their predictions.

Solo Exploration
Encourage students to use this predictogram to plan their own writing. They can collect their ideas in the box and sort them according to literary feature as a prewriting strategy. **(writing)**

Predictogram Literary Features

(Title) _____

Look at the selection title above and this list of words and phrases to write
sentences that predict who and what this story might be about.

_____

Characters: _____

_____

Setting: _____

_____

Problem: _____

_____

Events: _____

_____

_____

Outcome: _____

_____

Mystery Words or Phrases: _____

_____

Predictogram Asking Questions

About the Strategy

Predictograms ask students to use what they know about words and phrases from a selection to make predictions about its content and structure. Prediction activities involve students in the text, engage their attention, and give them a stake in the outcome of a story.

Look at the following example.

Predictogram Asking Questions

(Title) __A Ribbon for Baldy__

Look at the title of the selection above and the words or phrases below. Can you think of any questions to ask about this selection?

1

project	Why is a project important in this story?
posture	
Little Baldy	
cone-shaped	
broom-sedge	
fire	
corn row	
corkscrew	

Choose one of your questions and write a paragraph answering it.

3

Question: _____
_____

Answer: _____
_____
_____
_____
_____
_____
_____

Step ❶

Choose eight words or phrases from the selection that will help students write questions to predict what a story will be about.

Step ❷

Encourage students to use the title as they make their predictions.

Step ❸

Remind students to think about what they already know about the words and phrases as they answer the question.

Skills and Strategies: *predict outcomes, activate prior knowledge, draw conclusions*

Keep in Mind

- Choose appropriate words, phrases, and topical cues, such as titles or key words, to help students write their questions.
- Model one prediction before individuals begin.
- Be sure students return to their predictograms after reading to confirm their predictions.

Buddywork

Suggest to students that they use the glossary at the end of a chapter in their social studies book to create an asking questions predictogram. They can use their predictograms to help them set purposes for reading the chapter. (**cross-curricular connection**)

Predictogram Asking Questions

(Title) _____

Look at the title of the selection above and the words or phrases below. Can you think of any questions to ask about this selection?

Choose one of your questions and write a paragraph answering it.

Question: _____

_____

Answer: _____

_____

_____

_____

_____

_____

Predictogram Using Quotations

About the Strategy

Predictograms ask students to use what they know about words and phrases from a selection to make predictions about its content and structure. Prediction activities involve students in the text, engage their attention, and give them a stake in the outcome of a story.

Look at the following example.

A using quotations predictogram works well with any fictional piece in which characters can be identified by their words.

Predictogram Using Quotations

(Title) Becky and the Wheels-and-Brake Boys

Look at the title above and the descriptions of each character below. Can you predict who might have said each of the following? Write the quotation next to the character who might have said it.

①

"D'you think you're a boy?"

"I can't get rid of it, mam.

"What am I going to do?"

Character	Quotation
② **Becky:** a young girl who wants a bike	**③**
Mum: Becky's mother	

Now write a paragraph about one of the characters using the quotations above.

_____

_____

_____

_____

Step ①

Choose three to ten quotations from the selection that will help students predict what a story will be about.

Step ②

Choose two main characters and write a brief description of each.

Step ③

Ask students to match the quotations with the characters who might say them.

Skills and Strategies: *predict outcomes, activate prior knowledge, draw conclusions*

Keep in Mind

• Choose identifying quotations and topical cues, such as titles or key words, to help students make associations.
• Model one prediction before individuals begin.
• Be sure students return to their predictograms after reading to confirm their predictions.

All Together Now

Students could take turns reading the quotations with differing inflections. The class could predict how each sentence might be said in the context of the story. While reading they can check their predictions.

Predictogram Using Quotations

(Title) _____

Look at the title above and the descriptions of each character below. Can you predict who might have said each of the following? Write the quotation next to the character who might have said it.

Character	Quotation

Now write a paragraph about one of the characters using the quotations above.

_____

_____

_____

_____

K-W-L Chart

About the Strategy

K-W-L is a strategy for reading expository text that helps students use their prior knowledge to generate interest in a selection. K-W-L also helps students set purposes for reading by encouraging them to express their curiosity for the topic they will be reading about. K-W-L encourages group members to share and discuss what they know, what they want to know, and what they learn about a topic.

List selections for which you would like to use a K-W-L chart.

Step ❶
Students brainstorm what they know or think they know about the topic.

Step ❷
Students list questions they hope to have answered as they read.

Step ❸
Students list what they learn as they read.

K-W-L Chart

Topic: Abraham Lincoln

What We **K**now	What We **W**ant to Know	What We **L**earned
Lincoln was president of the United States. Lincoln grew up poor.	What was Lincoln's childhood like? How was Lincoln educated? What kind of person was Lincoln?	Lincoln was born in a log cabin and was poor as a child. Lincoln went to school when he could and read everything he could find. Lincoln was a good wrestler and runner and loved to tell jokes and stories.
❶	❷	❸

Skills and Strategies: *activate prior knowledge, generate questions, set purpose, summarize facts*

Idea Exchange

Keep in Mind
• If students are unsure of a fact they listed in column one, they can turn it into a question in column two.
• Encourage students to find out the answers to any unanswered questions.

Solo Exploration
Students can use a K-W-L chart to set purposes for reading a daily newspaper. Before reading, students should think about what they know (e.g., the weather forecast from listening to the radio) and what they want to know. **(cross-curricular connection)**

K-W-L Chart

Topic: _____

What We **K**now	What We **W**ant to Know	What We **L**earned

Plot Structure Map

About the Strategy

A plot structure map helps students recognize the structure, or grammar, of a fictional selection. Identifying story grammar enhances comprehension by helping students identify important characters, predict events, and be better prepared to summarize a selection.

A plot structure map works well with any story that has rising action, a clear climax, and a resolution.

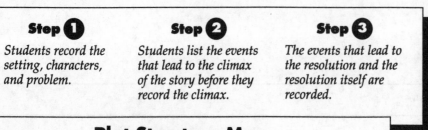

Step ❶
Students record the setting, characters, and problem.

Step ❷
Students list the events that lead to the climax of the story before they record the climax.

Step ❸
The events that lead to the resolution and the resolution itself are recorded.

Plot Structure Map

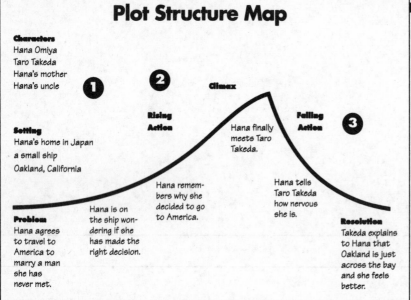

Characters
Hana Omiya
Taro Takeda
Hana's mother
Hana's uncle

Setting
Hana's home in Japan
a small ship
Oakland, California

Problem
Hana agrees to travel to America to marry a man she has never met.

❶

❷

Climax

Rising Action

Hana is on the ship wondering if she has made the right decision.

Hana remembers why she decided to go to America.

Hana finally meets Taro Takeda.

Falling Action

❸

Hana tells Taro Takeda how nervous she is.

Resolution
Takeda explains to Hana that Oakland is just across the bay and she feels better.

Skills and Strategies: *understand characters, note setting, identify plot, summarize*

Idea Exchange

Solo Exploration
Invite students to use a plot structure map to create an outline for a short story based on an incident in their life. Then, students can develop their outlines into stories. **(writing)**

Buddywork
Pairs of students can work together to create a plot structure map for a story with a flashback or for a story with subplots. Invite students to share their maps with the rest of the class.

Plot Structure Map

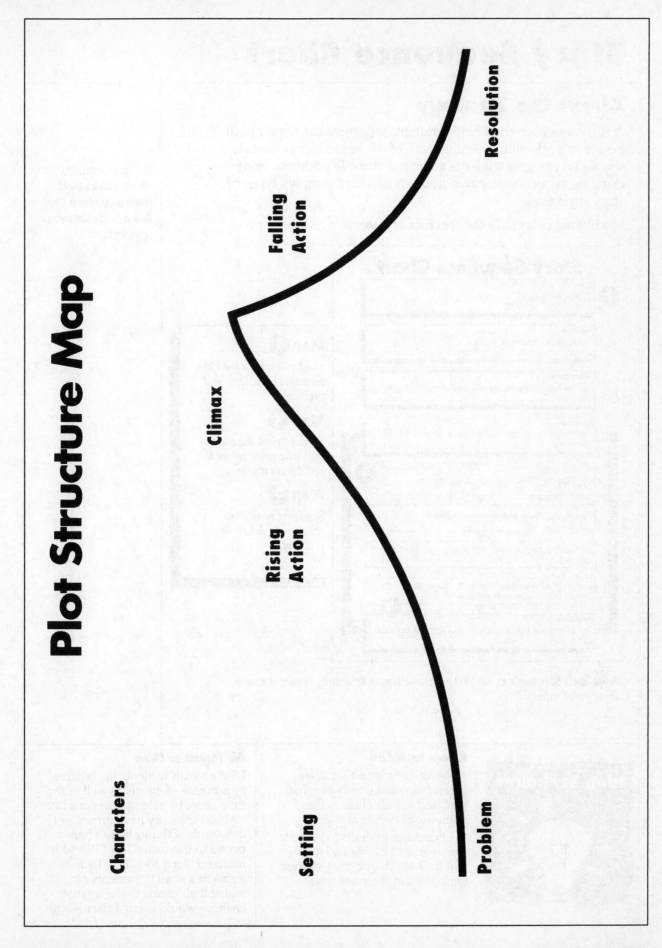

Characters

Setting

Rising Action

Climax

Falling Action

Resolution

Problem

Story Sequence Chart

About the Strategy

A story sequence chart helps students recognize the sequence of events in a selection. Keeping track of the sequence of events is a simple way to give students a sense of story. In addition, understanding sequence prepares students for more complex types of story structures.

Modify the chart to fit the specifics of a story.

A story sequence chart works well with any story that has a clear sequence of events.

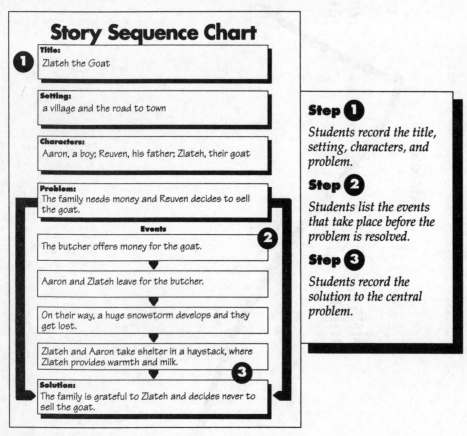

Story Sequence Chart

1
Title:
Zlateh the Goat

Setting:
a village and the road to town

Characters:
Aaron, a boy; Reuven, his father; Zlateh, their goat

Problem:
The family needs money and Reuven decides to sell the goat.

Events

2
The butcher offers money for the goat.

Aaron and Zlateh leave for the butcher.

On their way, a huge snowstorm develops and they get lost.

Zlateh and Aaron take shelter in a haystack, where Zlateh provides warmth and milk.

3
Solution:
The family is grateful to Zlateh and decides never to sell the goat.

Step 1
Students record the title, setting, characters, and problem.

Step 2
Students list the events that take place before the problem is resolved.

Step 3
Students record the solution to the central problem.

Skills and Strategies: *understand characters, note setting, sequence events, identify plot, summarize*

Idea Exchange

Keep in Mind

• Remind students that dates, time of day, and words like *first*, *next*, and *last* are clues to the sequence of events in a story.

• Encourage students to look for clue words like *while* and *during* that indicate two or more events happening at the same time.

All Together Now

Discuss with students the relative importance of events as well as the time order by asking questions like "Would the story have turned out differently if things hadn't happened in this order?" or "Would it matter if 'such and such' hadn't happened at all?" Students can adjust their charts to show what changes would occur. **(discussion)**

Story Sequence Chart

Title:

Setting:

Characters:

Problem:

Events

Solution:

Story Triangle

About the Strategy

A story triangle is a creative way to think about and summarize a story. Like a traditional story map, the story triangle helps students recognize story elements. However, a story triangle allows students to respond personally to a story since students must describe rather than just list characters, events, and problems.

The following model is based on the story "Seventh Grade."

Story triangles work well with all types of fiction, including realistic and historical fiction.

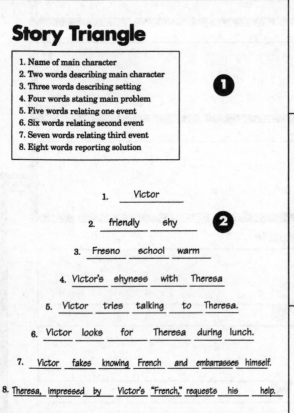

Story Triangle

1. Name of main character
2. Two words describing main character
3. Three words describing setting
4. Four words stating main problem
5. Five words relating one event
6. Six words relating second event
7. Seven words relating third event
8. Eight words reporting solution

1

1. Victor
2. friendly   shy   **2**
3. Fresno   school   warm
4. Victor's   shyness   with   Theresa
5. Victor   tries   talking   to   Theresa.
6. Victor   looks   for   Theresa   during   lunch.
7. Victor   fakes   knowing   French   and   embarrasses   himself.
8. Theresa,   impressed   by   Victor's   "French,"   requests   his   help.

Step ①
Students follow the directions at the top of the page to fill in the story triangle.

Step ②
Encourage students to be creative as they choose words, phrases, and sentences.

Skills and Strategies: *understand characters, note setting, identify plot, summarize*

Idea Exchange

Keep in Mind
• If students get stuck in the middle, encourage them to start with the last line and work backward.
• When using a story triangle with another story, be sure to change the guidelines to match the story.

Solo Exploration
After students complete their story triangles, they can circle any vague words they used. Encourage students to choose synonyms that are more interesting and specific to replace the vague words.

Story Triangle

1. Name of main character
2. Two words describing main character
3. Three words describing setting
4. Four words stating main problem
5. Five words relating one event
6. Six words relating second event
7. Seven words relating third event
8. Eight words reporting solution

1. _____

2. _____ _____

3. _____ _____ _____

4. _____ _____ _____ _____

5. _____ _____ _____ _____ _____

6. _____ _____ _____ _____ _____ _____

7. _____ _____ _____ _____ _____ _____ _____

8. _____ _____ _____ _____ _____ _____ _____ _____

Story-Within-a-Story Map

About the Strategy

A story-within-a-story map helps students identify the plot events of this complex text structure. Keeping track of plot events enhances comprehension by helping students recognize the change in narrative that is part of this structure.

Story-within-a-story maps work well with fiction in which the plot includes a story within the story.

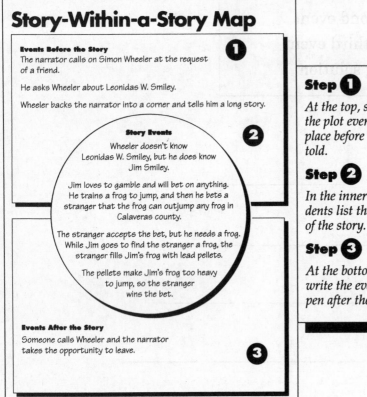

Story-Within-a-Story Map

Events Before the Story **①**

The narrator calls on Simon Wheeler at the request of a friend.

He asks Wheeler about Leonidas W. Smiley.

Wheeler backs the narrator into a corner and tells him a long story.

Story Events **②**

Wheeler doesn't know Leonidas W. Smiley, but he does know Jim Smiley.

Jim loves to gamble and will bet on anything. He trains a frog to jump, and then he bets a stranger that the frog can outjump any frog in Calaveras county.

The stranger accepts the bet, but he needs a frog. While Jim goes to find the stranger a frog, the stranger fills Jim's frog with lead pellets.

The pellets make Jim's frog too heavy to jump, so the stranger wins the bet.

Events After the Story **③**

Someone calls Wheeler and the narrator takes the opportunity to leave.

Step ①

At the top, students write the plot events that take place before the story is told.

Step ②

In the inner circle, students list the plot events of the story.

Step ③

At the bottom, students write the events that happen after the story is told.

Skills and Strategies: *use story elements, use text structure/genre, sequence*

Idea Exchange

Keep in Mind

If students are having difficulty recognizing this text structure, have them reread to look for the point in the story when the narrative shifts.

Solo Exploration

Suggest that students do a story-comparison map for the story and the story within the story to look for similarities and differences between them.

Story-Within-a-Story Map

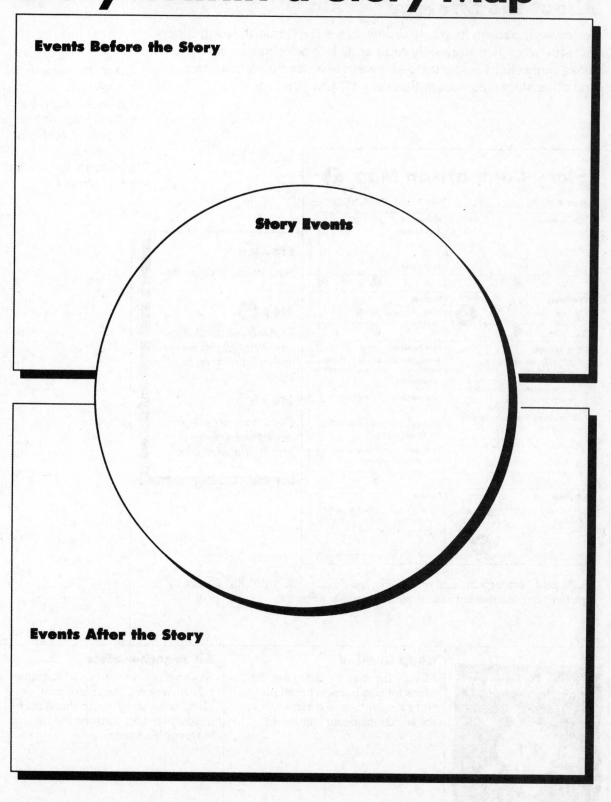

Events Before the Story

Story Events

Events After the Story

Story-Comparison Map

About the Strategy

A story-comparison map helps students see the similarities and differences between two stories. By comparing two selections, students can make connections across texts—between text structures, characters and other story elements, authors' styles, and points of view.

A story-comparison map works well with selections by the same author or selections that have unique story elements but similar text structures.

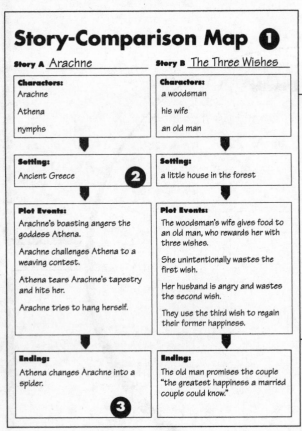

Story-Comparison Map ❶

Story A <u>Arachne</u>   Story B <u>The Three Wishes</u>

Characters:
Arachne
Athena
nymphs

Characters:
a woodsman
his wife
an old man

Setting:
Ancient Greece

❷

Setting:
a little house in the forest

Plot Events:
Arachne's boasting angers the goddess Athena.

Arachne challenges Athena to a weaving contest.

Athena tears Arachne's tapestry and hits her.

Arachne tries to hang herself.

Plot Events:
The woodsman's wife gives food to an old man, who rewards her with three wishes.

She unintentionally wastes the first wish.

Her husband is angry and wastes the second wish.

They use the third wish to regain their former happiness.

Ending:
Athena changes Arachne into a spider.

Ending:
The old man promises the couple "the greatest happiness a married couple could know."

❸

Step ❶
Students write down the titles.

Step ❷
Students list the characters, settings, plot events, and endings for both stories.

Step ❸
Discuss together the similarities and differences between the selections.

Skills and Strategies: *recall prior reading experience, use story elements, use text structure/genre, compare and contrast, make connections across texts*

Idea Exchange

Keep in Mind

Modify the map by changing the items for comparison based on the story elements or text structures of the selections being compared.

All Together Now

Ask students to read two biographical articles on the same person. Then, use a story-comparison map to compare and contrast the two biographies. **(genre)**

Story-Comparison Map

Story A _____   **Story B** _____

Characters:	**Characters:**
Setting:	**Setting:**
Plot Events:	**Plot Events:**
Ending:	**Ending:**

Cause-Effect Frame

About the Strategy

A cause-effect frame helps students identify what happened and why it happened in both fictional and nonfictional texts. When students can see that there are causal relationships between events or ideas in text, they can make generalizations about other causal relationships in new texts and in life situations.

Cause-effect frames work well with any selection that has clear cause-and-effect relationships.

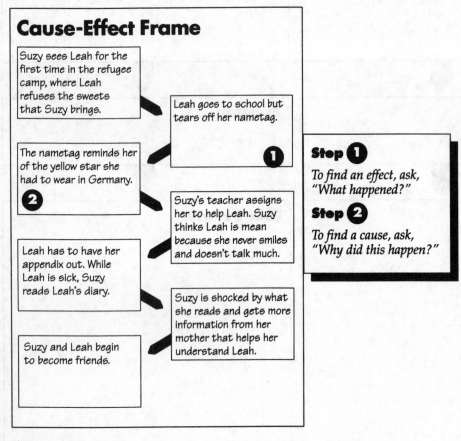

Cause-Effect Frame

Suzy sees Leah for the first time in the refugee camp, where Leah refuses the sweets that Suzy brings.

Leah goes to school but tears off her nametag. **1**

The nametag reminds her of the yellow star she had to wear in Germany. **2**

Suzy's teacher assigns her to help Leah. Suzy thinks Leah is mean because she never smiles and doesn't talk much.

Leah has to have her appendix out. While Leah is sick, Suzy reads Leah's diary.

Suzy is shocked by what she reads and gets more information from her mother that helps her understand Leah.

Suzy and Leah begin to become friends.

Step 1
To find an effect, ask, "What happened?"

Step 2
To find a cause, ask, "Why did this happen?"

Skills and Strategies: *summarize, sequence, cause-effect, make inferences*

Idea Exchange

Keep in Mind
• Suggest that students look for clue words, such as *since, as a result, consequently, therefore,* and *thus.*
• Remind students that some causes are not stated in the text. Students will have to figure out the cause by looking at what happened and asking themselves, "Why might this have happened?"

Solo Exploration
Help students see that they can use cause-effect frames as a way to organize their writing. Students can choose an important school issue and use a cause-effect frame to outline the main point. Ask students to place the outlines in their portfolios to use for future writing. **(portfolio)**

Cause-Effect Frame

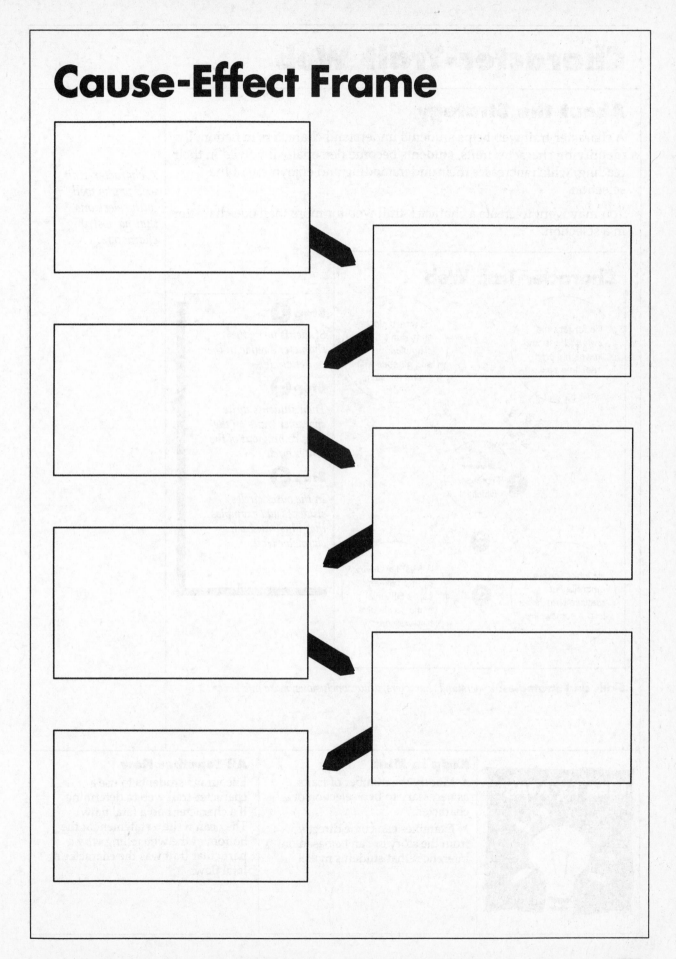

Character-Trait Web

About the Strategy

A character-trait web helps students understand characters in fiction. By identifying character traits, students become personally involved in their reading, which increases their understanding and enjoyment of the selection.

You may want to create a character-trait web for more than one character in a selection.

A character-trait web works well with selections that have strong characters.

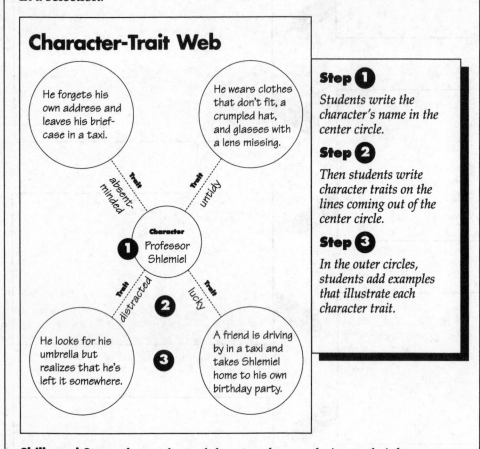

Character-Trait Web

He forgets his own address and leaves his briefcase in a taxi.

He wears clothes that don't fit, a crumpled hat, and glasses with a lens missing.

Trait absent-minded

Trait untidy

Character 1 Professor Shlemiel

Trait distracted

Trait lucky

2

3

He looks for his umbrella but realizes that he's left it somewhere.

A friend is driving by in a taxi and takes Shlemiel home to his own birthday party.

Step 1
Students write the character's name in the center circle.

Step 2
Then students write character traits on the lines coming out of the center circle.

Step 3
In the outer circles, students add examples that illustrate each character trait.

Skills and Strategies: *understand characters, draw conclusions, make inferences*

Idea Exchange

Keep in Mind
• Modify the number of traits as necessary to fit a selection or character.
• Examples can come directly from the story or can be based on inferences that students make.

All Together Now
Encourage students to use a character-trait web to determine if a character had a fatal flaw. They can write a statement at the bottom of the web telling why a particular trait was the character's fatal flaw.

Character-Trait Web

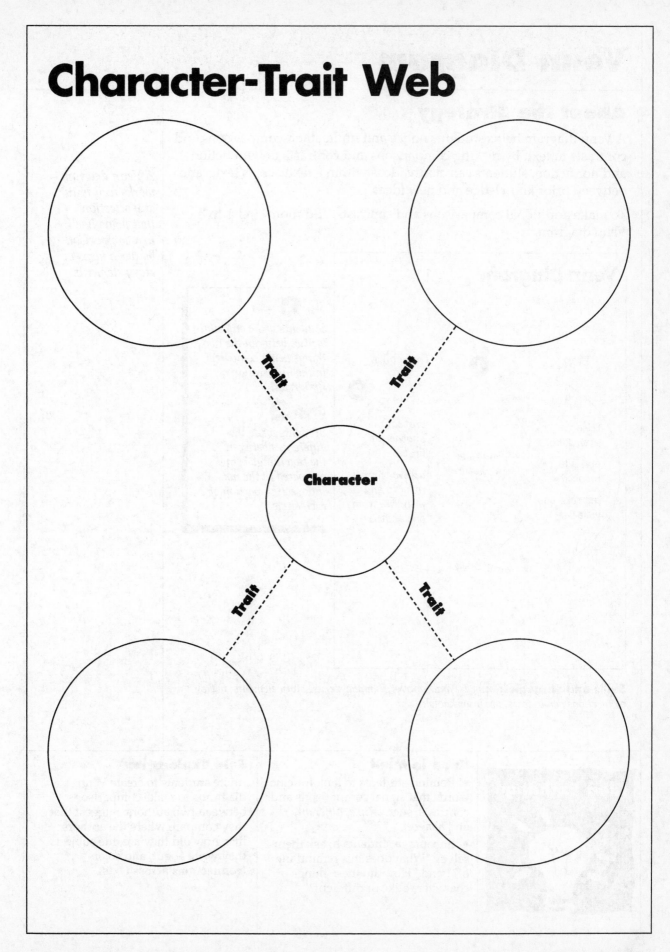

Venn Diagram

About the Strategy

A Venn diagram helps students notice and understand comparisons and contrasts in text. By making comparisons and contrasts in both fiction and nonfiction, students can clarify ideas within a text, across texts, and between prior knowledge and new ideas.

To make additional comparisons and contrasts, add more circles to the Venn diagram.

A Venn diagram works well with any selection that lends itself to a comparison between ideas or story elements.

Venn Diagram

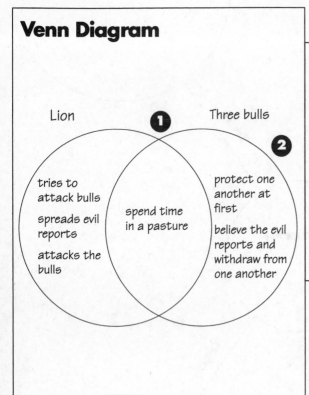

Lion — Three bulls

1

2

- tries to attack bulls
- spreads evil reports
- attacks the bulls

spend time in a pasture

- protect one another at first
- believe the evil reports and withdraw from one another

Step ❶

Students write any similarities between the two things being compared in the intersection of the circles.

Step ❷

Students write the differences between the two things being compared in the non-intersecting portion of each circle.

Skills and Strategies: *compare and contrast, summarize, use story elements, make connections across texts, use prior knowledge*

Idea Exchange

Keep in Mind

- Remind students to look for clue words that signal comparisons and contrasts, such as *like*, *different*, and *however*.
- Encourage students to ask themselves "What does this remind me of?" and "How are these things or characters alike or different?"

Solo Exploration

Invite students to create Venn diagrams to make comparisons between two authors. Suggest that they compare where the authors live, how old they are, the subjects they write about, and so on. **(connections across texts)**

310 Reading Kit

Venn Diagram

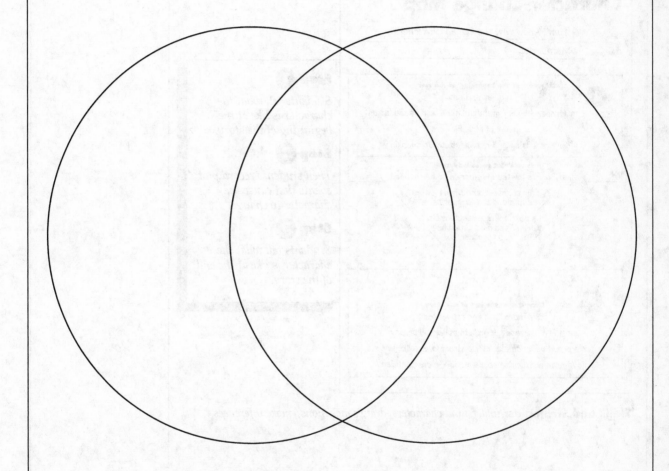

Character-Change Map

About the Strategy

A character-change map helps students understand characters in fiction. By analyzing a character over the course of a story, students can see how a character changes in response to plot events.

The following character-change map is modeled using an excerpt from *I Know Why the Caged Bird Sings*.

A character-change map works well with selections that have dynamic characters.

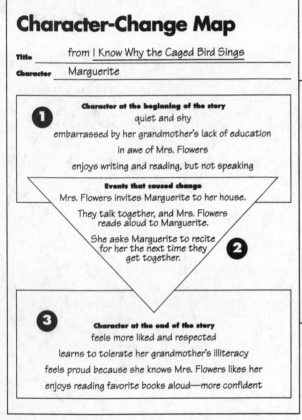

Character-Change Map

Title _____ from I Know Why the Caged Bird Sings

Character _____ Marguerite

1 — Character at the beginning of the story
quiet and shy
embarrassed by her grandmother's lack of education
in awe of Mrs. Flowers
enjoys writing and reading, but not speaking

Events that caused change
Mrs. Flowers invites Marguerite to her house.
They talk together, and Mrs. Flowers reads aloud to Marguerite.
She asks Marguerite to recite for her the next time they get together. **2**

3 — Character at the end of the story
feels more liked and respected
learns to tolerate her grandmother's illiteracy
feels proud because she knows Mrs. Flowers likes her
enjoys reading favorite books aloud—more confident

Step 1
Students tell what the character is like at the beginning of the story.

Step 2
Then students record plot events that cause the character to change.

Step 3
Students tell what the character is like at the end of the story.

Skills and Strategies: *understand characters, draw conclusions, make inferences*

Idea Exchange

Keep in Mind
You may want to ask students to map the changes in more than one character in a selection.

Solo Exploration
To help students see that cause-and-effect relationships are often a part of change, suggest that they create a cause-and-effect map for the changes a character goes through in a story.

Character-Change Map

Title _____

Character _____

Character at the beginning of the story

Events that caused change

Character at the end of the story

Details Web

About the Strategy

A details web helps students organize information in fictional or non-fictional text when many details are centered around one key or main idea. By completing the web, students see the relationship between the key or main idea and the details that support it.

A details web works well with informational selections.

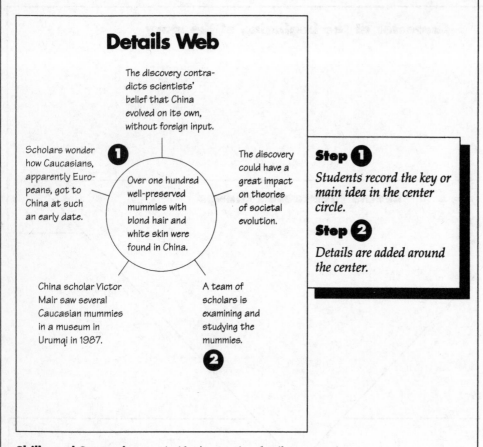

Details Web

The discovery contradicts scientists' belief that China evolved on its own, without foreign input.

Scholars wonder how Caucasians, apparently Europeans, got to China at such an early date.

1

Over one hundred well-preserved mummies with blond hair and white skin were found in China.

The discovery could have a great impact on theories of societal evolution.

China scholar Victor Mair saw several Caucasian mummies in a museum in Urumqi in 1987.

A team of scholars is examining and studying the mummies.

2

Step 1
Students record the key or main idea in the center circle.

Step 2
Details are added around the center.

Skills and Strategies: *main idea/supporting details, summarize*

Idea Exchange

Keep in Mind
• If there is more than one key or main idea in a selection, create a separate details web for each idea.
• Help students identify the main idea of a nonfictional selection by asking "What is the most important idea in the selection?"

Solo Exploration
Encourage students to create details webs to help organize their thoughts for a panel discussion or debate. Students can write the discussion/debate topic in the center of the web and brainstorm ideas in support or opposition. **(discussion)**

Details Web

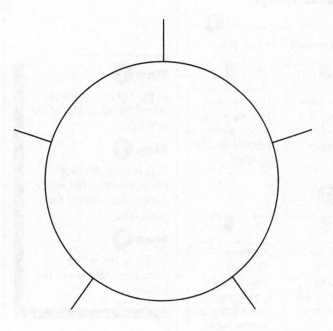

Main Idea Map

About the Strategy

A main idea map helps students recognize the main idea of a nonfictional selection and distinguish between the main idea and supporting details. Students determine the relative importance of what they read by organizing and reorganizing information from the text.

Main idea maps work well with any nonfictional selection that is organized around one main idea supported by major and minor details.

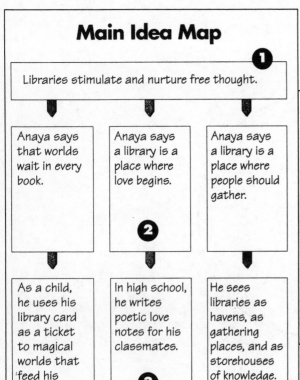

Main Idea Map

1 Libraries stimulate and nurture free thought.

Anaya says that worlds wait in every book.

Anaya says a library is a place where love begins.

Anaya says a library is a place where people should gather. **2**

As a child, he uses his library card as a ticket to magical worlds that feed his imagination.

In high school, he writes poetic love notes for his classmates. **3**

He sees libraries as havens, as gathering places, and as storehouses of knowledge.

Step 1

In the top box, students record the main idea of the selection.

Step 2

In this second row of boxes, students list major details that support the main idea.

Step 3

Students list minor details or examples in the bottom row.

Skills and Strategies: *main idea/supporting details, summarize, analyze information*

Idea Exchange

Keep in Mind
- Encourage students to think about the most important idea in the selection to figure out the main idea.
- Remind students that the main idea is not always stated in the text. Sometimes students will have to state the main idea in their own words.
- Sometimes it's easier to see a main idea *after* listing the details.

Solo Exploration
Invite students to use the information in a main idea map to create a pie chart showing the importance of the details. Each detail becomes a slice of the pie, with more important details making up the larger slices. **(cross-curricular connection)**

Main Idea Map

Time Line

About the Strategy

A time line helps students organize both fictional and nonfictional events in sequential order along a continuum. Not only do students see the events in order, but they are also exposed to the overall time frame in which the events occurred.

Time lines work well with any fictional or nonfictional selection in which understanding the order of events would help comprehension.

Step ❶
Students record the first event.

Step ❷
Students add the remaining events, placing them on the time line relative to the other events.

Time Line

| After church, Pepys goes to a meeting to talk about ways to keep the plague from growing. ❶ | Alderman Hooker tells the story of a man and his wife who took their last surviving child from an infected house in London. | Pepys mentions the good news that there has been a decrease of over five hundred in the number of new cases of the plague. | Pepys is very sad to hear of the people he knows who have lost someone to the plague or are sick themselves. | Jane, one of Pepys' maids, wakes him and his wife in the middle of the night to tell them about a great fire in the city. ❷ | Pepys goes out to track the progress of the fire, then goes to Whitehall to make a report. | As the fire continues to burn, Pepys and his family are forced to pack up their belongings and evacuate their home. |

| Sept. 3, 1665 | | Sept. 14, 1665 | | Sept. 2, 1666 | | |

Skills and Strategies: *summarize, sequence*

Idea Exchange

Buddywork
Invite pairs of students to create time lines into the future. They can list events that they imagine will occur before people live on the moon. Students might place their time lines in their portfolios to use for future writing. **(portfolio)**

All Together Now
As a class, make a list of the clue words in a selection organized by chronological, or time, order. You can add to the list as you read other selections organized by time order. Remind students to include clue words that indicate simultaneous order (*meanwhile, during,* etc.).

Time Line

Enumerative Text Frame

About the Strategy

An enumerative article states a main idea and lists examples to support the main idea. Students can use an enumerative text frame to help them recognize this type of expository text structure. Becoming aware of this and other expository text structures improves students' reading, particularly in the content areas.

An enumerative text frame works with selections that are organized according to this text structure.

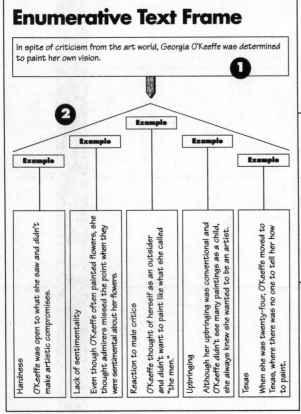

Enumerative Text Frame

In spite of criticism from the art world, Georgia O'Keeffe was determined to paint her own vision. **1**

2

Example
Example
Example
Example
Example

Hardness
O'Keeffe was open to what she saw and didn't make artistic compromises.

Lack of sentimentality
Even though O'Keeffe often painted flowers, she thought admirers missed the point when they were sentimental about her flowers.

Reaction to male critics
O'Keeffe thought of herself as an outsider and didn't want to paint like what she called "the men."

Upbringing
Although her upbringing was conventional and O'Keeffe didn't see many paintings as a child, she always knew she wanted to be an artist.

Texas
When she was twenty-four, O'Keeffe moved to Texas, where there was no one to tell her how to paint.

Step 1
Students fill in the main idea at the top of the graphic organizer.

Step 2
Students list examples that support the main idea.

Skills and Strategies: *main idea/supporting details, use text structure/genre, use text features, analyze information*

Idea Exchange

Keep in Mind
If students are having difficulty recognizing this text structure, suggest they look for clue words such as *first*, *next*, and *finally*.

Solo Exploration
Try using this graphic organizer to help students make predictions. After telling students the main idea of an enumerative article, suggest that they fill in examples they predict will be used to support the main idea. Remember to have students return to their predictions after reading.

Enumerative Text Frame

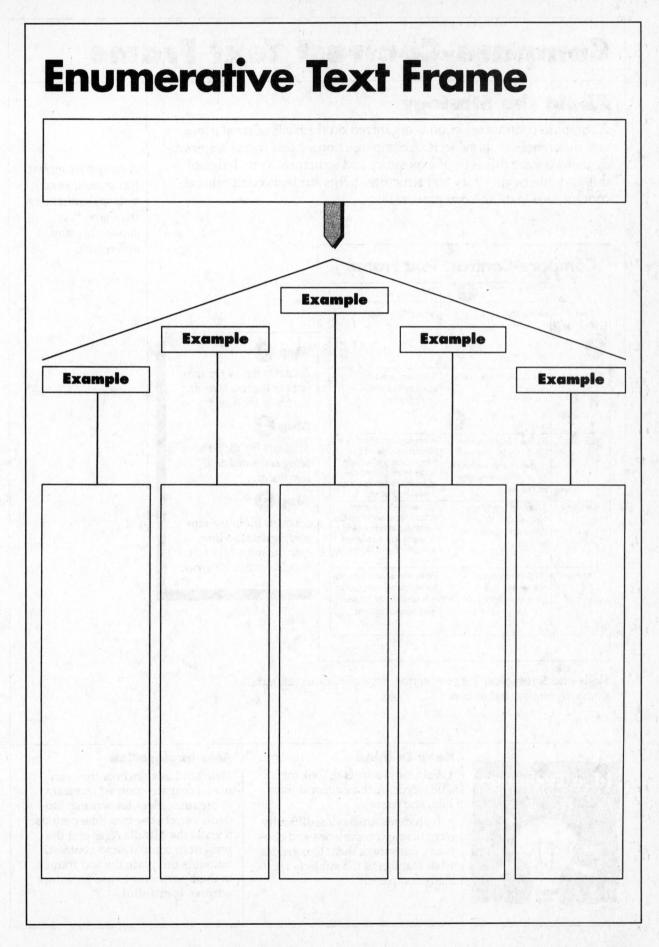

		Example		
	Example		Example	
Example				Example

Compare-Contrast Text Frame

About the Strategy

A compare-contrast selection is organized on the basis of similarities and differences of its subjects. A compare-contrast text frame helps students recognize this type of expository text structure. Knowledge of this and other expository text structures helps students comprehend content-area texts and compare texts.

A compare-contrast text frame works well with selections that have clear similarities and differences.

Compare-Contrast Text Frame

	"A Problem" **1**	"Luck"
Main Character **2**	Sasha Uskov	Arthur Scoresby
Setting	The study of the Uskov home	A military academy and a battle in the Crimean War **3**
Conflict	Sasha has disgraced his family by getting into debt and cashing a false promissory note at the bank.	Scoresby is really a blundering soldier, but every military situation works in his favor and he becomes famous and highly decorated.
Denouement	After his family has forgiven him, Sasha demands money from his uncle.	Scoresby wins a great victory because he makes a mistake and moves his regiment left instead of right and forward instead of back.
Theme	Forgiveness does not always lead to responsibility.	Those who create heroes, like the clergyman, can be held responsible for the false heroes' actions.

Step 1

Students record the subjects or the two texts at the top of the frame.

Step 2

Students list the features being compared and contrasted.

Step 3

Students fill in the supporting details telling how the subjects or texts are alike and/or different.

Skills and Strategies: *compare-contrast, draw conclusions, use text structure/genre, use text features*

Idea Exchange

Keep in Mind
• Remind students to look for clue words, such as *different from*, *alike*, and *resemble*.
• If students are having difficulty recognizing comparisons and contrasts, encourage them to consider what features of the subjects are being compared.

Solo Exploration
Help students see how they can use a compare-contrast text frame to organize ideas for writing. Students can choose two time periods such as the Middle Ages and the present to compare and contrast. Students can place the text frames in their portfolios to use for future writing. **(portfolio)**

Compare-Contrast Text Frame

Cause-Effect Frame Multiple Causes

About the Strategy

This type of cause-effect frame helps students identify what happened and multiple reasons why it happened in both fictional and nonfictional texts. When students can see that there are causal relationships between events or ideas in text, they can make generalizations about other causal relationships in new texts and in life situations.

This cause-effect frame works well with any selection that has clear cause-and-effect relationships with multiple causes.

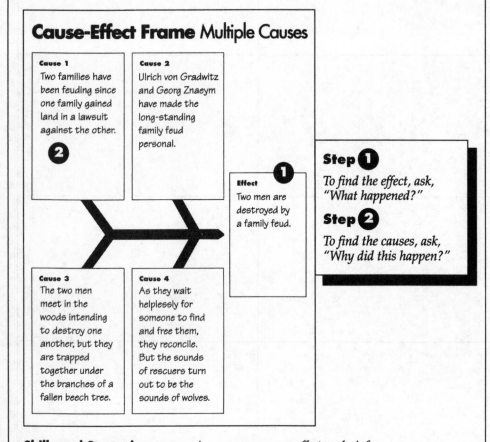

Cause-Effect Frame Multiple Causes

Cause 1
Two families have been feuding since one family gained land in a lawsuit against the other.
2

Cause 2
Ulrich von Gradwitz and Georg Znaeym have made the long-standing family feud personal.

Effect **1**
Two men are destroyed by a family feud.

Cause 3
The two men meet in the woods intending to destroy one another, but they are trapped together under the branches of a fallen beech tree.

Cause 4
As they wait helplessly for someone to find and free them, they reconcile. But the sounds of rescuers turn out to be the sounds of wolves.

Step 1
To find the effect, ask, "What happened?"

Step 2
To find the causes, ask, "Why did this happen?"

Skills and Strategies: *summarize, sequence, cause-effect, make inferences*

Idea Exchange

Keep in Mind
• If students have trouble identifying cause-and-effect relationships, suggest they look for clue words, such as *since, as a result, consequently, therefore,* and *thus.*
• Remind them that not all causes are stated directly in the text.

All Together Now
Try posing a question for students, such as "What would life be like if freedom of the press were not guaranteed under the First Amendment?" Ask students to suggest possible effects.
(cross-curricular connection)

Cause-Effect Frame Multiple Causes

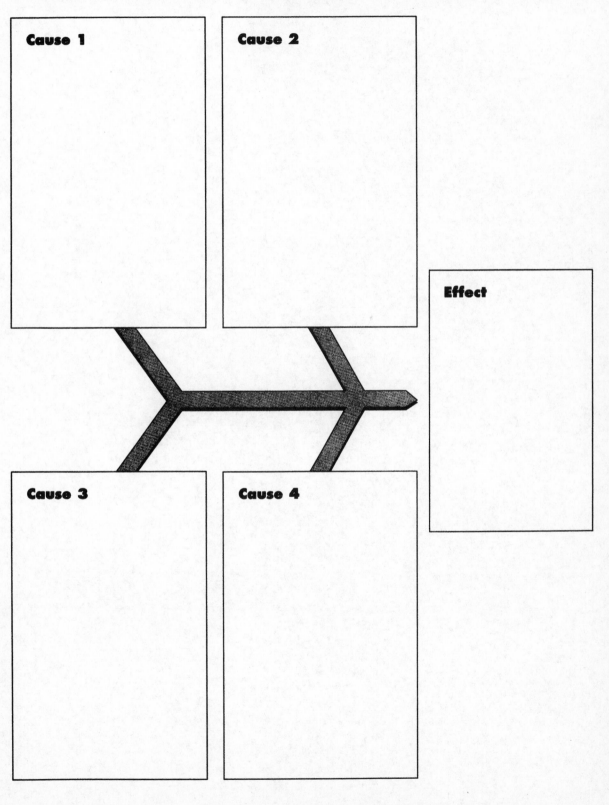

Classroom Management for Differentiated Instruction

The Challenge of Academic Text Reading

Most students enter classrooms woefully underprepared to independently navigate their reading assignments across the subject areas. While they may be able to tackle recreational reading of teen novels and magazines with relative ease, they often lack the academic language and strategic knowledge necessary for comprehending and studying concept and data rich texts. The challenging narrative and non-fiction selections students will be assigned in the course of an academic year are meant to be approached as learning tasks, not recreational activities. As such, these texts must be read multiple times with a clear learning purpose in mind.

Such an approach to reading is far from typical of adolescents engaging today's standards-driven Language Arts curricula. It is absolutely essential for teachers to assume an active instructional role, responsibly preparing students with the linguistic and strategic tools necessary for this potentially daunting task.

Strategies for Structuring Reading

The worksheets that follow offer strategies a teacher can draw on in taking this active role. The following worksheets give concrete formats for structuring students reading:

- Choral Reading
- Oral Cloze
- Silent Independent Rereading
- Structured Partner Reading

Sophisticated texts require rereading, and scaffolding the types of reading students do on each pass is essential to bringing them into a more sophisticated engagement with the text. Here is one recommended way of using these strategies to scaffold readings:

First Reading—Oral Cloze with broad task
Second Reading—Silent rereading with detailed task
Conclude—Class discussion/debriefing

Strategic Questioning

In traditional content-area reading instruction, the teacher assigns independent reading followed by an end-of-text question and answer session, in which the teacher and a handful of students dominate the discussion, leaving struggling readers disengaged and confused. Research suggests that struggling readers need explicit guidance in emulating the behaviors of competent readers.

This guidance must include breaking the reading into manageable chunks, approaching each section of text with a concrete question or purpose, and rereading sections for different levels of details. Teachers should pose increasingly complex questions while modeling a more active and strategic approach to reading.

The following worksheets give strategies to assist struggling readers in formulating appropriate reading questions and in connecting their guide questions to concrete tasks.

- Preparing-to-Read Questions
- Reading Guide Questions
- A Range of Appropriate Questions
- Question Frames

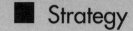

■ Strategy

A common primary-grade practice, choral reading can also work very well with older readers. Choral reading is effective because it requires that each student, regardless of level or proficiency in English, actively engage in attending to the text while it provides a nonthreatening atmosphere in which to practice. Many teachers find it helpful to use choral reading one row or group at a time. This modification tends to be less demanding and more manageable for diverse learners.

Tips to ensure success with choral reading:

- Request students to "Keep your voice with mine" to discourage them from racing ahead.

- Choose relatively short passages (e.g., 300–500 words).

- Follow with a silent rereading. Now that all students have basic access to the text, a second reading can elicit deeper understanding, supply an opportunity to apply previously taught strategies, answer inductive questions, and so on, while reinforcing the message that "constructing meaning is your job. I am here to help, not to do it for you."

Oral Cloze

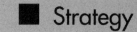

The oral cloze is a choral reading adaptation of a commonly used reading-comprehension assessment process, in which words are selectively deleted from a brief passage, and students are prompted to fill-in reasonable word choices. In the oral cloze, the teacher reads aloud while students follow along silently. The teacher occasionally omits selected words, which the students chime in and read aloud together. The oral cloze is useful in guiding students in an initial read of a difficult passage, thereby insuring that struggling readers will have access to the text. Often during teacher read-alouds, students listen passively, read ahead, or remain off-task. This strategy keeps students on their "reading toes" by giving them a concrete job while allowing teachers to check participation.

Tips to ensure success with cloze reading:

- To begin, demonstrate the oral cloze by contrasting it with a traditional read-aloud. Read a few sentences aloud without assigning students a role or task. Clarify the importance of being an active, thoughtful reader when the goal is accountable reading to learn, often with an assessment (e.g., quiz or paper). Explain that you will be reading aloud, and their job is to follow along, reading at the same pace and chorally chiming in when a word is occasionally omitted. Then reread the same sentences leaving out 2–3 words so that students see the contrast and grasp their active role.

- Choose to leave out meaningful words (e.g., nouns, verbs, adjectives) that most students can easily pronounce (prepositions and other connecting words do not work well).

- Take care to not distract students by leaving out too many words, not more than one per sentence (e.g., in a 50-word paragraph, delete 2–3 words).

- Pick words that come at a natural pause.

- Pick words (if any) that you have pretaught, providing students with a meaningful context for the new word.

- Provide students with an additional concrete active-reading task or question directing their attention to the content of the passage. On the first read, this task should be fairly broad and easy (e.g., Circle two adjectives describing how the character felt).

- In a mixed-ability class with many struggling readers, consider guiding students' reading with two rounds of the oral cloze before assigning a silent reading task. On the second reading, omit different words and pick up the pace a bit while providing an additional focus question or task.

After facilitating students in their first reading of a challenging passage using the oral cloze, prepare them for an active independent rereading of the passage.

The essential element here, as with both choral and cloze reading, is to make sure the students have a job, a task during reading that increases their attentiveness, cognitive focus, and accountability. Rereading silently to answer a question previously posed to the class as a whole efficiently meets this goal. Teachers may pose useful questions that the class reads silently to answer. Over time, students are taught to construct a range of questions themselves before such class reading (moving from literal to inferential).

After each section is read, engage students in a brief discussion to clarify questions and vocabulary and to ensure common understanding of essential big ideas in the text. You may choose to guide students in mapping or note-taking from the text at this point as well.

Tips to Get the Most From Structured Silent Rereading

- Chunk the text into 1–4 paragraph sections within which students silently reread and actively identify information necessary to respond to the teacher's focus question.

- Request that anyone who finishes before you convene the discussion go back and reread the section to look for additional details in the text.

- The first few times, model how one thinks while reading to find answers to a question. Think aloud to give students a "window" on this sophisticated cognitive task.

- Encourage students to discuss their thinking, as well as their answers, during whole-class discussion. For example, focus on such issues as *"How did you know?"* or *"Why did you think that?"*

Research has consistently pointed to partner reading as a potent strategy to increase the amount of actual reading students engage in, while providing access for all students to key ideas in the text. Partner reading is an excellent way to ensure that all students are actively engaged in the text and accountable for doing their jobs.

Tips to get the most from structured partner reading:

- Rank-order students by overall literacy and proficiency in English. In a group of 30 students, for example, students #1 and #15 are the first readers and #16 and #30 are the first coaches.
- Ensure that activities are fully reciprocal—students should spend equal time in the roles of reader and coach.
- Provide specific directions and demonstrate the roles of reader and coach (e.g., "First reader: Whisper-read the first paragraph, coaches follow along, fix mistakes, and ask the comprehension questions.").

The Reader

The reader reads a paragraph or a page or reads for a given amount of time. Touching under the words may be helpful if the students have extremely limited literacy.

The Coach

The coach encourages and supports the reader.

1. If the reader asks for a word, the coach will say the word.

2. If the reader makes a mistake, the coach will correct the error using the following steps:

   a. Point to the word and say, *"Can you figure out this word?"*
   b. If the reader cannot figure out the word in five seconds, say *"This word is __."*
   c. Have the reader repeat the word and then reread the sentence.

   Why reread the entire sentence?

   • Improve comprehension.
   • Practice the word again—read it fluently in context.
   • Hold students accountable for reading more carefully.

After students have mastered the basic sequence, add various comprehension strategies, such as retelling main ideas after each page or section.

Summarize/paraphrase. State the main idea in ten words or less. (Using only ten words prompts students to use their own words.)

Predict and monitor. Reader predicts what will happen next, reads a paragraph/section and then determines if the prediction was accurate, revises as needed, summarizes, and predicts again, continuing for a set amount of time.

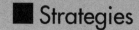

Provide focused questions to guide students before reading.

If students have background knowledge regarding the subject, it is very helpful to pose a few open-ended questions to elicit a lively brainstorming session prior to reading. Cueing students to examine any related visual support, as well as the title, can assist students in focusing their thinking more productively.

> What are the possible effects of eating too much junk food?
> Take a look at this school lunch menu in the photograph and identify with your partner two healthy and two unhealthy foods.

Instructional Tip: *Guide students to share answers with a teacher-selected partner; take care to designate roles (1s and 2s) to insure ALL are active participants.*

When students lack critical background knowledge related to a topic, brainstorming alone is often insufficient. Students will benefit from carefully formulated questions before and during each reading segment to focus their attention on the most important information. Without a concrete purpose when tackling each segment of a text, less proficient readers are apt to get mired in confusing details and distracted by unfamiliar yet non-essential vocabulary. Thus, it is essential to provide students a very specific question to guide their initial reading.

> What are the three most important reasons cited by the author in favor of recycling? How can recycling actually save money?

Provide questions during the reading process.

It is critical that teachers guide less proficient students in reading each segment of text at least twice, providing a clear task each time. Posing a thoughtful question before students read challenging text will help them understand the active and focused approach necessary for reading to learn. Global questions are most appropriate for initial reading, followed by questions that require more careful analysis and attention to detail in subsequent reading.

> 1st **read:** What is this section in our article on teen health mainly about?
> **Task:** Identify a word or phrase that names our topic (e.g., *teen diet*).
>
> 2nd **read:** Why is the author so concerned about adolescent diet?
> **Task:** Identify two reasons stated by the author.
>
> 3rd **read:** Since the snack foods provided at school are a major cause of poor adolescent health, why do you think schools continue to sell them?
> **Task:** Write down a specific reason you think schools still make candy, sodas, and chips so easily available in vending machines.

Instructional Tip: *Complement the guide question with a concrete task to increase student accountability and increase focus and attention.*

There are common text elements that teachers can utilize to frame reading guide questions and model an alert and strategic reading process for students.

Use headings and topic sentences to generate reading guide questions.

Model for students how to turn a heading into a reading guide question for the initial reading of a passage. Be sure to prompt them to translate the question into a concrete task for which they will be held accountable in subsequent class discussion.

> Subheading: Recycling Saves Money
>
> Guide question: How does recycling save money?
>
> Task: "I need to identify two ways that recycling helps people save money."

Students need to approach each paragraph within a section of text with a clear sense of what they need to attend to in and extract from their reading. While a heading often provides the overall topic for a section of text, topic sentences provide a more specific focus for developing reading guide questions for discrete paragraphs.

> Subheading: Recycling Saves Money
>
> Topic sentence, paragraph one: "Because of the recent downturn in the auto industry, Smithville has come up with a creative recycling program to support their cash-strapped schools."
>
> Guide Question: What is Smithville's recycling program?
>
> Task: I need to identify the key features of Smithville's recycling program.

Helping struggling students develop genuine competence in formulating and applying reading guide questions is rather labor intensive. Students who are accustomed to approach all forms of reading material in a generic, unfocused manner will require considerable hand-holding through a gradual release process that moves systematically from "I'll do it" (teacher modeling) to "We'll do it" (unified class with teacher guidance) to "You'll do it" (partner practice) to "You do it on your own" (independent practice).

Provide questions after reading a passage.

After students have navigated a demanding text and achieved basic comprehension, they are well positioned to extend their thinking by responding to higher-order questions requiring greater reflection and application. These questions are the interesting and provocative ones that teachers long to pose but that fall flat unless students have been prepared.

> How could we set up a viable recycling program in our school community?
>
> If you had two minutes to address the school board, what are the three best arguments you would provide to support the development of a district wide recycling program?

Begin with "on the surface" questions.

Why? Struggling readers must be able to identify the most essential information in the reading *before* they are guided in grappling with more abstract analysis/interpretation. Otherwise, many students will not have the cognitive tools to benefit from the discussion.

What? Ask questions that require literal, factual recall and text-based answers that students can point to, underline, or circle.

> What is an endangered species? What are two examples of endangered species mentioned in this article? How are environmentalists working with oil companies to protect the red-tailed hawk?

Include "under the surface" questions.

Why? To comprehend challenging reading material, students must go beyond the factual basics of the text. Getting the gist certainly is no small feat for many struggling readers. However, it is important to help less proficient students acquire a more in-depth understanding and the strategic know-how required for mature comprehension.

What? Ask questions that require students to make inferences from or to analyze and synthesize text-based information, as well as to make inferences connecting new ideas from the text with prior knowledge.

> Why has it been difficult for environmentalist and oil companies to work together in protecting the red-tailed hawk? What environmental factors are placing some animal species in danger in your community?

Teach students the questions for reading to learn.

Why? Less proficient readers have often spent their early literacy development with relatively undemanding stories. In the classroom, they have largely responded to the "who, where, and when" questions appropriate for stories, leaving them ill equipped to reply to the "why, how, and what" demands of information text comprehension.

What? Teachers need to teach specific tasks involved in responding to questions associated with informational texts. Students need to understand that when asked a "why question" (e.g., Why have many schools outlawed soft drink sales?), they need to read, looking for specific reasons. It is not enough simply to model the questions; students must understand what prompted you to ask that specific question and the kind of information the question suggests.

> Why? = For what reasons? What are the reasons?
> How? = What was the process? What was the sequence?
> What? = Definition (What is _____?)
> What? + signal word   What are the <u>benefits</u> of _____?
> What was the <u>reaction</u> to _____?

■ Strategy

Teaching students how to generate their own questions is an important comprehension-enhancing element of structured silent reading. Underprepared readers are often overly dependent on teachers and have not learned to self-question as they read. According to the research of Taffy Raphael,[1] students who understand how questions are written are more capable of analyzing and answering them than students who lack this understanding. One useful model, derived from Bloom's *Taxonomy*,[2] was developed by Stiggins[3] using Question Frames for different levels of questions to provide initial support for students during self-questioning:

Recall (Literal) ("I can put my finger on the answer in the text.")
What is the name of _____?
Define _____.
Identify the _____.
Who did _____?

Analysis (Inferential) ("I combine my knowledge with the author's information to understand.")
What is the main idea?
The most important part of _____ is _____ because _____.
The essential parts are _____.

Compare/Contrast ("I analyze similarities and differences.")
Compare the motives of _____ to those of _____.
What are the most important differences/similarities between _____ and _____?

Prediction ("I predict based on the evidence so far.")
What do you think will happen in the next _____?
Predict what you think _____ will do. Why?
What would happen if _____?

Evaluation ("I make and defend judgments.")
What is your opinion of _____?
What is the best solution to the problem of _____?
Defend why _____ is a better solution than _____.

Question Frames are helpful when teaching diverse learners to ask questions beyond simple recall/literal questions. Teacher modeling and well-supported initial practice are key to assisting all students in generating different types of questions.

---

1. Raphael, T. "Teaching Learners About Sources of Information for Answering Questions." *Journal of Reading* (1984), vol. 28(4), 303–311.
2. Bloom, B. *Taxonomy of Educational Objectives.* New York: Longmans, Green, 1956.
3. Stiggins, R. "Improving Assessment Where It Means the Most: In the Classroom." *Educational Leadership* (1985), 43, 69–74.

Vocabulary

To succeed in narrowing the language divide, a school-wide comprehensive academic vocabulary program must include the following four components:

1. **Fluent, wide reading.** Vocabulary for academic purposes grows as a consequence of independent reading of a variety of texts (in particular, informational texts) and increasing reading volume.

2. **Direct scaffolded teaching of critical words.** Students learn new words via various explicit, teacher-directed instructional strategies.

3. **Teaching word-learning strategies.** When taught the tools to exploit context, analyze prefixes, and various other strategies, students can independently learn new word meanings while reading independently.

4. **Daily participation in structured, accountable contexts for daily speaking and writing.** Academic language develops when students are engaged in rigorous and meaningful application of newly acquired vocabulary and syntax in structured speaking and writing tasks.

The following group of worksheets, marked with the triangle icon, provide concrete strategies for addressing many of these objectives for vocabulary development:

- Preteaching Vocabulary: Convey Meaning
- Preteaching Vocabulary: Check Understanding
- Vocabulary Development
- Choosing Vocabulary Words
- Possible Sentences
- Word Analysis/Teaching Word Parts
- Assessing Vocabulary Mastery

Concept development goes hand in hand with vocabulary enrichment. The following worksheets, also labeled with the triangle icon, provide strategies for concept development:

- List-Group-Label
- Concept Mapping/Clarifying Routine
- Using Concept Maps

The remaining worksheets in Part 3, marked with the circle icon, offer strategies for structuring academic discussion and writing.

- If your goal is simply to familiarize students with a word to help them recognize and comprehend it in a reading, follow steps 1–4.

1. Pronounce the word (and give the part of speech).

This article focuses on an *ecstatic* moment in a high school student's life.

2. Ask students to all repeat the word.

Say the word *ecstatic* after me. (ec stat' ic)

3. Provide an accessible synonym and/or a brief explanation.

Ecstatic means "extremely happy."

4. Rephrase the simple definition/explanation, asking students to complete the statement by substituting aloud the new word.

If you are extremely happy about something, you are _____ (students say *ecstatic*).

- If your goal is to familiarize students with a word that is central to comprehending the reading and that you also want them to learn, continue with step 5, then check for understanding.

5. Provide a visual "nonlinguistic representation" of the word (if possible) and/or an illustrative "showing" sentence.

Showing image: a picture of a man happily in love.
Showing sentence: Julio was *ecstatic* when Melissa agreed to marry him.

Have students fill out a vocabulary worksheet as you preteach the words; doing so involves them more directly and provides them with a focused word list for later study and practice.

Sample Vocabulary Note-Taking

Term	Synonym	Definition/ Example	Image
ecstatic, *adj.*	extremely happy	feeling very happy, excited, or joyful *Julio was <u>ecstatic</u> when Melissa agreed to marry him.*	
distraught, *adj.*	extremely worried and upset	feeling very worried, unhappy, or <u>distressed</u> *Mark was <u>distraught</u> to learn that the camp bus had left without him.*	

Preteaching Vocabulary: Check Understanding

1. Focused Questions

Ask focused questions to see if students seem to grasp the word's meaning (as opposed to questions such as *Any questions? Do you understand?* or *Is that clear?*). Questions may be initially directed to the unified group for a thumbs-up or thumbs-down response; to teams using Numbered Heads; or to pairs using Think-Pair-Share, followed by questions to individuals.

> • Would you be ecstatic if you won the lottery?
> • Would you be ecstatic if you were assigned a 20-page report to complete over the Spring break?
> • Would you be ecstatic if you won two front-row tickets to a concert given by your favorite band?
> • Would you be ecstatic if your mother bought your favorite brand of breakfast cereal?

2. Images

If the word is crucial (for the lesson and their academic vocabulary tool kit), consider asking students to generate their own relevant images or examples.

> • Turn to your partner and ask what has happened recently that made him/her ecstatic. Or ask what would make him/her ecstatic. Be prepared to share one example with the class.
> • What other images might we associate with *ecstatic?* Think of one or two, turn to your partner and discuss, and then be prepared to share one of your images with the class.

Vocabulary Development

▼ Strategies

Words that are new to students but that represent familiar concepts can be addressed using a number of relatively quick instructional tactics. Many of these (e.g., synonyms, antonyms, examples) are optimal for prereading and oral reading, which call for more expedient approaches.

Brief Strategies for Vocabulary Development (Stahl[4])

- **Teach synonyms.** Provide a synonym that students know (e.g., link *stringent* to the known word *strict*).

- **Teach antonyms.** Not all words have antonyms, but for those that do, thinking about their opposites requires students to evaluate the critical attributes of the words in question.

- **Paraphrase definitions.** Requiring students to use their own words increases connection-making and provides the teacher with useful informal assessment—"Do they really get it?"

- **Provide examples.** The more personalized the example, the better. An example for the new word *egregious* might be *Ms. Kinsella's 110-page reading assignment was egregious indeed!*

- **Provide nonexamples.** Similar to using antonyms, providing nonexamples requires students to evaluate a word's attributes. Invite students to explain why it is not an example.

- **Ask for sentences that "show you know."** Students construct novel sentences confirming their understanding of a new word, using more than one new word per sentence to show that connections can also be useful.

- **Teach word sorting.** Provide a list of vocabulary words from a reading selection and have students sort them into various categories (e.g., parts of speech, branches of government). Students can re-sort words into "guess my sort" using categories of their own choosing.

---

4. Stahl, S. A. *Vocabulary Development.* Cambridge, MA: Brookline Books, 1999.

340 Reading Kit

© Pearson Education, Inc., publishing as Pearson Prentice Hall.

Restrict your selections to approximately six to eight words that are critical to comprehending the reading passage/segment you intend to cover in one lesson (e.g., one Science chapter section; a three-page passage from a six-page short story.)

- Choose **"big idea"** words that name or relate to the central concepts addressed in the passage (in subject areas outside of English Language Arts, these central lesson terms are typically highlighted by the publisher).

- Choose high-use, widely applicable **"academic tool kit"** words that student are likely to encounter in diverse materials across subject areas and grade levels (e.g., *aspect, compare, similar, subsequently*).

- Choose high-use **"disciplinary tool kit"** words for your subject area that you consider vital for students to master at this age and proficiency level (e.g., *metaphor, policy, economic, application, species*).

- Choose **"polysemous"** (multiple meaning) words that have a new academic meaning in a reading in addition to a more general, familiar meaning (e.g., "wave of immigrants" in U.S. History vs. a greeting or an ocean wave).

- Identify additional academic words, not included in the reading selection, that students will need to know in order to engage in **academic discourse** about the central characters, issues, and themes (especially for literary selections).

- Be careful not to overload students with low-frequency words that they are unlikely to encounter in many academic reading contexts, especially words that are not essential to comprehend the gist of the text.

Possible Sentences

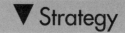

Possible Sentences (Moore and Moore[6]) is a relatively simple strategy for teaching word meanings and generating considerable class discussion.

1. The teacher chooses six to eight words from the text that may pose difficulty for students. These words are usually key concepts in the text.

2. Next, the teacher chooses four to six words that students are more likely to know something about.

3. The list of ten to twelve words is put on the chalkboard or overhead projector. The teacher provides brief definitions as needed.

4. Students are challenged to devise sentences that contain two or more words from the list.

5. All sentences that students come up with, both accurate and inaccurate, are listed and discussed.

6. Students now read the selection.

7. After reading, revisit the Possible Sentences and discuss whether they could be true based on the passage or how they could be modified to be true.

Stahl[7] reported that Possible Sentences significantly improved both students' overall recall of word meanings and their comprehension of text containing those words. Interestingly, this was true when compared with a control group and when compared with Semantic Mapping.

---

6. Moore, P. W., and S. A. Moore. "Possible Sentences." In E. K. Dishner, T. W. Bean, J. E. Readence, and P. W. Moore (eds.). *Reading in the Content Areas: Improving Classroom Instruction*, 2nd ed. Dubuque, IA: Kendall/Hunt, 1986, pp. 174–179.

7. Stahl, op. cit.

Word Analysis/Teaching Word Parts helps many underprepared readers who lack basic knowledge of word origins or etymology, such as Latin and Greek roots, as well as discrete understanding of how a prefix or suffix can alter the meaning of a word. Learning clusters of words that share a common origin can help students understand content-area texts and connect new words to those already known. For example, a secondary teacher (Allen[8]) reported reading about a character who suffered from amnesia. Teaching students that the prefix *a-* derives from Greek and means "not," while the base *-mne-* means "memory," reveals the meaning. After judicious teacher scaffolding, students were making connections to various words in which the prefix *a-* changed the meaning of a base word (e.g., *amoral, atypical*).

The charts below summarize some of the affixes worth considering, depending on your students' prior knowledge and English proficiency.

Prefix	Meaning	Percentage of All Prefixed Words	Example
un-	not; reversal of	26	uncover
re-	again, back, really	14	review
in-/im-	in, into, not	11	insert
dis-	away, apart, negative	7	discover
en-/em-	in; within; on	4	entail
mis-	wrong	3	mistaken
pre-	before	3	prevent
a-	not; in, on, without	1	atypical

Suffix	Meaning	Percentage of All Suffixed Words	Example
-s, -es	more than one; verb marker	31	characters, reads, reaches
-ed	in the past; quality, state	20	walked
-ing	when you do something; quality, state	14	walking
-ly	how something is	7	safely
-er, -or	one who, what, that, which	4	drummer
-tion, -sion	state, quality; act	4	action, mission
-able, -ible	able to be	2	disposable, reversible
-al, -ial	related to, like	1	final, partial

---

8. Allen, J. *Words, Words, Words: Teaching Vocabulary in Grades 4–12.* York, ME: Stenhouse, 1999.

Following are three meaningful and alternative assessment formats that require relatively little preparation time:

1. Select only four to six important words and embed each in an accessible and contextualized sentence followed by a semicolon. Ask students to add another sentence after the semicolon that clearly demonstrates their understanding of the underlined word as it is used in this context. This assessment format will discourage students from rote memorization and mere recycling of a sample sentence covered during a lesson.

   Example: Mr. Lamont had the most <u>eclectic</u> wardrobe of any teacher on the high-school staff.

2. Present four to six sentences, each containing an underlined word from the study list, and ask students to decide whether each word makes sense in this context. If yes, the student must justify why the sentence makes sense. If no, the student must explain why it is illogical and change the part of the sentence that doesn't make sense.

   Example: Mr. Lamont had the most <u>eclectic</u> wardrobe of any teacher on the high-school staff; rain or shine, he wore the same predictable brown loafers, a pair of black or brown pants, a white shirt, and a beige sweater vest.

3. Write a relatively brief passage (one detailed paragraph) that includes six to ten words from the study list. Then, delete these words and leave blanks for students to complete. This modified cloze assessment will force students to scrutinize the context and draw upon a deeper understanding of the words' meanings. Advise students to first read the entire passage and to then complete the blanks by drawing from their study list. As an incentive for students to prepare study cards or more detailed notes, they can be permitted to use these personal references during the quiz.

Because these qualitative and authentic assessments require more rigorous analysis and application than most objective test formats, it seems fair to allow students to first practice with the format as a class exercise and even complete occasional tests in a cooperative group.

List-Group-Label (Taba[5]) is a form of structured brainstorming designed to help students identify what they know about a concept and the words related to the concept while provoking a degree of analysis and critical thinking. These are the directions to students:

1. Think of all the words related to _____. (a key "big idea" in the text)
2. Group the words listed by some shared characteristics or commonalities.
3. Decide on a label for each group.
4. Try to add words to the categories on the organized lists.

Working in small groups or pairs, each group shares with the class its method of categorization and the thinking behind its choices, while adding words from other class members. Teachers can extend this activity by having students convert their organized concepts into a Semantic Map that becomes a visual expression of their thinking.

List-Group-Label is an excellent prereading activity to build on prior knowledge, introduce critical concepts, and ensure attention during selection reading.

---

5. Taba, H. *Teacher's Handbook for Elementary Social Studies.* Reading, MA: Addison-Wesley, 1988.

Concept Mapping/Clarifying Routine

Research by Frayer et al.[9] supports the strategy of teaching by Concept Mapping:

1. identifying the critical attributes of the word.
2. giving the category to which the word belongs.
3. discussing examples of the concept.
4. discussing nonexamples.

Others have had success extending this approach by guiding students through representation of the concept in a visual map or graphic organizer. The Clarifying Routine, designed and researched by Ellis,[10] is a particularly effective example:

1. Select a critical concept/word to teach. Enter it on a graphic clarifying map like the sample for *satire*.
2. List the clarifiers or critical attributes that explicate the concept.
3. List the core idea—a summary statement or brief definition.
4. Brainstorm for knowledge connections—personal links from students' world views/prior knowledge (encourage idiosyncratic/personal links).
5. Give an example of the concept; link to clarifiers: "Why is this an example of —————————?"
6. Give nonexamples. List nonexamples: "How do you know ————————— is not an example of —————————
7. Construct a sentence that "shows you know."

Term: SATIRE		
Core Idea: Any Work That Uses Wit to Attack Foolishness		
Example • A story that exposes the acts of corrupt politicians by making fun of them **Nonexample** • A story that exposes the acts of corrupt politicians through factual reporting **Example sentence** • Charles Dickens used satire to expose the problems of common folks in England.	**Clarifiers** • can be oral or written. • ridicule or expose vice in a clever way. • can include irony, exaggeration, name-calling, understatement. • are usually based on a real person or event.	**Knowledge Connections** • Political cartoons on the editorial pages of our paper • Stories TV comics tell to make fun of the President— as on *Saturday Night Live* • My mom's humor at dinner time!

9. Frayer, D. A., W. C. Frederick, and H. J. Klausmeier. *A Schema for Testing the Level of Concept Mastery* (Technical Report No. 16). Madison, WI: University of Wisconsin Research and Development Center for Cognitive Learning, 1969.
10. Ellis, E. *The Clarifying Routine*. Lawrence, KS: Edge Enterprises, 1997.

Students benefit from graphic presentations of the connections between the ideas they are learning. Each Unit Resources booklet includes Concept Maps—graphic organizers that illustrate the logical relationship among the skills taught in a Part or a Unit. In Grades 6 through 10, the Concept Maps focus on the Literary Analysis, Reading Skill, and Academic Vocabulary skills in each Part. In Grades 11 and 12 and in *World Masterpieces,* each Map connects the Literary Analysis skills in a Unit to the trends and themes of the period covered.

Steps

1. Review the Concept Map and identify the skills you will cover.

2. Distribute copies of the Concept Map to students. Identify those skills and concepts you will teach and have students circle or otherwise note them. Elicit from students any prior knowledge they may have about the ideas you have introduced. In addition, you may wish to ask them about their own interests in connection with the ideas. In later classes, you can make connections to students' prior knowledge and interests as relevant.

3. Briefly note the connections between ideas on the Concept Map. For example, you might explain that the "Big Picture" or "Main Idea" in the Part is the short story. Using the Concept Map, explain that a plot is an important part of a short story.

4. Emphasize for students that the skills you have identified represent a goal for the class: Everyone will be working toward mastery of those skills.

5. In succeeding lessons, refer students to their Concept Maps at appropriate junctures. As you introduce a selection, review the relevant portion of the Concept Map with students so that they clearly grasp the goals you are setting.

6. As you conclude teaching the selection, review the Concept Map with students to see how the skills are connected with other concepts they have learned. Have students add the name of the selections they have completed to the appropriate blanks. Have students log the additional assignments they complete, such as Extension Activities, in the Learning Log on the chart.

7. As you conclude instruction for a Part or for a Unit, review with students the skills they have covered and the logical connections among the skills.

Grateful acknowledgment for the idea of the Concept Map is made to B. Keith Lenz and Donald D. Deshler, who develop the idea in their book *Teaching Content to All: Evidence-Based Inclusive Practices in Middle and Secondary Schools* (New York: Pearson Education, Inc., 2004).

Idea Wave

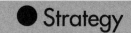

- Students listen while the teacher poses a question or task.

- Students are given quiet time to consider what they know about the topic and record a number of possible responses. This may be a simple list of words and phrases or a focused quick-write. It is also helpful to provide students with a series of response prompts to complete prior to being asked to share aloud. In this way, less proficient academic language users will have a linguistic scaffold to bolster their linguistic output along with their confidence in sharing aloud.

  For example, if students are being asked to make predictions about what will happen in the next chapter of *The Joy Luck Club*, they might be provided with these sentence prompts to complete:

  I predict that Waverly's mother will be (disappointed in / proud of) her daughter's behavior because . . .

  Based on Waverly's relationship with her mother, I assume that her mother will react very (positively / negatively) because . . .

- The teacher whips around the class in a relatively fast-paced and structured manner (e.g., down rows, around tables), allowing as many students as possible to share an idea in 15 seconds or less.

- After several contributions, there tends to be some repetition. Students point out similarities in responses using appropriate language strategies (e.g., *My idea is similar to / related to . . .*), rather than simply stating that their ideas have already been mentioned. This fosters active listening and validation of ideas.

- The teacher can record these ideas for subsequent review or have students do a quick-write summarizing some of the more interesting contributions they heard during the discussion.

Numbered Heads

- Students number off in teams, one through four.
- The teacher asks a series of questions, one at a time.
- Students discuss possible answers to each question for an established amount of time (about 30 seconds to 90 seconds, depending on the complexity of the task).
- The teacher calls a number (1–4), and all students with that number raise their hand, ready to respond.
- The teacher randomly calls on students with the specified number to answer on behalf of their team.
- Students are encouraged to acknowledge similarities and differences between their team's response and that of other teams (e.g., *We predicted a very different outcome. Our reaction was similar to that of Ana's group.*).
- The teacher continues posing questions and soliciting responses in this manner until the brainstorming or review session is finished.

Think-Write-Pair-Share

- Students listen while the teacher poses a question or a task.
- Students are given quiet time to first answer the question individually in writing.
- Students are then cued to pair with a neighbor to discuss their responses, noting similarities and differences. Students encourage their partners to clarify and justify responses using appropriate language strategies:

    How did you decide that?

    In other words, you think that . . .

- It is often helpful to structure the roles (first speaker, first listener) and designate the time frames:

    First speakers, you have 90 seconds to share your answers with your partner.

- After rehearsing responses with a partner, students are invited to share with the class.
- The teacher asks a series of questions, one at a time.
- Students discuss possible answers to each question for an established amount of time (about 30 seconds to 90 seconds, depending on the complexity of the task).

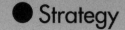

Students who bring special learning needs to the writing process are more likely to internalize the assignment expectations if the task is first clearly outlined on the board or in a handout. They must, in turn, hear the assignment described and, subsequently, have the opportunity to paraphrase what they understand the actual assignment expectations to be—ideally, orally to a partner and in writing to the teacher. If all students are then encouraged to turn in two clarification questions about the assignment, less proficient writers will have a safe and structured venue for monitoring their comprehension and articulating instructional needs. In so doing, passive or apprehensive students are more likely to vocalize any misunderstandings about the task in a timely and responsible manner, rather than realizing the night before the paper is due that they are unsure how to proceed.

Sample Description of a Writing Assignment

Writing Assignment Guidelines:
A Color That Has Special Significance

Write a detailed expository paragraph providing specific reasons that your chosen color has special meaning in your life. Your justification paragraph must include these qualities of effective expository writing:

- An appropriate title (e.g., *Jade Green: A Link to My Heritage*)
- A topic sentence that lets the reader know that you will be discussing the relevance of a particular color to specific aspects of your life
- Transition words that introduce each of your new points about your chosen color (e.g., *first of all, in addition, furthermore, moreover*)
- Specific reasons for selecting this color, including details and relevant commentary that help the reader easily understand the color's special significance
- A visible effort to include new vocabulary from this unit
- An effort to use subordinating conjunctions to join related ideas
- A concluding statement that thoughtfully wraps up your paragraph
- Proofreading goals for the final draft:
  - complete sentences (no fragments or run-on sentences)
  - correct verb tenses
  - correct spelling

Your first draft is due on _____. Please bring two copies of your draft for a peer-response session

---

Using Sentence Starters

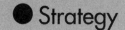

As demonstrated in your *Prentice Hall Literature* Teacher's Edition, one concrete way to structure linguistic equity and to scaffold the vocabulary demands of a challenging writing assignment is to provide students with an array of sentence starters, including practical vocabulary options relevant to the specific writing task and topic. Another equally important scaffold for students writing in a second language or second dialect is a word-form chart that highlights important forms of a base word germane to the assignment.

Following is a list of sentence starters and a relevant word-form chart for a writing assignment on a personally significant color.

Sentence Starters to Discuss a Color You Value

_____ is my favorite color because I associate it with _____. (my future career, my love of nature, my personality, my hobby)

This color reflects/represents/is associated with my interest in _____. (salsa dancing, R & B music, physical fitness, environmental protection)

This color symbolizes/is a symbol of _____. (my culture, my ethnicity)

I have included/selected/chosen the color _____ because _____.

The color _____ is meaningful/valuable/significant to me because _____.

I appreciate/value/like/am fond of the color _____ because/since _____.

Sample Word-Form Chart

Noun	Adjective	Verb	Adverb
symbol	symbolic	symbolize	symbolically
meaning	meaningful		meaningfully
value	valuable	value	valuably
relevance	relevant		relevantly
importance	important		importantly
relationship	related	relate	
association	associated	associate	
significance	significant	signify	significantly
preference	preferred; preferable	prefer	preferably
fondness	fond		fondly

Language Arts Instruction—
Professional Articles

Introduction

The number of children in the country who can be classified as diverse learners because of the special circumstances they bring to public education is growing at a pace that currently outstrips educators' abilities to keep up. Unless significant educational changes are made in response to the dramatic changes occurring in classrooms throughout the country, including the development and utilization of instructional strategies that address the needs of diverse learners, the number of children who "fall through the cracks" in public education will continue to rise.[1]

The 2000 census confirmed what demographers had been documenting for the previous decade: America is more diverse than ever. Certainly, the diversity of our population is a significant asset to our nation in many ways; however, it also places considerable stress on our educational system to effectively accommodate the range of learning needs found in students today. A typical high-school classroom includes students who are diverse in terms of their experiential, linguistic, cultural, socioeconomic, and psychological backgrounds. The range of student needs, interests, motivation, and skill levels often presents heightened challenges to both curriculum and instruction. It should be clearly acknowledged that the individual needs of some students require additional specialized support in basic reading skills, English language development, study skills, and behavioral/emotional/social domains. However, the goal of a comprehensive Language Arts program remains the provision of "universal access" for all students to an intellectually rich and challenging language arts curriculum and instruction, in addition to whatever specialized intervention may be required.

Universal access exists when teachers provide curriculum and instruction in ways that allow all learners in the classroom to participate and to achieve the instructional and behavioral goals of general education, as well as of the core curriculum. Teachers will succeed in providing universal access if they teach in heterogeneous, inclusive classrooms and consistently

---

1. Kame'enui, Edward, and Douglas Carnine. *Effective Teaching Strategies That Accommodate Diverse Learners.* Upper Saddle River, NJ: Prentice Hall, 1998.

and systematically integrate instructional strategies that are responsive to the needs of typical learners, gifted learners, less proficient readers, English language learners, and students who are eligible for and receiving special education services.

Although each student population represented in the classroom may require specific interventions and supports, these learner populations also share many common characteristics, such as the need to build on prior knowledge, the need for systematic vocabulary development, and the need for systematic instruction in strategic reading approaches, to name a few key curricular and instructional areas. Through identification of these shared needs and the implementation of teaching and learning strategies responsive to these needs, the general education teacher, with the support of specialists and other staff, can make significant inroads in designing inclusive lessons that are responsive to the learning and behavioral needs of all learners.

This book provides numerous suggestions to assist teachers in designing English Language Arts lessons that strive for universal access. The suggestions focus specifically on the instructional needs of students who are less proficient readers, students who are English language learners, and students with identified special education needs. The next section describes the reading process and what it takes to be a proficient reader. The remaining sections explore the specific needs of the three focus student populations: English language learners, less proficient readers, and students with special education needs.

A clear consensus has emerged in the field of reading education supporting the notion that reading is a complex process of constructing meaning from text. Successful readers must bring an array of interrelated skills, knowledge, and strategies together in order to understand written English. Skillful readers are able to decode the words accurately and fluently, connect their meanings to prior knowledge, and continually monitor their emerging understanding as they read. In other words, successful readers are active, thoughtful, and strategic learners able to make meaning from what they are reading.

Factors That Affect Reading Success

Successful reading is largely determined by the elaborate interaction of four factors: learner characteristics, skill and instructional variables, demands of the text, and nature of the classroom environment. To better understand these elements, we will examine each in turn, as well as the way they interact to affect successful reading.

Learner Characteristics

Each learner brings unique characteristics to the learning experience. For example, students who are less proficient readers may experience attention and memory issues that make reading especially challenging. English language learners may be highly capable students who, because of limited vocabulary or experiences in their new country, lack the schema for understanding the ideas encountered in text. Students with disabilities may experience cognitive, behavioral/social, and/or physical challenges that make the development of reading skill more challenging.

Skill and Instructional Factors

Reading success is largely determined by the particular skills an individual reader brings to the reading act. For example, the ability to fluently and accurately decode the words in a given reading selection is a necessary but not sufficient condition for successful reading. In addition, the ability to activate and build prior knowledge along with the related ability to connect what one is reading to existing knowledge are essential for proficient comprehension. Moreover, comprehension is significantly determined by a student's level of English acquisition, vocabulary, and skillful use of various reading comprehension strategies such as summarization or self-questioning.

An essential personal aspect of successful reading is the extent to which a reader is actively engaged in the reading, has a clear purpose for reading, and is interested in the content being explored. Skillful readers have learned helpful mental habits such as perseverance, managing and directing attention, being aware of and monitoring their thoughts and feelings as they read. Skilled readers are active participants in the reading act—reading is not a spectator sport.

Instructional interventions provided in the classroom play a significant role in students' development of these skills. Explicit, systematic instruction in decoding and fluency, the incorporation of activities that build and enhance prior knowledge, the provision of explicit vocabulary instruction, and the direct teaching, modeling, and practicing of comprehension strategies will lead to students' skill development and their enhanced engagement and interest in the complexities of the reading act.

Text-Based Factors

It is immediately apparent that the types of texts encountered by students vary widely and create different levels of challenge for different readers. Just as the make and model distinguish one automobile from another, text-based factors differentiate one text from another. While some of these factors may be largely cosmetic in nature, others, such as sentence length, novel vocabulary, density of the concepts, or clarity of the organizational pattern, can have a significant influence on reader comprehension. For example, the presence of well-designed reader aids, including pictures, charts, graphs, and focus questions, can provide additional support to naive readers.

Perhaps the most fundamental distinction in text-based factors affecting reading success is that of narrative (story) reading vs. expository (informational) reading. Expository texts are generally written to inform or persuade the reader using very different organizational patterns from those typically utilized in narratives. For example, information in content-area reading, such as in science and social studies, is often arranged according to structures such as chronological sequence, comparison and contrast, cause and effect, main idea and supporting details, and so forth. Many students are quite comfortable reading stories but find themselves ill equipped to deal with the demands of informational content-area texts.

Classroom Environment

The classroom environment affects everything and everyone within it, including the nature of the reading/literacy program. Specifically, the classroom environment can be viewed as composed of both physical and social-psychological dimensions.

Research suggests that students learn best in a friendly, respectful setting where

- they feel a sense of safety/order and are comfortable taking risks.
- they understand the purpose of and value the tasks at hand.
- they have high expectations/goals for learning.
- they feel accepted by their teacher and peers.

These general factors are of particular import when thinking about what accounts for successful reading. Students will often have significant gaps in their skill, knowledge, proficiency in English, and be self-conscious concerning their lagging literacy.

It is important to be respectful and truthful with students about what it will take to significantly improve their abilities in the Language Arts: It takes PRACTICE, and lots of it. Literacy cannot be "done to" students—it is a collaborative enterprise that is "done with" students. To be sure, teachers provide excellent direct instruction, guided practice, specific feedback, coaching, and more, yet students must understand their roles as active self-directed learners. The intentional design of a caring yet "on purpose" classroom climate creates the condition within which the hard work of improving literacy can take place.

Summary

Understanding that successful reading comprises a complex interaction of factors—learner, skills and instruction, text, and environment—provides a template for thinking about how classrooms can provide universal access to a rich core curriculum for the diverse range of learners in today's high-school classrooms. Secondary students need a balanced Language Arts program based on their individual needs. All students require a firm foundation in fluent/automatic decoding, broad background knowledge of various subjects, ever-expanding vocabularies, all coupled with an array of comprehension strategies to fit the purpose for reading as well as the type of text being read.

In the following section, we examine strategies for developing lesson plans that support diverse learners in meeting rigorous grade-level standards in the Language Arts.

English Language Learners

The number of immigrant, migrant, and refugee students in the United States who have little knowledge of the English language is growing exponentially. In fact, students who are learning English as an additional language are the fastest-growing segment of the school-age population. While the number of English language learners (ELLs) nationwide has skyrocketed, their academic achievement trails behind that of their native English-speaking peers. National studies of English language learners have shown that they are likely to come from disadvantaged socioeconomic backgrounds, attend low-income schools, and have parents with limited English proficiency. These students are also judged by their teachers to have weaker academic abilities, receive lower grades, and score well below their classmates on standardized tests of mathematics and reading.[1] Moreover, in a large-scale California study, secondary schools reported that even long-term resident ELLs entered high school with only fourth to sixth grade academic competencies.[2]

Differential Preparation for Second-Language Schooling

Secondary-school curricula are based on assumptions about basic reading and writing skills and elementary subject matter foundations. However, the growing population of secondary English language learners is tremendously diverse, particularly with regard to their educational backgrounds. These students enter U.S. schools with varying degrees of curricular preparation and a vast range of language proficiencies, in English and their native language. At times, it may seem that the one thing these diverse students have in common is the need to accelerate their English language and literacy acquisition in order to participate more fully in their secondary schooling.

Although some have parents with impressive levels of formal education and professional job experiences, many come from less privileged families, challenged by limited functional literacy even in their native language. Newcomers from war-torn regions and rural areas of developing countries are apt to arrive severely under-schooled, with fragmented native language literacy training and weak subject matter foundations.

1. Moss, M., and M. Puma. *Prospects: The Congressionally Mandated Study of Educational Growth and Opportunity.* Washington, DC: U.S. Department of Education, 1995.
2. Minicucci, C., and L. Olsen. "Programs for Secondary Limited English Proficiency Students: A California Study." *Focus*, Vol. 5. Washington, DC: National Clearinghouse for Bilingual Education, 1992.

These youths predictably require compassion, considerable time, and patient modeling simply to adjust to basic school routines and expectations before they can ever begin to concentrate on phonemic awareness lessons, let alone literary analysis.

On the other hand, more fortunate immigrant youths have benefited from rigorous and sustained elementary schooling in their native country and make the transition to American classrooms more effortlessly. Literate in their home language, these second-language learners have already internalized critical scripts for schooling and often function above equivalent grade levels in math or science. However, these traditionally educated newcomers still face a daunting transition to daily instruction in a language they have only begun to study, along with curriculum content, teaching practices, and skills that may not have been emphasized in their native schooling.

Our secondary schools also serve increasing numbers of students who have been raised and educated entirely in the United States but who speak a language other than English at home. These continuing English language learners were either born in the United States or arrived here as very small children. Many of these long-term U.S. residents are not literate in their home language and remain struggling English readers well into the upper grades and beyond. They may demonstrate a comfortable handle on the social domain of both languages but flounder with grade-level reading and writing tasks.

In summary, with regard to prior schooling, secondary English language learners tend to fall into one of three general and frequently overlapping categories:

1. Recent adolescent immigrants who have received continuous native language schooling prior to immigration to the United States and are prepared with relatively strong academic and study skills to apply to new subject matter

2. Language minority students continuing into secondary schools from U.S. elementary schools with insufficient English fluency and literacy to compete in challenging academic areas

3. Immigrant, refugee, and migrant students with sporadic or no prior schooling who consequently enter lacking basic literacy and elementary curricular foundations.

Second-Language Literacy Development

Statistics on the academic achievement of English language learners demonstrate a dire need for informed attention devoted to literacy, the cornerstone of all academic abilities.

Nonetheless, given the extreme variability in these students' educational histories, they must be offered different pathways to eventual academic success. One approach to literacy instruction will not fit all English language learners. However, the instructional practices outlined in this chapter and throughout this manual should greatly assist them in participating more fully in a heterogeneous secondary Language Arts classroom.

Those with significant gaps in their elementary educational backgrounds will require a thoughtful and sustained literacy intervention program, complemented by a substantive and protracted English language development program. Their acute and compelling academic needs cannot be accommodated solely within the confines of the general education Language Arts classroom, an after-school tutorial, or a reading intervention program.

Similarly, literate and academically prepared newcomers will still need a viable English language development program to enable them to transfer the knowledge and skills they acquired in their native language schooling to the curricula they are studying in the United States. Literate adolescents who are virtual beginners in English will also benefit from a separate reading support class, to help them readily acquire the basic phonology, morphology, and syntax of English and to more efficiently transfer the reading skills they have already mastered in their native language. Students who can already read relatively fluently in their first language will make an easier transition to English decoding than bilingual classmates who are nonreaders. These literate second-language learners will therefore need to move more rapidly than struggling ELL readers, from initial skill-building lessons that focus on decoding, word recognition, and pronunciation to explicit instruction in comprehension strategies such as prediction, questioning, and summarizing that will help them deal more productively with the reading demands of content-area classrooms.

Reading in a Second Language

Research findings suggest that reading processes in a second language are not significantly different from those in a first language.[3] For example, both rely on the reader's background knowledge regarding the topic and text structure to construct meaning, and both make use of cueing systems (graphic,

---

3. Grabe, W. "Current Developments in Second Language Reading." *TESOL Quarterly* (1991), 25, 375–406.

syntactic, phonological, semantic) to allow the reader to predict and confirm meaning.

While literacy processes in first and second languages may be quite similar, two crucial areas of difference must be addressed. First, initial reading and writing in English will be slower and more painstaking for second-language learners because of their lack of overall fluency. The second-language learner is often in the process of acquiring basic oral language while simultaneously developing literacy skills in English. Limited proficiency in a second language can cause a proficient reader in the native language to revert to poor reading strategies, such as reading word by word. Also, some students may not even have the native language literacy skills to transfer concepts about print and strategies to the second language.

Secondly, ELL students are likely to have less prior knowledge and relevant vocabulary to process new information while reading academic English assignments. Furthermore, readers' background knowledge is often culture-bound and may not match the content needed for a given reading text. ELL students with a limited range of personal and educational experiences on a reading topic will therefore have little to draw upon to construct meaning from a selection even if they are able to accurately decode.

Academic Language Development

Many adolescent ELL students come to school with sufficient social language for everyday classroom interactions yet are severely lacking in the academic English foundations to tackle a poem or follow the instructions on a standardized test. This is because academic vocabulary is primarily developed through school-based reading and repeated exposure during content-based classroom activities.

The average native English-speaking student enters elementary school with an internalized understanding of the syntax and phonology of English, plus a working vocabulary of several thousand words. This vocabulary base is enhanced each year through new school experiences and reinforced in home and community settings. In striking contrast, the language minority student enters U.S. schooling with a tenuous grasp of the phonology and syntax of the English language, a scant working English vocabulary, and rare opportunities for practice and expansion of this knowledge outside the classroom. As a consequence, they must develop content-specific language and literacy skills along with conceptual foundations, all the while competing with native English-speaking classmates who may also be challenged by grade-level Language Arts curricula, but who at least operate from a relatively firm foundation in basic academic English and years of exposure to high-frequency social English vocabulary.

Implications for English Language Arts Instruction

A number of implications for instruction can be drawn from these descriptions of the academic language and literacy challenges of ELL students. Novice English readers will require extensive and dynamic instructional "front-loading" in order to effectively grapple with challenging literacy tasks. Teachers all too often concentrate their energies on the damage-control phase, when it becomes clear that students either failed to comprehend or felt too overwhelmed to even try to tackle a reading task. Explaining critical concepts and language after the fact does little to engender reader confidence or competence for the next task. The students may walk away with a better grasp of the plot development in *The Joy Luck Club* but have no sense of how to proceed with the next chapter. Instead, conscientious literacy mentors essentially "teach the text backwards" by devoting far more instructional time to the preparation and guidance phases of lessons. Since a second-language reader may be approaching an assignment with impoverished background knowledge and weak English vocabulary, it makes sense to concentrate on classroom activities that build strong conceptual and linguistic foundations, guide them into the text organization, model appropriate comprehension strategies, and provide a clear purpose for reading. This responsible preparation will in turn help to create the kind of nurturing affective and cognitive arena that communicates high expectations for their literacy development and encourages them to persist and take risks.

Instructional Considerations When Preparing Lessons to Support English Language Learners

All of the instructional practices detailed in Part 3 of this booklet will support ELL students in making strides in their second-language literacy development and in becoming vibrant members of the classroom community of learners. Following are some additional reminders of ways in which you can support ELL students at various stages of your lesson planning to deal more productively with the reading and writing demands of English Language Arts curricula.

Phase 1: Preteach

- Pull out a manageable number of key concepts.

- Identify vocabulary most critical to talking and learning about the central concepts. Don't attempt to cover all of the vocabulary words you anticipate they will not know. Do more than provide synonyms and definitions. Introduce the essential words in more meaningful contexts, through simple sentences drawing on familiar issues, people, scenarios, and vocabulary. Guide students in articulating the meanings of essential terms through these familiar contexts and hold them responsible for writing the definitions in their own words.

- Present key words when they occur within the context of the reading selection or activity. Make the words as concrete as possible by linking each to an object, photo, drawing, or movement.

- Post the new essential vocabulary in a prominent place in the classroom to create a word bank of organized lesson terminology.

- Examine your lesson to see what types of language functions students will need to participate in various activities. For example, if they are being asked to make predictions about upcoming paragraph content in an essay based on transition words (e.g., *therefore, in addition, consequently*), students will need to be taught some basic sentence patterns and verbs to express opinions (e.g., "I predict that . . ."; "Based on this transition word, I conclude that . . ."). If being asked to agree or disagree with the arguments in a persuasive article, students will need to learn some sentence patterns and verbs to convey agreement or disagreement (e.g., "I don't agree with the author's argument that adolescents don't have a work ethic because . . .").

- Engage students in prereading activities that spark their curiosity and involve them in all four language modes.

- Assess students' prior knowledge related to key concepts through participation structures and collaborative group discussions with realia (e.g., photographs, objects) serving as a visual trigger.

- Utilize realia and visuals needed to make the concepts less abstract.

- Use multimedia presentations such as CD-ROM and videos to

familiarize students with the plot, characters, and themes of a narrative text prior to reading, but don't use it as a replacement for reading.

- Provide a written and oral synopsis of the key content prior to actually asking students to read a selection if the sentence structures and vocabulary are particularly demanding.

- Use graphic organizers and semantic maps to help students grasp the central content in an accessible manner prior to reading.

- Lead a quick text prereading, or "text tour," focusing student attention on illustrations; chapter title and subtopics; boldface words; summary sections; and connection of chapter to theme, previous chapters, activities, and concepts.

- When possible, build in opportunities for "narrow reading," allowing students to read more than one selection on the same topic, to build concept and vocabulary recognition that will support their reading more fluently and confidently.

Phase 2: Teach

- Clearly establish a reading purpose for students prior to assigning a manageable amount of text.

- Describe and model strategies for navigating different kinds of text. Provide a convincing rationale for each new strategy and regularly review both the purpose and process.

- Familiarize students with a manageable tool kit of reading comprehension and study strategies and continue practicing these selective strategies. In this way, students end the school year with a viable approach unattainable through sporadic practice with a confusing array of new reading behaviors.

- Introduce a new strategy using a text that isn't too difficult in order to build credibility for the strategy and ensure student success. Otherwise, if a selection is too difficult and the strategy fails to deliver for students, they will have little faith in experimenting with the new strategy on future texts.

- Whenever possible, get students physically involved with the page, using highlighters, self-sticking notes, and a small piece of cardboard or heavy construction paper to focus and guide their reading from one paragraph or column to the next.

- Alternate between teacher-facilitated and student-dominated reading activities.
- Do "think-aloud" reading to model your cognitive and metacognitive strategies and thought processes.
- Assign brief amounts of text at a time and alternate between oral, paired, and silent reading.
- Guide students through the process of reading and comprehending a passage by reading aloud to them and assisting them in identifying the text organization and establishing a clear reading purpose.
- Allow students to read a passage while listening to an audiotape recorded by a classmate, cross-age tutor, or parent volunteer.
- Have students engage in "repeated readings" of the same brief passage to build word recognition, fluency, and reading rate.
- Provide some form of study guide in order to focus their reading on the critical content and prevent them from getting bogged down with nonessential details and unfamiliar vocabulary. A partially completed outline or graphic organizer is more task based and manageable than a list of questions to answer, which often results in simple scanning for content without really reading and comprehending material.
- Demonstrate your note-taking process and provide models of effective study notes for students to emulate.

Phase 3: Assess

- Prepare both text-based and experientially based questions, which lead students from simply getting the gist of a selection to establishing a personal connection to the lesson content.
- Build in task-based and authentic assessment during every lesson to ensure that ELL students are actually developing greater proficiency with new content and strategies. Quick writes, drawings, oral and written summaries, and collaborative tasks are generally more productive indicators of lesson comprehension than a closing question/answer session.
- Provide safe opportunities for students to alert you to any learning challenges they are experiencing. Have them submit

anonymous written questions (formulated either independently or with a partner) about confusing lesson content and process, and then follow up on these points of confusion at the end of class or in the subsequent class session.

- Ask students to end the class session by writing 3–5 outcome statements about their experience in the day's lesson, expressing both new understandings and needs for clarification.

- Make sure that assessment mirrors the lesson objectives. For example, if you are teaching students how to preread expository text, it isn't relevant to assess using comprehension questions. A more authentic assessment of their ability to apply this strategy would be to provide them with a photocopy of an expository selection and ask them to highlight and label the parts one would read during the actual prereading process. It would be relevant, however, to ask them to identify two reasons for engaging in a text prereading before tackling the entire selection.

- Build in opportunities for students to demonstrate their understandings of texts that draw upon different language and literacy skills: formal and informal writing assignments, posters, small-group tasks, oral presentations, and so on.

- Don't assign ELLs tasks that require little or no reading or lesson comprehension. For example, don't allow them to simply draw a picture while other students are writing a paragraph. Instead, make sure that you have adequately scaffolded the task and equipped them with a writing frame and model to guide them through the process. While one might argue that this is multimodal and tapping into multiple intelligences, it is actually conveying expectations for their development of academic competence in English.

- Make sure that students understand your assessment criteria in advance. Whenever possible, provide models of student work for them to emulate, along with a nonmodel that fails to meet the specified assessment criteria. Do not provide exemplars that are clearly outside their developmental range. While this may be an enriching reading task, it will not serve as a viable model. Save student work that can later serve as a model for ELLs with different levels of academic preparation.

- Develop accessible and relevant rubrics for various tasks and products that are customized to the task rather than generic assessment tools. Introduce a rubric in tandem with exemplars of successful and less productive work to help them internalize the assessment criteria. Guide students in identifying the ways in which sample work does or does not meet established grading criteria.

Phase 4: Extend

- Consider ways in which students can transfer knowledge and skills gleaned from one assignment/lesson to a subsequent lesson.
- Build in opportunities for students to read a more detailed or challenging selection on the same topic in order to allow them to apply familiar concepts and vocabulary and stretch their literacy muscles.
- Recycle pre- and postreading tasks regularly, so students can become more familiar with the task process and improve their performance. If they are assailed with curricular novelty, ELLs never have the opportunity to refine their skills and demonstrate improved competence. For example, if you ask them to identify a personality trait of an essential character in a story and then support this observation with relevant details in an expository paragraph, it would make sense to have them shortly afterwards write an identical paragraph about another character.
- Discuss with students ways in which they can apply new vocabulary and language strategies outside the classroom.
- Praise students' efforts to experiment with new language in class, both in writing and in speaking.
- Demonstrate the applicability of new reading and writing strategies to real-world literacy tasks. Bring in potentially more engaging reading selections that will pique their interest and provide a more compelling rationale for applying a new strategic repertoire. Design periodic writing tasks for an authentic audience other than the teacher: another class, fellow classmates, and so on.

Characteristics of Less Proficient Learners

Every classroom has a number of less proficient students, individuals who begin the year one, two, or more years below grade level yet who do not qualify for special education services and may not be English language learners. It is important to keep in mind that most accommodations made for English learners and special needs students will be helpful for all kinds of diverse learners, including less proficient learners. However, it is worthwhile to briefly examine some of the learner characteristics of less proficient students in comparison with their average achieving peers. An appreciation of these distinctions will provide a useful foundation for understanding the importance of using the various "universal access" strategies described throughout this section and incorporated into the Prentice Hall Literature program.

Attention and Memory

Research suggests that underachieving students have difficulty in organizing and categorizing new information during instruction. Typically, less skillful students do not effectively order, classify, and arrange information in meaningful ways during learning, frequently leaving them confused and missing the "big picture." Long-term memory is often adversely affected due to the lack of meaningful connections established and difficulty with noticing how new information relates to prior knowledge. In addition, underprepared students frequently do not know how to focus their attention on the important aspects of a classroom presentation, demonstration, or reading selection. In either case, the intentional use of explicit strategies coupled with interactive review and extension activities can make a significant difference in providing poorly prepared students full access to the Language Arts curriculum.

Lesson Planning and Instructional Accommodations
for Attention and Memory

Phase 1: Preteach

- Gain attention requesting a simple physical response (e.g., "Everyone, eyes on me please," "Touch number one," and so forth). Students need to show you they are ready.

- Keep the lesson pace moving along briskly—a "perky not pokey" pace is helpful.

- Clarify or introduce critical "big ideas" or conceptual anchors that the reading or lesson or activity is built around (e.g., an example, a metaphor, a demonstration).

- Use brief choral responses when the answer is short and identical (e.g. "Everyone, the answer to number one is _____.").

- Use brief partner responses when the answer is open-ended and longer (e.g., "Ones, tell twos the most important new information revealed in the last paragraph.").

- After students have had a chance to rehearse or practice with a partner, randomly call upon them to build prior knowledge or raise questions the text may answer.

- Use graphic organizers, charts, and concept maps to assist students with focusing on critical concepts as well as categorizing and organizing information to be studied/learned.

Phase 2: Teach

- Engage students in a "read/reflect/discuss/note" cycle of filling out the graphic organizers/concept maps collaboratively as you progress through the reading or lesson.

- Do a brief oral review using partners (e.g., think-write-pair-share) to ensure that all students are firm on the big ideas/critical concepts.

- Cue students to take special note of crucial information and explore why this information is so critical.

- Engage students in the active use or processing of the new information (e.g., paraphrase, give an example, write a response).

- Emphasize connections between new and known information.

- Connect new learning to student's personal experience (e.g., coach students to create analogies or metaphors using prior knowledge).

Phase 3: Assess

- Ask students to explain their graphic organizer/concept map to a partner. Monitor selected students and determine their level of understanding—reteach/provide additional examples as necessary.

- Provide students the opportunity to reorganize, prioritize, and otherwise reflect on the key aspects of the lesson.

- Systematically monitor retention of key information or "big ideas" over time using "quick writes" (brief written summaries to a prompt), random questioning, observing student interactions, written assignments, and so on. Reteach, provide additional examples, invite students to elaborate, and so on, as necessary.

Phase 4: Extend

- Have students design investigations or projects using the information in new ways.

- Design homework assignments that require students to go beyond the text to apply lessons learned to their lives or to other circumstances.

- Challenge students to organize information in novel ways, come up with different categories, and otherwise elaborate the information being studied.

- Draw explicit connections and prompt students to induce connections between information studied earlier in the term and new ideas encountered in the current reading selection.

Learning Strategies and Use

Perhaps the most ubiquitous characteristic of less proficient students is their lack of effective and efficient strategies for accomplishing various academic tasks, from writing a persuasive essay to taking notes during a lecture to responding to a piece of literature. Less skillful students tend to have a very limited repertoire of learning strategies and have little awareness of how to monitor the use of learning strategies during reading, writing, and other academic activities. In contrast, successful learners are active, "strategic," and flexible in their employment of appropriate learning strategies tailored to the demands of a particular academic task or assignment.

Kame'enui and Carnine[4] suggest three critical design principles teachers need to keep in mind when addressing the issue of learning strategies with underprepared or diverse learners.

---

4. Kame'enui, Edward and Douglas Carnine, op. cit.

1. Important learning strategies must be made overt, explicit, and conspicuous.

2. Strong verbal and visual support, or "scaffolding," should be provided to ensure that diverse learners understand when, where, and how to use the strategies.

3. Judicious review of new learning strategies is required to allow less prepared students enough practice to incorporate the new strategy into their learning routines.

It is important to note that differences between less proficient students and average achievers in their use of learning strategies is not based on organic or biological differences. In other words, it is their lack of experience and preparation that is the critical difference. Fortunately, less proficient learners are quite capable of acquiring effective learning strategies and significantly improving their academic performance when provided with direct instruction in the "what-why-how-when" of strategy use in a highly focused educational setting.

Lesson Planning and Instructional Accommodations for Learning Strategies

Phase 1: Preteach

- Clarify the rationale for learning the new strategy in terms, examples, and results the students value (e.g., "Where in school or life would it be useful to know how to write a persuasive essay?").
- Brainstorm for examples of successful strategy usage with interactive tactics such as "give one, get one" to involve all students (e.g., each student lists as many ideas as possible in 3–4 minutes and then has 3–5 minutes to compare with a peer and "give one" idea to them as well as "get one" from them to extend their brainstormed list).
- Provide personal examples of how you have used this strategy to your academic advantage.
- Directly teach any "pre-skills," or prerequisite skills, students need to perform the strategy.

Phase 2: Teach

Explicitly model the use of the strategy, including a significant focus on thinking aloud during the execution of each step in the strategy.

- Provide students with a brief summary of the strategy steps or an acronym to facilitate retention of the strategy.

    Example:

    POWER: **P**repare, **O**rganize, **W**rite, **E**dit, **R**evise

    (Archer & Gleason 2000)

- Guide students in practicing the strategy using less demanding content that allows students to focus on the new strategy. Gradually transition to more difficult content.

- Break the strategy down into explicit steps, ensuring that students are able to perform each step and combine steps to use the whole strategy.

- Structure partner-mediated practice in which students take turns practicing the strategy and providing feedback to one another (e.g., taking turns reading a paragraph or page and paraphrasing the gist in 12 words or less).

Phase 3: Assess

- Monitor partners during strategy practice to observe competence, areas for review, and so forth.

- Randomly call on students to informally demonstrate their strategy knowledge.

- Include explicit use of strategies taught as part of the quiz, paper, report, project, and other formal assessments.

Phase 4: Extend

- Discuss with students where else in or out of school they could use the strategy.

- Provide extra credit or some other incentive to encourage the use of the strategy in other content area classes.

- After they have gained some degree of mastery, encourage students to modify and otherwise personalize the strategy to better fit their learning style or needs.

Vocabulary and Reading Fluency

Vocabulary differences between struggling and average students are apparent from the primary years in school and tend to get worse over time. It is not surprising that less prepared learners engage in far less reading in and out of school, resulting in substantially impoverished vocabularies.

In addition, their ability to read fluently and accurately is often diminished, further compounding the issue and rendering reading a frustrating and defeating experience.

There is no shortcut, or "quick fix," for vocabulary building, but teachers can make a tremendous difference by sustained attention to the following practices:

- Directly teaching key conceptual vocabulary using strategies that take students beyond simple memorization
- Teaching students how to learn words and concepts from context
- Encouraging wide reading in and out of school; students who have serious fluency problems (e.g., reading below 100 words per minute in grade-level text) will require sustained practice daily in repeated reading of instructional level/age-appropriate texts

Lesson Planning and Instructional Accommodations for Vocabulary and Fluency

Phase 1: Preteach

- Select conceptually rich, critical vocabulary for more detailed instruction before reading.
- Choose age- and level-appropriate passages for students to use repeated reading strategies (e.g., on prerecorded tapes, partner reading, choral reading with small groups).

Phase 2: Teach

- Directly teach the meanings of critical, conceptually rich vocabulary required for full understanding of the passage or lesson.
- Pick vocabulary strategies that take students beyond simple repetition of the definition to prompt active construction of new connections between the concept and their prior knowledge. Such strategies include
  —creating semantic maps showing how words are related
  —using the words in sentences that "show you know" the meaning
- Define the critical attributes of the concept in short bulleted phrases and create examples and nonexamples of the concept, prompting students to explain why the exemplar does or does not have the attributes of the concept under consideration (a graphic organizer showing the attributes and examples/nonexamples can be very useful).

- Engage students in word sorts: Provide 10–20 vocabulary words for students to place into preset categories (e.g., parts of speech, words descriptive of the character or not, and so on).

- Pair students at similar instructional levels for repeated reading practice; have the more proficient student read a paragraph or a page and then have the less proficient student reread the same section.

- Practice repeated reading of instructional-level passages of 150–200 words in length with prerecorded tapes, set goals, and individually graph and monitor fluency daily, finishing with a written retelling of the passage.

- Teach students important generative word roots (e.g., Latin and Greek) and common affixes. Practice sorting and combining to examine how they work (e.g., -spec-: *spectrum, spectacle, inspection, speculation*).

- Model and practice the use of context in predicting word meanings during reading, thinking aloud to demonstrate to students how textual cues direct your thinking.

Phase 3: Assess

- Randomly call on students to provide examples of the vocabulary word under examination.

- Monitor students during partner discussion of selected critical vocabulary words.

- Evaluate students during small-group discussion, written products, and so on.

- Directly monitor the fluency of selected students via one-minute timings. Note rate, accuracy, and expression.

Phase 4: Extend

- Encourage students to informally use recently taught vocabulary words in "show you know" sentences during classroom conversations, written products, and so on.

- Intentionally revisit newly acquired vocabulary during discussion, while thinking aloud during demonstrations, and so on.

- Encourage students to practice fluency building via repeated reading at home, appropriate CD-ROM technology, and cross-age tutoring of younger students, in which the target student must prepare a story to read fluently with his or her tutee.

Motivation and Academic Identity

Motivation is complex and difficult to define, but most experts agree that it is significantly related to how much success or failure one has experienced relative to the activity in question. Less proficient secondary students typically do not see themselves as capable of sustained reading, inquiry, or writing in a challenging academic setting. The old cliché "Nothing succeeds like success" is relevant to this discussion. To build motivation and encourage the development of a productive "academic identity," it is important to engage less proficient students in challenging lessons while simultaneously incorporating adequate support or instructional scaffolding to increase the likelihood students will experience success. In addition, helping students to explore their thinking as they read and write through structured dialogues and thinking aloud can be very helpful. Noted reading researcher David Pearson calls this process a "metacognitive conversation," allowing less proficient students to gain an understanding of how successful readers and writers think as they work. In a manner of speaking, teachers can provide less proficient students with an academic or cognitive role model. For example, modeling a simple self-monitoring strategy during writing such as "remember your audience" can assist students in keeping multiple perspectives in mind as they compose.

Lesson Planning and Instructional Accommodations for Motivation and Academic Identity

Motivation and academic identity do not lend themselves to the Preteach, Teach, Assess, and Extend lesson format. In a sense, motivation is more "caught than taught" and will be the result of successfully engaging students in the curriculum. However, there are a number of general strategies that are useful to consider including:

- **Self-selected reading** Allow less proficient students regular opportunities to read material they are interested in, at their instructional level.
- **Goal setting** Engage students in setting personal goals for various academic tasks, such as pages/chapters read per week, strategy usage, words read per minute during fluency practice, and so forth.

- **Metacognitive dialogues** Ask students to informally share their perceptions, approaches, and fears regarding various school-related challenges. Students and teachers then share their thoughts and feelings about how they used various strategies to become more successful.
- **Book clubs, book reviews, newsletter reviews, e-mail postings** These provide an audience for students' opinions about books they have read.
- **Partnerships** Have students build partnerships with peers and with younger students, community members, and business personnel.
- **Negotiated choices** As appropriate, involve students in negotiating alternative assignments, options, and novel ideas to reach common goals.
- **Model an "academic identity"** Invite teachers/students/ other adults into the classroom to share how they developed as literate citizens.

Summary

Less proficient high-school students are underprepared for the academic challenges of a rigorous grade-level Language Arts program in a variety of ways. Many of their difficulties can be linked to difficulties with attention and memory, learning strategies, vocabulary and reading fluency, and motivation/academic identity. Secondary Language Arts teachers can have an extremely beneficial effect on the learning of less proficient students by the sustained focus on appropriate strategies for preteaching, teaching, assessment, and extension beyond the lesson.

Students With Special Needs

Students with special education needs are a highly diverse student group. Although their learning needs vary greatly, a majority of children identified as special education students will experience mild to severe difficulties in becoming proficient and independent readers and writers. Through instruction that incorporates adaptations and modifications and is delivered in collaborative ways, students with disabilities can gain literacy skills and be active participants in general education Language Arts curricula and instruction.

Characteristics of Special Education Learners

Eligibility for Special Education

Federal law IDEA '97 (Individuals with Disabilities Education Act, P.L. 105–17) specifies the disabling conditions under which students are found eligible to receive special education services. These disabling conditions may be clustered into the two broad categories of high incidence and low incidence disabilities (see chart on the following pages for descriptions of disabling conditions). Each student with a disability may experience specific cognitive, communicative, behavioral/social/emotional, physical, and learning issues. Students may exhibit all, or some combination, of the characteristics listed for their particular disability and, in the case of some students, have more than one disability (e.g., a student identified as having a learning disability may also have a communicative disorder). Because of the heterogeneity of the special education student population, even within categories of disability, an Individualized Education Program (IEP) is created for each student found eligible to receive special education services.

Disabling Conditions

High Incidence Disabilities	Descriptors	Reading Instruction Consideration
• *Speech or Language Impairment*	• Speech disorders include difficulties in articulation, voice, and fluency. • Language impairments may include difficulties in phonology, morphology, syntax, semantics, and pragmatics.	• When possible, provide opportunities for intensive instruction in decoding and word-recognition skills (e.g., computer drill and practice programs; flash cards of frequently encountered words). • Provide time for students to read the text multiple times to gain fluency (e.g., repeated readings; paired reading). • Explicitly teach vocabulary and provide strategies for dealing with unknown words (e.g., teaching syllabification skills; teaching meaning of prefixes and suffixes). • Explicitly teach more complex language patterns (e.g., compound sentences) and literary elements (e.g., idioms; metaphors).
• *Learning Disabilities*	• Students exhibit average to above-average intelligence combined with uneven academic performance patterns (i.e., perform at an average to above-average level in some academic subjects, while experiencing significant difficulties in others). • Students experience processing difficulties (e.g., have difficulty taking in oral and print information and in expressing ideas orally and in writing). • Students may experience attention and social/behavioral challenges.	• Preteach "big ideas" and vocabulary. • Provide multiple opportunities for students to read text to gain fluency. • Explicitly teach vocabulary using activities that are multisensory and require active participation (e.g., acting out meanings of words; drawing images to represent word meanings; tape-recording words and word meanings; using computer software programs). • Explicitly teach comprehension strategies by modeling the steps, guiding the students through the steps, and monitoring for implementation (e.g., webbing and outlining; predicting; summarizing). • Provide multiple avenues for demonstrating comprehension of text (e.g., writing, drawing, speaking, acting out scenes).
• *Emotional Disturbance*	• Students experience difficulty learning that is not due to cognitive, sensory, or health factors. • Students may have difficulty forging and maintaining interpersonal relationships.	• Make students accountable during large-group, small-group, and paired reading (e.g., have them take notes and make and check predictions; ask questions of all group members, not just a spokesperson; have students complete individual quizzes to check for understanding).

continued

	• Students may display inappropriate behaviors or feelings under normal circumstances. • Students may experience feelings of unhappiness or depression. • Students may have physical symptoms or fears associated with personal or school problems.	• Explicitly teach skills for working in groups (e.g., how to ask questions; how to state an opinion; how to disagree with another person's ideas). • Provide structure and establish routines for reading activities and transitions (e.g., specify expectations during large-group reading; establish routines for how students are to complete comprehension activities). • Become familiar with the student's behavior plan and systematically implement it in the classroom (e.g., use the reinforcers and consequences identified in the plan to build consistency for the student).
• *Mental Retardation*	• Students will demonstrate subaverage (in students with mild/moderate mental retardation) to significantly subaverage (in students with severe mental retardation) intellectual functioning. • Students will demonstrate overall low performance in adaptive behavior domains (e.g., taking care of personal health needs).	• Preteach and reteach vocabulary and concepts as needed. • Make concepts concrete by linking concepts to the students' daily lives. • Explicitly model what is expected, and when able, provide examples of completed projects. • Provide multiple avenues for students to engage with text (e.g., books on tape, paired reading, passages in hypertext format). • Provide multiple exposures to the same text and its key vocabulary. • Provide multiple ways for students to demonstrate understanding of text.
• *Low Incidence Disabilities*	**Note:** Students with low incidence disabilities may have average to above-average intelligence or may experience cognitive impairments ranging from mild to severe.	**Note:** Students with low incidence disabilities may have average to above-average intelligence or may experience cognitive impairments ranging from mild to severe.
• *Deaf/Hard of Hearing*	• Students who are deaf or who have some degree of hearing loss	• Present ideas visually. • Capture key ideas from discussions in written form on the overhead or chalkboard. • Use FMI systems when available. • When orally reading text, reduce background noise as much as possible; when conducting small-group or paired reading activities, consider having the groups move to other rooms or spaces. • Work with the interpreter or special education staff to identify adaptations and modifications.

continued

• *Blind/Low Vision*	• Students who are blind or who have some vision	• Present ideas auditorially and through tactile modes to support student access. • Work with the special education teacher to secure large-print text, Braille text, books on tape, and AAC reading devices. • Work with the special education staff to identify specific adaptations and modifications.
• *Deaf/Blindness*	• Students who have concomitant hearing and visual impairments	• Work with the special education staff to identify specific adaptations and modifications. • Gain understanding and a level of comfort in using the AAC devices the student is using in the classroom.
• *Other Health Impaired*	• Students with health conditions that limit strength, vitality, or alertness (e.g., heart condition, sickle cell anemia, epilepsy, AIDS)	• Work with the special education staff to identify adaptations and modifications. • Gain understanding of the child's condition and day-to-day and emergency medical needs. • Develop plans for dealing with students' absences.
• *Orthopedic Disabilities*	• Students with physical disabilities (e.g., club-foot, bone tuberculosis, cerebral palsy)	• Work with the special education staff to identify specific adaptations and modifications. • Work with the special education staff to secure adapted materials and AAC devices, as appropriate (e.g., book holder; computer voice-recognition system that allows student to dictate written assignments). • Adapt routines and activities to take into consideration the student's physical needs (e.g., room arrangement that allows for mobility in a wheelchair; procedures for distributing and collecting materials; procedures for forming work groups.)
• *Autism*	• Students experience difficulty in verbal and nonverbal communication • Students experience difficulties in social interactions • Is commonly referred to as a "spectrum disorder" because of the heterogeneity of the group	• Work with the special education staff to identify specific adaptations and modifications. • Structure group and paired activities to take into consideration the child's needs; teach social skills and supports for working in small group and paired situations. • Connect concepts and vocabulary to the interests of the student. • Work with the special education staff to implement behavioral/social plans to provide consistency. • Establish and maintain routines to ensure predictability within the classroom.

continued

• *Traumatic Brain Injury*	• Students who experience an acquired injury to the brain • Injury results in total or partial functional disability or psychological impairment (e.g., cognition, language, memory, attention, reasoning)	• Work with the special education staff to identify specific adaptations and modifications. • Adapt routines and activities to take into consideration the student's physical needs (e.g., room arrangement that allows for mobility in a wheelchair). • Take into consideration student's language, memory, and attention skill needs when constructing class assignments and activities. • Preteach and reteach concepts and vocabulary as appropriate.

Individualized Education Plan

The IEP serves to guide general and special education teachers, related service providers, and parents in designing and delivering educational programs that maximize students' school participation and learning. The IEP includes goals, objectives, and benchmarks that outline what an individual student is expected to learn and achieve during the course of the academic year, as well as the types of services and special adaptations and modifications that are to be put into place to support the educational achievement of the student. For example, in the area of Language Arts instruction, a student's IEP may include the following goal and objectives:

Goal: Jamal will improve in reading comprehension skills as measured by the district-adopted standardized test.

Objective: Given narrative passages written at the seventh-grade level, Jamal will correctly write the name(s) of the main character(s) and outline, in writing, the main events of the passages in correct sequence for three out of four passages by December.

Objective: Given expository passages written at the seventh-grade level, Jamal will correctly write the main idea of the passages and at least three supporting details for three out of four passages by February.

The IEP goes on to identify specific services the student will need in order to achieve these goals and objectives. A range of services is available to students with disabilities through their IEP. Services fall along a continuum and include the option of students receiving instruction in general education classrooms with special education supports and participating in specialized instruction delivered by special education teachers in special education classrooms for one or more periods a day. The type of service delivery to be provided is determined individually for each student through the IEP meeting. The general education teacher, in partnership with the special education staff and the student's parents and, when appropriate, the student, determine the type of service delivery that is most appropriate for a student based on his or her learning needs.

Many students with disabilities are educated in general education classrooms alongside their general education peers. Service-delivery models that support student participation in general education classrooms go by various names, including mainstreaming, integration, and inclusion. All have the underlying same intent—to provide for the needs of students with disabilities in the least restrictive environment, alongside their general education peers.

In the case of Jamal, the service delivery option selected and specified in his IEP may look something like this:

> Student will participate in the general education Language Arts class and in one period of special education reading resource support each day. The special education teacher will team with the general education Language Arts teacher at least two days per week to provide instruction in the general education Language Arts class.

IEPs also specify the types of curricular, instructional, and behavioral adaptations and modifications that are to be put into place to support the student's achievement. For Jamal, the following adaptations and modifications may be specified in the IEP:

> The student will receive instruction in learning strategies to identify characters, story sequence, and main ideas and supporting details. The student will be provided a story map for identifying the main character(s) and for sequencing story events. The student will be provided a main idea/supporting details map when working with expository passages.

The IEP is a guide that details the types of goals, educational program, and adaptations and modifications a special education student is to receive. The IEP is developed by a team and is reviewed at least annually. General education teachers, special education professionals, administrators, parents, and students all have a voice in the development of the individual IEP.

Lesson Planning and Instructional Accommodations

When developing Language Arts lesson plans for inclusive classrooms of general and special education learners, teachers will want to consider the addition of teaching and learning strategies that will support universal access to the content. Teachers will need to be familiar with the unique learning needs and requirements of the students and their goals, objectives, and benchmarks and, through collaboration with other IEP team members, incorporate those needs and strategies into the classroom.

This process does not need to be as intimidating as it sounds because there are some common, relatively unintrusive teaching and learning strategies that can be implemented in the classroom to address students' specific needs, as well as support the learning of the other students present in the classroom. For example, students with disabilities can greatly benefit from activities that preteach and reteach concepts, that explicitly link lesson content with prior experience and knowledge, that directly teach the meaning of critical vocabulary words, and that explicitly model how tasks are to be completed. This is true for other learners as well, including less proficient readers and students who are English language learners. Lesson plans that include explicit instruction in behavioral and social expectations also help to ensure student participation and learning. Pacing is also an issue. Some students with disabilities will require a somewhat slower pace or an ongoing review of key concepts if they are to grasp key understandings and skills. Also, activities need to be considered in light of the students' disabilities. For example, will special materials be needed (such as materials with enlarged print for students with low vision or adapted manipulatives that can be used by a student with a physical disability)? If participating in student-mediated instruction (e.g., small-group learning), what type of preparation will students receive for participating in these activities? Will the activities provide necessary supports to ensure student participation (e.g., will directions be explicit and in writing as well as presented verbally)?

There are a number of other simple adaptations and modifications general education teachers can implement in the classroom to directly address the literacy learning needs of students with disabilities. In fact, in many cases, these adaptations and modifications will assist all learners in the classroom, including typically developing readers, English learners, and less proficient readers. A beginning list of suggestions for meaningfully including students with disabilities in the general education Language Arts curriculum is presented in the chart at the end of this section. Although presented in terms of disabling conditions, the suggestions apply across conditions.

It is also helpful to think of instructional considerations that specifically apply to the four phases of instruction: Preteach, Teach, Assess, and Extend. A beginning list of suggestions is provided below.

Phase 1: Preteach

- Identify the most critical and high-utility vocabulary words for comprehension of the passage. Provide explicit instruction in the meaning of these words that incorporates instruction in the understanding of prefixes, suffixes, word roots, synonyms, and antonyms.
- Provide an overview of key ideas and concepts presented in the text using study guides, outlines, or maps.
- Explicitly connect text content with the students' lives.
- Preteach key concepts.

Phase 2: Teach

- Present all ideas orally and visually and, when possible, incorporate tactile and kinesthetic experiences as well.
- Stop often to discuss key ideas and check for understanding.
- Limit the presentation of information or discussion of key topics to short periods of time (no more than ten minutes) to enhance attention.
- Require students to demonstrate that they are listening and following along (e.g., taking notes, running a finger along the text).
- Incorporate active reading strategies (e.g., choral reading, paired reading) to assist students in maintaining attention.
- Provide necessary adaptive materials as appropriate (e.g., enlarged print).
- Incorporate the same comprehension and learning strategies over extended periods to allow for mastery. This will provide students with multiple opportunities to practice a strategy and to become comfortable in its application. This will also prevent "strategy clutter," which can occur when a student has too many strategies to draw from and is not facile enough with any to allow for ease of use.

- Provide specific and step-by-step instructions. Model what the students are to do, step-by-step.

Phase 3: Assess
- Go beyond questioning techniques to assess students' understanding by having them write questions about what they have learned, identify those sections they find are unclear or confusing, or complete short writes of the key points.
- When having students work in groups or pairs, set up procedures that maintain individual student accountability (e.g., students each having to write, draw, or state a response).
- When appropriate, have students self-manage and chart their performance. Academic performance, homework and assignment completion, and behavior could be charted.

Phase 4: Extend
- Provide examples of completed projects.
- Allow students to work in pairs or small groups.
- Provide outlines of what is to be done, with suggested dates and timelines for project completion.

Collaboration as a Key to Student Achievement
One of the most critical things a general education teacher can do is to collaborate with the special education teachers and staff. Special education staff have extensive expertise in working with students with disabilities and are there to support each student with an IEP. These professionals are available as support systems for general education teachers and parents. The chart that follows presents a brief list of potential special educators that you may want to contact when working with students with disabilities in your general education classroom.

General education teachers can do a great deal to ensure that students with disabilities are meaningfully included in the life of the classroom. The attributes listed on the next page are impor-tant to all classrooms, but they play a key role in the creation of a classroom culture and climate that supports the participation and achievement of students with disabilities.

- Exploring differences and the importance of the acceptance of differences
- Setting clear expectations for all students that take into consideration students' learning styles and needs
- Providing students with reasonable choices
- Setting up instructional activities that foster the development of relationships between students and between students and teachers
- Demonstrating mutual respect, fairness, and trust

For example, in the case of Jamal, you could work with the special education teacher to identify those learning strategies you are already teaching in the classroom that will assist Jamal. You may want to invite the special education teacher into the classroom to provide instruction in other critical learning strategies that would assist all of your students in becoming better readers and writers, including Jamal. Because Jamal is receiving resource-room support one period per day, you may want to discuss with the special education teacher the type of instruction he is receiving during the support period and together work to develop a plan that links the curriculum of the two learning environments. You will most likely be involved in assessing whether Jamal is achieving his goals and objectives and in providing instruction to support their achievement.

Summary

Students with disabilities are a highly heterogeneous group of learners. Their cognitive and behavioral, social, and physical needs can present unique challenges in the classroom, but through careful and strategic planning and collaboration among professionals and parents, these students can be contributing and vital members of the classroom community, as well as readers and writers. It is the professionals' responsibility, in consultation with the parents, to ensure universal access to the curriculum for these students. Lesson planning and the inclusion of adaptations and modifications within lessons are beginning points for achieving the goal of universal access for students with disabilities.

Special Education Teachers and Service Providers

Support Provider	Roles	How They Can Support the General Education Teacher
Special Education Teacher • resource teacher • itinerant teacher • special-day class teacher • inclusion specialist	• Is intimately familiar with students' IEP goals, objectives/benchmarks, and the students' academic, communicative, and behavioral/emotional needs • Has expertise in how to adapt and modify curriculum and instruction to meaningfully include students with disabilities in general education classrooms and curriculum • Has expertise for providing remedial support and intensive intervention services for students with disabilities	• Can answer questions about students' learning needs • Can explain the students' IEP and what can be done in the general education class to support student achievement of IEP goals and objectives/benchmarks • Can help you develop ways to adapt and modify instruction that will help students learn • Can work with you in the classroom to support the students' participation and achievement
Para-professional	• May be assigned to "shadow" a student in the general education classroom • Can assist in adapting and modifying curriculum and instruction for the particular student(s) • May serve to monitor students' academic and behavioral/emotional needs and intervention plans • May assist students in meeting physical, mobility, and health needs	• Can assist you in addressing the student's needs (e.g., can provide a one-on-one explanation that you may not be able to furnish because of the other students in the classroom) • Can be responsible for adapting and modifying instructional activities and assignments, with guidance from you and the special education teachers • Can oversee the implementation of specialized intervention plans • Can be responsible for the student's physical, mobility, and health needs
Audiologist	• Expertise in measuring students' hearing levels and evaluating hearing loss	• Can give you suggestions for how to work with students who have partial or total hearing loss • Can give you suggestions for how to deal with a student who refuses to wear his or her hearing aids in class

Physical and Occupational Therapist	• Physical therapist generally focuses on gross motor development (e.g., walking, running) • Occupational therapist generally focuses on fine motor development (e.g., using writing tools)	• Can give you suggestions for how to modify requirements to take into consideration students' motor and physical needs
School or Educational Psychologist	• Expertise in educational testing administration and interpretation • May also have training in counseling and working with students in crisis situations	• Can help you understand testing results and may be able to come into the classroom to observe and give you suggestions for working with a particular student • Can help you work with a student who is in crisis (e.g., divorce, death)
Augmentative and Alternative Communicative Specialist	• Expertise in assessing students' AAC needs • Expertise in developing programs that assist students in using alternative means for communicating verbally and in writing (e.g., communication boards; using speech synthesizer software)	• Can explain to you how a student's AAC device works • Can give you suggestions for how to make adaptations and modifications that support the student's use of the AAC device in the classroom (e.g., physical arrangement of the learning environment; assignment adjustments)
Educational Therapist	• Expertise in assessment and remediation for students experiencing learning problems • May serve as a case manager and build communicative links between school, home, and related service providers	• Can give you suggestions for how to adapt instruction to meet the student's needs • Can give you suggestions for communicating with parents and for working with the special education staff

ANSWERS

Unit 1

Reading: Context Clues

Practice, p. 2

1. smaller; 2. lives; 3. dollars; 4. disasters;
5. law; 6. spills; 7. life; 8. winter;
9. navigate; guide; 10. storms

Assess, p. 3

A 1 B; 2 C; 3 C; 4 B; 5 A; 6 C

B 1 C; 2 E; 3 G; 4 A; 5 D; 6 B; 7 F

Literary Analysis: Narration

Practice, p. 4

1. Next; 2. then; 3. after; 4. At first; 5. then;
6. Meanwhile; 7. Finally

Assess, p. 5

Correct order: 4; 6; 2; 5; 1; 7; 3
After a while, Noni neared home, dragging the sled. Even before he arrived, he could hear the sled dogs barking. Then, as Noni came close to the cabin, he panicked. Smoke was coming from a side window near the stove. Immediately he rushed past the dogs and stormed into the cabin. Then he ripped flaming curtains from the wall. At last, he rushed out the front door with them, flinging them into the snow.

Literary Analysis: Point of View

Practice, p. 6

1. T-P; 2. F-P; 3. F-P; 4. T-P; 5. T-P

Assess, p. 7

A 1. A; 2. B; 3. A; 4. B

B 1. First person point of view

2. Students should state that readers do not know whether the narrator's view of Daniel is correct. In the first-person point-of-view readers only get information from the narrator; the information may not be correct.

3. Third-person point of view

Literary Analysis: Fiction and Nonfiction

Practice, p. 8

A 1. yes; 2. no
B 1. fiction; 2. nonfiction
C 1. nonfiction; 2. fiction; 3. fiction

Assess, p. 9

A 1. fiction; 2. nonfiction; 3. nonfiction

B 1. nonfiction: use of facts such as "a group of two or more families was known as a clan." 2. fiction: the words *once upon a time*, a mermaid living in a city under the sea; 3. nonfiction; use of facts such as "at 21 stories high, the Cape Hatteras lighthouse. . . is the tallest one in the United States"; 4. either fiction or nonfiction; winter snow is realistic, but this could be a real person and a real event, or a fictional character and event.

Vocabulary: Word Origins

Practice, p. 10

1. reveal; 2. significance; 3. verify; 4. context;
5. revelation

Assess, p, 11

A 1. B; 2. C; 3. D; 4. A
B 1. verify; 2. context; 3. reveal; 4. significance

Grammar: Common and Proper Nouns

Practice, p. 12

A 1. proper noun; 2. common noun; 3. common noun; 4. proper noun

B 5. Edison-proper noun; inventions-common noun;
6. inventor-common noun; America-proper noun;
7. laboratory-common noun; New Jersey-proper noun;
8. phonograph-common noun; Europe-proper noun;
9. Thomas Edison-proper noun; movies-common noun

C 10. inventions; 11. inventor; 12. laboratory;
13. phonograph; 14. movies; 15. Edison;
16. America; 17. New Jersey; 18. Europe;
19. Thomas Edison

Assess, p. 13

A 1. proper noun; 2. common noun; 3. proper noun; 4. common noun; 5. proper noun;
6. common noun; 7. common noun

B 8. people-common noun; boats-common noun; river-common noun
9. home-common noun; family-common noun; Buckingham Palace-proper noun
10. Queen Elizabeth-proper noun; Windsor Castle-proper noun; family-common noun
11. castles-common noun; England-proper noun
12. stations-common noun; trains-common noun; Victoria Station-proper noun
13. Fleet Street-proper noun; destination-common noun; travelers-common noun;

14. People-common noun; tea-common noun; afternoon-common noun; 15. citizens-common noun; nations-common noun; traditions-common noun; English-proper noun

Grammar: Possessive Nouns

Practice, p. 14
A 1. library's-singular; 2. children's-plural; 3. adult's-plural; 4. books'-plural; 5. book's-singular; 6. author's-singular; 7. town's-singular

B 8. laboratory's; 9. chemists'; 10. computer's; 11. men's; 12. day's; 13. chemist's

Assess, p. 15
A 1. years, Alaska's; 2. mines', miners; 3. miners, inhabitants, territory's; 4 states

B 5. ocean's; 6. waves; 7. chairs; 8. passengers'; 9. ship's; 10. cabins; 11. Jones's; 12. engines; 13. navigators; 14. sun's

Grammar: Incorrect Forms of Plural Nouns

Practice, p. 16
A 1. girls; 2. glasses; 3. ponies; 4. tomatoes; 5. elves; 6. teeth; 7. birches; 8. foxes; 9. lashes; 10. monkeys; 11. sheep; 12. hobbies

B 13. persons, shadows; 14. Centuries, children; 15. men, woman; 16. Guesses, days; 17. Clocks, watches

Assess, p. 17
A 1. potatoes; 2. chiefs; 3. branches; 4. valleys; 5. boxes

B 1. books; 2. bunches; 3. feet; 4. allergies; 5. thieves 6. aluminum; 7. halves; 8. spaghetti; 9. lunchboxes; 10. heroes

C 1. Zoos, cities, animals; 2. Foxes, monkeys, ropes; 3. Sea lions, seals, pools

Writing: Comparison-and-Contrast Essay

Practice, p. 18
Sample Answers:
A 1. Tennis and baseball are being compared.
   2. Students should offer another point of comparison, such as there are baseball teams and tennis teams in high school; that both boys and girls like both sports.

B 1. Students should pick two reasonable things to compare.
   2. Students should point out two similarities of their chosen topics.
   3. Students should point out two differences between their two choices.

Assess, p. 19
Sample Answers:
   1. Students should name a specific topic for comparison.
   2. Students should list at least three accurate facts or details about each subject.
   3. Students should list both similarities and differences.
   4. Students' paragraphs should point out clear similarities and differences.

Writing: Hyperbole

Practice, p. 20
A 1. C, 2. A
B 1. F, 2. T, 3. F, 4. T

Assess, p. 21
   1.–3. Students should write appropriate examples of overstated description.
   4. Students should explain that they would use hyperbole in their writing to be entertaining and to give their readers a strong impression. They should indicate that hyperbole would best used in creative writing, and might mention personal narrative, short stories, tall tales, or poetry.

Writing: Descriptive Essay

Practice, p. 22
A Details will vary.
B Details will vary but should follow the guideline provided.

Assess, p. 23
A 1. sight
   2. touch
   3. sound
   4. taste
   5. smell
   6. touch

B 2. the loud music from a nearby car radio; I would exclude this detail because it doesn't add to the beauty of calm lake.

C
Sample Answers:
   1. From the roots at the bottom to the leaves at the top.
   2. From one speaker to another.
   3. From opening the soda to taking a big gulp to finishing it.

Reading: Author's Purpose

Practice, p. 24

1. to inform
2. Students should list any two details that are informative.
3. to entertain
4. Students should list any two details from the paragraph that are entertaining.

Assess, p. 25

A 1. to persuade
2. Students should list persuasive language, "wherever and whenever. . . you should wear a helmet," and the use of statistics, or other details that they found persuasive.

B 1. B; students should explain why the article is informative.
2. D; students should understand that this writer is trying to persuade, to inform, and to entertain all at once in his negative review of the movie.
3. D; students should state that though this author has the opposite opinion, he does have the same purpose—to persuade, to inform, and to entertain all at once.

Reading: Web Site's Purpose

Practice, p. 26

1. B
2. A
3. D

Assess, p. 27

1. C
2. D
3. B
4. A

Literary Analysis: Setting

Practice, p. 28

A 1. A; 2. C; 3. A
B 1. B; 2. C; 3. B
C 1. D; 2. A; 3. C; 4. B

Assess, p. 29

A 1. B, C; 2. A, B; 3. A, C
B 1. A; 2. B
C 1. true; 2. false; 3. false; 4. true

Literary Analysis: Historical Context

Practice, p. 30

Sample Answers

Then: job is exhausting, takes all day, little contact with friends, happy to help out

Now: job is easy, takes two hours, easy to have contact with friends, happy to help out

Assess, p. 31

A 1. false; 2. false; 3. true; 4. false
B 1A. unhappy; 1B. "I would like to go, too."
"I have no choice but to stay home."; 2. A; 3. B

Literary Analysis: Author's Purpose/Tone

Practice, p. 32

1. A
2. Students might underline any of the entertaining details, including details about Postmistress Perkins or Uncle Al's April Fool's Day trick.
3. B
4. Students might underline any or all of the sentences showing the author's opinion. <u>I think we learned a lot during that playing time. We learned how to negotiate and how to compete. We learned how to manage bullies and how to take care of our friends. We learned real-life lessons. It is harder for children today, with their busy schedules and organized activities, to get the kind of experience that we took for granted.</u>

Assess, p. 33

Sample Answers

1. B
2. The author's purpose in passage I is to inform.
3. Students might list facts such as "walking is easily the most popular form of exercise. . . Walking burns approximately the same amount of calories per mile as does running."
4. The author's purpose in passage II is to persuade.
5. The writer wants people to take an action, joining a club. He or she uses peppy language such as "Come on, everybody, put down your remotes and your game controllers and get moving!"

Vocabulary: Prefixes *re-* and *pre-*

Practice, p. 34

A 1. Prearrange
2. precook
3. preschool
4. prepay
5. pretest

B 1. to go backward
  2. to pay back
  3. to put back in place
  4. to find again

Assess, p. 35

A 1. prejudge
  2. precaution
  3. resell
  4. premature
  5. prefabricated

B
Sample Answers:
  1. a passage at the beginning of a written work
  2. a feeling that something bad is going to happen
  3. cooked ahead of time
  4. know beforehand

Grammar: Personal Pronouns

Practice, p. 36

A 1. I, my, you; 2. We, yours, me; 3. your, his; 4. I, it, mine, my; 5. You, it, us; 6. Its, I, your, it, 7. she, we, our; 8. you, our; 9. They, they, their

B 1. The class saw Denise do <u>her</u> first magic trick. friends, Denise
  2. <u>She</u> started <u>it</u> by borrowing Carmen's straw hat. Denise, trick
  3. "What are <u>you</u> going to do with <u>my</u> hat?" she asked. Denise, Carmen, Carmen
  4. Denise took off the ribbon and cut <u>it</u> into several pieces. Ribbon
  5. <u>She</u> told Carmen to put <u>them</u> into the hat and shake <u>it</u>. Denise, pieces, hat

Assess, p. 37

A 1. their; 2. his; 3. you; 4. his; 5. her; 6. their; 7. their; 8. yours; 9. his; 10. its

B 1. his; 2. my; 3. her; 4. its; 5. their; 6. his; 7. their; 8. her; 9. his; 10. her

Grammar: Possessive Pronouns

Practice, p. 38

A 1. His; 2. its; 3. Her; 4. its

B 1. I like their knitted hats.
  2. Have you ever seen hats as unusual as theirs?
  3. The pink scarf is hers, too.
  4. Which hat in that pile is hers?

C 1. his; 2. her; 3. their; 4. yours

Assess, p. 39

A 1. their; 2. your; 3. its; 4. theirs; 5. their

B 6. their; 7. his; 8. mine; 9. His; 10. her; 11. hers; 12. your; 13. they're; 14. your; 15. There's; 16. you're

Grammar: Pronoun-Antecedent Agreement

Practice, p. 40

A 1. Visitors; 2. government; 3. states; 4. woman; 5. Vermonters; 6. Tim and Joel; 7. mountains; 8. Ms. Brockman

B 1. their–mountains; 2. it–monument; 3. she–tourist; 4. he–tourist; 5. their– Vermonters; 6. I–visitor; 7. It–state;

Assess, p. 41

A 1. his; 2. them; 3. They; 4. our; 5. their; 6. His

B 7. Mr. Garcia; 8. seeds; 9. birds; 10. Mrs. Suzuki; 11. Mr. Garcia

C 12. it; 13. his; 14. it; 15. he; 16. their

Spelling: Homophones

Practice, p. 42

A 1. rows; 2. tow; 3. write; 4. sail; 5. hours; 6. sun

B 1. warn; 2. missed; 3. rain; 4. there; 5. sees; 6. road

C 1. through, mooed; tails; 2. horse, neighs; 3. mane, reins; 4. deer, herd, fowl

Assess, p. 43

A 1. Hour
  2. two
  3. week
  4. here
  5. won
  6. plane
  7. they're

B 1. A. hair; B. hare
  2. A. tail; B. tale
  3. A. by; B. buy
  4. A. whole; B. hole

C Sign should read: There is no fish today. Try again next week.

Writing: News Report

Practice, p. 44

  1. B
  2. B
  3. B
  4. B
  5. A
  6. A

Assess, p. 45

Students should write six specific questions for the author, covering Who? What? Where? When? and Why?

394 Reading Kit Answers

Writing: Letter/Letter of Proposal

Practice, p. 46
A 1. B; 2. C; 3. A
B 1. B; 2. A; 3. A
C In their letters, students should use a suitably formal greeting and closing. They should use appropriately formal and respectful language. They should describe their plan for a cleanup and explain why the idea is a good one.

Assess, p. 47
A 1. B; 2. C; 3. A
B 1. Students should select a topic for their letter of proposal.
2. Students should name an appropriate person or organization to whom they will send their letter. For example, if their topic is a new video-game system, they might name the president of an entertainment company.
C 3. In their letters, students should use a suitably formal greeting and closing. They should use appropriately formal and respectful language. They should describe their idea and explain why it is worth supporting.

Writing: Autobiographical Narrative (Writing Workshop)

Practice, p. 48
1. Times should be present-day or recent past. Settings should be real places.
2. Word webs should include personality traits as well as physical attributes.
3. Events should follow one another in logical order and the climax should be truly the highest point of interest.

Assess, p. 49
1. Beginning: In the morning, we could not find my white cat Boots.
   Middle: All day, we checked the apartment, the hall, and the street.
   End: that night, we found Boots cuddled in my new white scarf!
2. Students should write about an experience that they consider interesting, using details about setting, characters, problems and dialogue.

Unit 2

Reading: Predicting

Practice, p. 50
A Students' answers should indicate that the title leads them to predict that something will go wrong with the plans, or that something unexpected will happen.

B 1. B; 2. B; 3. A

Assess, p. 51
1. B
2. B
3. Students should predict that the next paragraph will be about Civil War music.
4. The clues students will use to make their predictions will be the title of the piece, "Hardtack and Music: Life of a Civil War Soldier." The first paragraph tells about hardtack. The next paragraph will probably discuss music.

Literary Analysis: Plot

Practice, p. 52
A The order is 3, 4, 1, 5, 2.
B A. 3; B. 1; C. 5; D. 4; E. 2

Assess, p. 53
A 1. true; 2. false; 3. true; 4. false
B The order is 2, 1, 4, 3.
C 1. D; 2. A; 3. C; 4. B

Literary Analysis: Character

Practice, p. 54
A 1. shy; 2. reckless; 3. clever; 4. kind; 5. brave
B 1. A. friendly; B. lonely
2. A. calm; B. restless

Assess, p. 55
Sample Answers
1. How the character looks
   O'Malley: dressed like an executive; looks good
   Junior: wore casual work shirts and blue jeans; looks "like one of the guys"
2. What the character does
   O'Malley: knows the business from working his way up through the company; chats with employees; knows everyone
   Junior: has only held high-paying jobs that his father, the owner, gave him; never visits mailroom or factory; has fine education
3. Character traits of each
   O'Malley: hardworking, knowledgeable, sincere
   Junior: privileged, out of touch, inexperienced

Vocabulary: Word Roots *-dict-*, and *-ver-*

Practice, p. 56

1. predict; 2. veracity; 3. dictator; 4. edict;
5. dictate; 6. veritable; 7. verify; 8. aver

Assess, p. 57

A 1. B; 2. C; 3. A; 4. C; 5. A; 6. D
B Sample Answers:
1. We checked in the atlas to <u>verify the</u> location of the Ural Mountains.
2. Miss Brown will <u>dictate</u> the spelling words and we will write them down.
3. Sergeant Davis always tells the truth, so he is known for his <u>veracity.</u>
4. The yellow traffic light will <u>indicate</u> that drivers should slow down.
5. It is difficult to <u>predict</u> the outcome of a well-written mystery story.

Grammar: Action Verbs and Linking Verbs

Practice, p. 58

1. action; 2. action; 3. linking; 4. linking;
5. action; 6. linking; 7. action; 8. linking;
9. linking; 10. action

Assess, p. 59

1. action; 2. action; 3. action; 4. linking;
5. action; 6. action; 7. action; 8. action;
9. linking; 10. linking; 11. action; 12. action;
13. action; 14. linking; 15. action; 16. linking

Grammar: Regular and Irregular Verbs

Practice, p. 60

A /t/: looked; helped; crushed; pushed
/d/: rained; named; called; turned
/ed/: landed; planted; shifted; sorted
B 1. built; 2. knew; 3. thought; 4. caught; 5. flew

Assess, p. 61

A 1. climbing; climbed; climbed; 2. buying; bought; bought; 3. cooking; cooked; cooked; 4. driving; drove; driven; 5. growing; grew; grown
B 1. wrote; 2 spoken; 3 thought; 4 said; 5 begun
C 1 spotted; 2 fallen; 3 rubbed; 4 went; 5 worn

Grammar: Verb Tenses

Practice, p. 62

A act; acted; will (or shall) act; have acted; had acted; will have (or shall have) acted
B 1. future; 2. present; 3. past; 4. present; 5. future; 6. present perfect; 7. past perfect

Assess, p. 63

A 1. past; 2. past; 3. present 4. present 5. future
B 1. washed; 2. raised; 3. needs; 4. is; 5. will do
C 1. The trumpet plays loudly.
2. The flute whistled sweetly.
3. The musicians will tune their instruments.
4. The piano player ran his hands across the keys.

Writing: Informative Article

Practice, p. 64

1. Changes in the American Colonies by the mid 1700s.; 2. students of American history; 3. examples of change, i.e., population, experience in self-government, increased productivity, less need for protection; 4. order of importance; 5. It could be more specific.

Assess, p. 65

1. Students should identify the audience for their informative article of their chosen topic. For example, "The basics of cheering," might have girls from elementary school through high school as its audience.
2. Students should write a topic sentence that states what the article is about.
3. Students should supply three supporting ideas or pieces of information for their articles.
4. Students should indicate a logical order in which they would use the ideas, for example, order of importance or chronological order.
5. Students should supply definitions for unfamiliar terms. For example in an article on the basics of cheering, names of specific jumps or stunts might be defined.

Writing: Journal Entry

Practice, p. 66

Answers will vary.

Assess, p. 67

Studens' journal entries should describe the next day in this sequence. Students should include feelings, thoughts, and descriptions in their journal entries.

Writing: Review of Short Story

Practice, p. 68

1. A, B, C, E, F, G, H, J
2. C
3. B

Assess, p. 69

1. A
2. C
3. F; Students should explain that a reader does not have to like a story in order to review it. The reader/reviewer needs to comment on the story and its elements but does not need to be positive in his or her response.
4. Students should choose any story and write two things that they like about it and two things that they do not like as well. They should mention story elements such as plot, character, action, dialogue, etc.

Reading: Make Inferences

Practice, p. 70

Sample Answers

A 1. scared and nervous
   2. <u>Rebecca jumped slightly</u>, <u>grabbed the back of the chair</u>, <u>biting her knuckle</u>
   3. Rebecca would probably like to get out of the situation she's in.

B 1. I would guess that my sister failed her history test.
   2. I can infer that my tire just went flat again and that my friend doesn't know tires as well as she thinks.

Assess, p. 71

1. a
2. The room was filled with kids; they all looked like they knew each other
3. a
4. [Sam] sat down in the back of the room; his eyes glued to the desk
1. b
2. create my masterpiece
3. a
4. she looked around in a bored way; useless glass

Reading: Generalization

Practice, p. 72

Sample Answers

1. Jim always has a great time at Luis's Halloween party.
2. Mark does not like fish fillet sandwiches.
3. Anna and Luke are a good team and always get good grades together.
4. Mr. Donner gives about half an hour of math homework each night.

Assess, p. 73

1. Students should make the generalization that walking is good exercise or that walking is good for your health.
2. Students should underline three bits of supporting evidence in the passage.

Literary Analysis: Conflict and Resolution

Practice, p. 74

1. internal conflict, resolution answers will vary
2. external conflict, resolution answers will vary

Assess, p. 75

1. A; 2. B; 3. B; 4. B; 5. A

Literary Analysis: Theme

Practice, p. 76

A 1. A; 2. B
B 1. B; 2. A

Assess, p. 77

A 1. false; 2. true; 3. true
B 1. B; 2. A; 3. B

Literary Analysis: Irony

Practice, p. 78

1. A; 2. D; 3. C

Assess, p. 79

1. Students' answers should show that they expected Leon to become a city dweller.
2. Answers will vary but might include the facts that Leon intended to move to the city, that he succeeded in everything he did including schoolwork and getting a job, and that his dream seemed to be coming true.
3. The actual ending of the story is that he had to move back to the country.
4. Situational irony.

Vocabulary: Prefixes *con-*, *sub-*, and *ob-*

Practice, 80

A 1. subordinate; 2. conclusion; 3. obstruction; 4. construction; 5. submarine
B 1. A; 2. C; 3. B; 4. B; 5. A

Assess, p. 81

1. subnormal; 2. concurrent; 3. objection; 4. conforming; 5. submarine
B 1. B; 2. C; 3. A; 4. A; 5. B

Grammar: Adjectives

Practice, p. 82

A 1. simple, young; 2. A, easy, many; 3. The, older, happy, funny; 4. every, a, dramatic, a, sad; 5. a, welcome; 6. a, delightful, a, recent; 7. the, hard, adventurous; 8. the, humorous, the, long; 9. several, the, frozen; 10. The, new, a, complete, the, poet's

B 11. An, a; 12. A, a; 13. An, a; 14. A, a; 15. An, a; 16. an, an

Assess, p. 83

A 1. A, a, an; 2. The, a, a; 3. A, a

B 1. The, model, metal, seventeen; 2. The, a, a, red; 3. a, miniature, an; 4. The, a, dark; 5. A, steel, realistic, the

C Answers will vary.

Grammar: Adverbs

Practice, p. 84

A 1. eagerly; 2. always; 3. wonderfully; 4. extremely; 5. here; 6. soon; 7. yearly; 8. very; 9. effectively; 10. very

B Arrows should be drawn to the verbs listed 1. is; 2. went; 3. saw; 4. beautiful; 5. closely; 6. perfect; 7. piloted

Assess, p. 85

A 1. later; 2. soon; 3. quite; 4. finally; 5. very; 6. very; 7. formerly

B 1. sneered; 2. continued; 3. thoroughly; 4. better; 5. flew; 6. reported; 7. successfully

Grammar: Degrees Of Adjectives and Adverbs

Practice, p. 86

1. quickly, more quickly, most quickly; 2. cold, colder, coldest; 3. tall, taller, tallest; 4. bright, brighter, brightest; 5. grumpily, more grumpily, most grumpily

Assess, p. 87

A 1. more steadily, most steadily

2. more beautiful, most beautiful

3. more tan, tannest

4. more gracefully, most gracefully

5. younger, youngest

6. more carefully, most carefully

7. spicier, spiciest

8. prettier, prettiest

9. sadder, saddest

10. more, most

B 1. A king loved one of his daughters most of all.

2. The best pie would win the contest.

3. The judge needed to determine which runner ran farther than the other.

4. Which vegetable do you like more: potatoes or beans?

5. The least used bicycle had new tires.

Spelling: Tricky or Difficult Words

Practice, p. 88

A 1. abundant; 2. careless; 3. brilliant; 4. weather; 5. surprise; 6. principal; 7. recommend; 8. guidance; 9. forty; 10. disappoint

B 1. sophomore; 2. consider; 3. appreciate; 4. concede; 5. C; 6. escape

Assess, p. 89

A 1. where

2. finally

3. friend

4. of

B 1. there

2. Where

3. through

4. off

5. favorite

6. They

C 1. there

2. their

3. they're

Writing: Anecdote

Practice, p. 90

A 1. B

B 1. Yes; Students may say that the uncle learned that his plans might backfire sometimes, or that being stingy doesn't always pay off.

2. Students should state two of the following reasons: the story is short; the story is amusing; a character does learn a lesson; the story has a beginning, a middle, and an end.

Assess, p. 91

Students should follow the guidelines and choose a topic to write their own anecdote.

Writing: Letter to the Editor

Practice, p. 92

A. Answers will vary but should include details that support the positions taken.

B. Student letters should be in a business letter format and clearly state the position taken and contain supporting details.

Assess, p. 93

A Answers will vary but should include details that support the positions taken.

B Student letters should be in a business letter format and clearly state the position taken and contain supporting details.

Writing: Short Story

Practice, p. 94

A 1. S
   2. S
   3. S
   4. P
   5. P

B 1. The setting is Kari's bedroom.
   2. The plot is Kari is looking for her new outfit.
   3. The conflict is that her younger sister Debbie has taken the outfit and Kari wants it back.

C Sample Answers:
   1. Pat and I are tied for third place.
   2. I am a great soccer player.
   3. I am learning to swim.

Assess, p. 95

A Sample Answers:
   1. first person point of view
   2. A. She is shy; she is 14 years old; she has long blond hair.
      B. She is shy and feels uncomfortable around the other students.
   3. a dense forest; huge ferns; thick fog covered the ground; a very large animal

B Sample Answers:

   Maria grabbed my hand. "What was that?" she said, her voice trembling.

   "I don't know, but it sounds big," I answered. "Maybe we should stay really quiet until it passes."

   "Is that the best you can think of," she said, her voice rising. "You're the one who got us into this mess. How do you plan to get us out?"

Unit 3

Reading Skill: Main Idea

Practice, p. 96

   1. C; 2. A; 3. The pyramid's bulk is enormous.

Assess, p. 97

A 1. D; 2. A

B Not only does it seem that everybody is juggling these days, they seem to be tossing around just about anything you can imagine.

Literary Analysis: Expository Essay

Practice, p. 98

A 2, 1, 4, 3, 6, 5, 7

B 1. E, 2. N, 3. E, 4. N, 5. E

Assess, p. 99

A 1. Chronological organization
   2. Cause-and-effect organization
   3. Comparison-and-contrast organization
   4. Problem-and-solution organization

B 1. Expository; chronological organization
   2. Not expository
   3. Expository; comparison-and-contrast organization
   4. Not expository.

Literary Analysis: Reflective Essay

Practice, p. 100

A The author admires her grandmother's hard work, patience, and self-reliance.

B 1. N, 2. R, 3. N, 4. R, 5. N

Assess, p. 101

A Sample Answers:
   1. The main purpose of this essay is to present the thoughts and feelings of the author about the backyard blackberry patch.
   2. My Backyard Blackberry Patch

B Sample Answers:
   1. The main purpose of this essay is to present the thoughts and feelings of the author about his or her most unforgettable teacher.
   2. My Most Unforgettable Teacher

Literary Analysis: Biography and Autobiography

Practice, p. 102

A Autobiography, as it is personal, is based on memory and emotion.

B Biography, as it is objective and based on research.

Assess, p. 103

   1. Biography, because it is objective and based on research. It is written in the third person.
   2. Autobiography, because it is based on a personal memory and uses the first person.
   3. Biography because it is objective and based on research. It is written in the third person.

Vocabulary: Prefixes *ir-* and *in-*

Practice, p. 104

A 1. irresistible; 2. indecisive; 3. inflexible;
4. irregular; 5. inexcusable; 6. irresponsible;
7. incompetent; 8. incoherent

B 1. incompetent; 2. irresponsible;
3. incoherent; 4. inflexible

Assess, p. 105

A 1. indecisive; 2. insufferable; 3. incompetent;
4. irresponsible; 5. incoherent 6. irregular
7. irreplaceable; 8. intangible

B Sample Answers

1. Spending long hours outside, she was <u>insensitive</u> to the heat and humidity.

2. The shipping charges were <u>irreversible</u> when the wrong product was returned.

3. Constant noise and traffic on the road made waiting for the bus <u>intolerable</u>.

Grammar: Coordinating Conjunctions

Practice, p. 106

A 1. and; 2. but; 3. and; 4. or; 5. and; 6. for;

B 1. and; 2. or; 3. nor; 4. so; 5. yet; 6. and;

Assess, p. 107

A bold indicates circled answers

1. <u>Alex</u> **and** <u>Ethan</u> live in the village.
2. I exercise <u>before breakfast</u> **or** <u>before dinner</u>.
3. We had <u>carrots</u> **and** <u>peas</u> with our meal.
4. <u>I would like to bake a cake</u>, **but** <u>I am missing a few ingredients</u>.
5. <u>I will be late coming home from school</u>, **for** <u>I have to go the library</u>.
6. You have a choice of <u>vanilla, strawberry</u>, **or** <u>chocolate</u> ice cream.
7. The weather report promised <u>blue skies</u> **and** <u>no rain</u>.
8. Ellen drew a picture of <u>horses</u> **and** <u>lamas</u>.
9. I forgot to get <u>milk</u> **and** <u>sugar</u> at the grocery.
10. <u>Cats</u> **and** <u>dogs</u> do not always fight when living in the same house.

B 1. and; 2. but; 3. and; 4. but; 5. or; 6. for;
7. yet; 8. and

Grammar: Prepositions and Prepositional Phrases

Practice, p. 108

A 1. The actress <u>with red hair</u> held a book <u>in her hand</u>.
2. She stood <u>in the very center</u> <u>of the huge stage</u>.
3. She was auditioning <u>for the director and the producer</u>.

4. The stage manager sat <u>inside the wings</u> <u>to the right</u>.
5. <u>Behind him</u> stood various members <u>of the cast</u>.

B Students should use the prepositional phrases listed on the worksheet to construct their own sentences.

Assess, p. 109

A 1. under; 2. to; 3. in, above; 4. During, at;
5. except, at; 6. within; 7. across, from; 8. after

B 1. over the river, through the woods, on our trip; 2. under the shelves; 3. beneath the large chestnut tree; 4. During the night; 5. in the music room; 6. on the class trip; 7. in large binders; 8. behind the curtain

C Student answers will vary but should include a prepositional phrase.

Grammar: Conjunctions

Practice, p. 110

Student responses may vary, but they should reflect correct usage of conjunctions to combine sentences.

Assess, p. 111

A Student paragraphs should reflect the correct usage of conjunctions to combine sentences.

B 1. although; 2. or, and; 3. because, and;
4. since, because; 5. but

Writing: Problem-and-Solution Essay

Practice, p. 112

Chart: Students should complete the entire chart.

1. Students should target the statement of the problem to the audience. The statement should clearly identify the problem.

2. Students should list the problem step by step, making sure to clearly describe each step.

3. Be sure students supply adequate examples for each of the solutions.

4. Concluding statements should provide a clear solution.

Assess, p. 113

A Students should complete the entire chart.

B 1. Students should target the statement of the problem to the audience. The statement should clearly identify the problem.

2. Students should list the problem step by step, making sure to clearly describe each step.

3. Be sure students supply adequate examples for each of the solutions.

4. Concluding statements should provide a clear solution.

Writing: Outline

Practice, p.114

Items 2 and 7 are sample answers.

1. I
2. Keep a record of your daily life
3. B.
4. C.
5. II
6. B.
7. Pick time to write

Assess, p. 115

Items 2 and 4–6 are sample answers.

1. I
2. Born in Georgia, 1944
3. B.
4. Youngest of eight children
5. Parents worked as sharecroppers
6. The family was poor but strong.
7. Career
8. Went to college
9. became a famous writer
10. Her novel *The Color Purple* won a Pulitzer Prize and was made into a movie.

Writing: How-to Essay

Practice, p. 116

1. Student topic sentences should reflect what the essay is trying to explain.
2. Details should include all of the materials as well as the steps in order.
3. Students can complete the chart to ensure they have remembered all of the steps and materials.
4. Concluding sentences should sum up the essay.

Assess, p. 117

1. This essay instructs the reader on how to make a peanut butter and jelly sandwich.
2. *First*, *next*, *then* all are transitional words used to show sequence.
3. Materials needed are two slices of bread, jelly or jam, and peanut butter. Equipment needed includes a plate and a butter knife.
4. 1) Gather materials.; 2) Place both slices of bread face down on a plate.; 3) Spread jelly or jam on the face of one slice of bread.; 4) Spread peanut butter on the face of the other slice of bread.; 5) Place both slices of bread together making sure the jelly or jam and the peanut butter face each other.; 6) Apply light pressure.
5. Students should write a concluding sentence

that sums up the process of making a peanut butter and jelly sandwich.

Reading: Fact and Opinion

Practice, p. 118

A 1. Fact; 2. Opinion; 3. Fact; 4. Opinion; 5. Fact

B 1. Fact, reliable Web site, encyclopedia; 2. Fact, reliable Web site, encyclopedia; 3. Opinion; 4. Opinion; 5. Fact, reliable Web site, encyclopedia

Assess, p. 119

A 1. You could check the facts in an encyclopedia or a reliable Web site

2. It is an opinion because it is about the future.

3. The second sentence contains both fact and opinion. You could prove whether "Several other artists . . . have also worked at the Disney studios." An encyclopedia or a reliable Web site would have this information. The middle part of the sentence, however, is an opinion. You could not prove "who are less wellknown" to be true or false.

4. The third sentence is a statement of fact. You could prove whether Frank Thomas and Ollie Johnston were artists who worked on those movies. An encyclopedia or a reliable Web site would have this information.

B 1. Fact; 2. Fact; 3. Fact; 4. Opinion; 5. Fact; 6. Fact

Reading: Check Facts

Practice, p. 120

1. Fact; encyclopedia, reliable Web site
2. Fact; almanac, encyclopedia, reliable Web site
3. Fact; atlas
4. Fact; reliable Web site

Assess, p. 121

A 1. reliable Web site—would include up-to-date information

2. almanac—provides information on climate that caused the recession

3. atlas—a collection of maps would provide the location

4. biographical dictionary—the question asks for the dates of his life, not the full background of his life and inventions

5. dictionary—includes the definition as well as the origin of words

Literary Analysis: Persuasive Essay

Practice, p. 122

1. appeal to emotion; <u>thrilled</u>; <u>jump in</u>; <u>we promise you</u>; <u>without a doubt</u>; <u>a week you will always remember</u>

2. appeal to reason; <u>more special events than ever before</u>; <u>The poll we took show that 80% of students have enjoyed each of these events in past years.</u>

3. appeal to authority; <u>Principal Norris</u>

Assess, p. 123

1. C
2. B
3. C
4. D
5. Students' topic sentences should use at least one persuasive technique.

Literary Analysis: Diction

Practice, p. 124

A 1. The diction is informal because the writer uses colorful language and contractions and is entertaining.

2. The writer may have wanted to provide characterization through the use of a character's description of an approaching storm. The writer's diction reveals a character who is not formal and possibly not well educated.

3. A threatening thunderstorm appeared in the southwestern sky.

B 1. I; 2. F; 3. I

Assess, p. 125

A Student responses should reflect correct usage of diction.

1. Formal to informal; 2. Formal to informal; 3. Informal to formal

B 1. The diction is formal because the writer uses descriptive poetic language which has no contractions or conversational elements.

2. The writer wanted to capture the quiet, peaceful feeling of a sunset. The writer's language is descriptive with visual images for readers.

3. The cold night air was chillin' the hot sandy beach.

Literary Analysis: Humorous Essay

Practice, p. 126

1. Chang finds himself in a situation of mistaken identity and ends up asking his grandmother to the dance.

2. Chang thinks he is calling Marilyn, but the reality is that he is calling his grandmother.

3. Student responses will vary but may include don't act rashly, take your time, check the number before calling.

4. Student responses will vary between the grandmother and Chang.

Assess, p. 127

A 1. A; 2. B; 3. A; 4. C; 5. C

B Student responses will vary but should include elements of a humorous essay.

Vocabulary: Borrowed and Foreign Words

Practice, p. 128

1. garage; 2. moccasins; 3. piano; 4. denim; 5. hurricane; 6. taco; 7. balcony; 8. canyon

Assess, p. 129

A 1. C; 2. G; 3. F; 4. A; 5. D; 6. H; 7. E; 8. B

B 1. garage; 2. denim; 3. moccasins; 4. piano; 5. taco; 6. balcony; 7. canyon; 8. hurricane

Grammar: Subjects and Predicates

Practice, p. 130

A Student responses should reflect the use of a subject and predicate that makes logical sense.

B Student responses should reflect the use of a subject and predicate that makes logical sense.

Assess, p. 131

A *Italics indicate double underscores.*

1. The <u>artist</u> *painted* in her studio all day.
2. <u>Alma</u> *ran* to the grocery store for milk.
3. The <u>aquarium</u> *was filled* with tropical fish.
4. The <u>ranger</u> *gave* an informative presentation about the meadow.
5. The <u>puppies</u> *barked* when we arrived.
6. The <u>notebook</u> *is* on the hall table.
7. <u>Raccoons</u> *are* nocturnal animals.
8. A large <u>turtle</u> *was* in the middle of the road.
9. Our <u>house</u> *is* blue with green shutters.
10. <u>Fred</u> *fed* the hamsters and the fish before leaving the house.

B Student responses should reflect the use of a complete subject and predicate that makes logical sense.

Grammar: Compound Subjects and Predicates

Practice, p. 132

A
1. <u>Baseball</u> and <u>football</u> are my favorite sports.
2. <u>Hikers</u> and <u>mountain biker</u>s often share the same trail.
3. The <u>rain</u> and <u>wind</u> caused flood damage.
4. <u>Doors</u> and <u>windows</u> need to be ordered for the house.
5. <u>Trout</u> and <u>pike</u> are in the lake.
6. <u>Canoes</u> and <u>rowboats</u> can be rented by the hour.
7. <u>Sandstone</u> and <u>shale</u> are found in our neighborhood.
8. <u>Books</u> and <u>tapes</u> are available at the library.

B
1. I went <u>snowboarding</u> and sprained my ankle.
2. The waves <u>crested</u> and <u>broke</u> against the rocks.
3. The ring <u>glistened</u> and <u>glimmered</u> in the sun.
4. The tourists <u>stopped</u> and <u>watched</u> the street performer.
5. Christopher <u>wrote</u> and <u>directed</u> the play.
6. The lettuce <u>wilted</u> and <u>drooped</u> on the counter.

Assess, p. 133

A
1. <u>Felix</u> and <u>Rex</u> went to the circus in town. compound subject
2. They <u>saw</u> many clowns and <u>ate</u> a lot of popcorn. compound predicate
3. <u>Lion</u>s and <u>tigers</u> are ferocious animals. compound subject
4. The homeowner <u>ordered</u> new rugs and <u>threw</u> out her old rugs. compound predicate
5. I <u>bought</u> a bicycle and <u>rode</u> it to school. compound predicate
6. I <u>collected</u> cans and <u>brought</u> them to the recycling center. compound predicate
7. <u>Blackberries</u> and <u>raspberries</u> grow by the house. compound subject

B Student responses should include correct use of compound subjects and compound predicates as well as logic.

Grammar: Usage in Adjective and Adverb

Practice, p. 134

A 1. I ate <u>only</u> a little bowl of ice cream.; 2. I played <u>badly</u> at the tennis tournament.; 3. I <u>just</u> made a huge birthday cake.; 4. correct

B Student responses should reflect correct placement of the modifiers.

Assess, p. 135

A 1. I wanted <u>badly</u> to play ball.; 2. Luis asked <u>fewer</u> questions than Shelia; 3. correct; 4. correct; 5. correct

B Student responses should reflect correct usage and logical placement of the modifiers.

Spelling: Tools for Checking Spelling

Practice, p. 136

A
1. high
2. dream
3. why
4. sleep
5. stay

B
1. ninety
2. believe
3. OK
4. said
5. OK

Assess, p. 137

A
1. OK
2. thief
3. cousin
4. Friday
5. OK
6. victim
7. batteries
8. drowned
9. OK
10. world

B
1. Sunday
2. beach
3. children
4. boats
5. enjoyed
6. water
7. great

Writing: Persuasive Letter

Practice, p. 138

1. Sample Answers:

Points	Persuasive Techniques
Ballot is a chance to decide the future	Appeal to emotion
Voting is right; secured by Declaration of Indep. and Bill of Rights	Appeal to reason and backed by facts
Corporations and public service groups spend money	Appeals to authority

2. The right to vote for all citizens was bought with the blood of patriots.

Assess, p. 139

1. Students should clearly state their position in a thesis statement.
2. All points should be listed and followed with the appropriate persuasive technique.
3. Students should state that they will use strong, forceful language to stir their readers.
4. Students' conclusions should reinforce their position statement.

Writing: Adaptation

Practice, p. 140

A Students should include details from the passage but adjust the word choice for the intended audience.

B 1. dictionary, thesaurus; 2. dictionary, history text, thesaurus

Assess, p. 141

A Student responses should have word choice and content suitable to the audience selection.

B 1. C; 2. A

Writing: Comparison-and-Contrast Essay

Practice, p. 142

1. Similarities: the goal of the game; the need for speed and stamina; teamwork. Differences: amount of action; ease in following the ball.
2. Both try to move the ball to the opponent's goal; both require speed and stamina.
3. There is more constant action in soccer; it is easier to follow the ball in a soccer game.

Assess, p. 143

Sample responses for "dogs or cats as pets":

1. personal attention; exercise; grooming
2. **Category:** personal attention; Dogs: must be petted and played with often; Cats: do not require as much attention. **Category:** exercise; Dogs: must be walked or exercised daily; Cats: Do not need to have supervised exercise. **Category:** grooming; Dogs: must be bathed regularly; Cats: keep themselves clean.
3. Millions of people in the United States have pets. Two of the most popular types of pets are dogs and cats. There are many similarities in having dogs and cats as pets. Both need to be fed and watered regularly. Both need to be taken to the veterinarian for checkups and shots. Both dogs and cats can be affectionate and can be good company.

While there are many advantages to owning dogs, I prefer cats as pets.

First of all, cats are much cleaner than dogs. Cats are constantly grooming themselves and never need a bath. Dogs have to be bathed regularly or they get very dirty and smelly. If dogs get into mud or dirt, they cannot clean themselves as cats do. Cats need only to be brushed regularly.

Unit 4

Reading: Draw Conclusions

Practice, p. 144

A 1. Details include a chestnut tree (hard, strong wood), a smith with large, strong hands and arms, muscles like iron bands. Details emphasize the smith's strength.

2. The details all refer to the smith's size and strength.
3. The smith is a large and physically powerful man.

B 1. Circled details include deep, windless wood, one leaf, afraid, dares, afraid. Details suggest intense fear in absolute quiet.

2. Students should conclude the poet uses the details to show the power of absolute fear in nature.

Assess, p. 145

1. B
2. C
3. A

Reading: Recognize Propaganda Techniques

Practice, p. 146

1. Buy their toothpaste tonight, get shiny teeth.
2. Loaded language: "A toothpaste that is out of sight," Bandwagon appeal: "Leaves everyone's teeth so clean and white."

Assess, p. 147

A 1. loaded language
2. bandwagon appeal
3. broad generalization
4. faulty reasoning
5. hidden message

B Student advertisements should contain one or more examples of propaganda techniques.

C Students should identify and list any propaganda techniques.

Literary Analysis: Forms of Poetry

Practice, p. 148

1. Lyric poem because it uses a single image of a traveler against the rising and falling of the tide; repeated language adds to musical quality.
2. Students should select an image and write a line from a haiku that contains the correct number of syllables.
3. Student explanations should logically support the image they selected.

Assess, p. 149

1. A
2. D
3. B
4. D
5. A
6. B

Literary Analysis: Figurative Language

Practice, p. 150

A 1. simile
2. personification
3. symbol

B Student responses should follow the definitions for each example of figurative language.

Assess, p. 151

A 1. simile
2. metaphor
3. simile
4. metaphor
5. simile

B 1. personification
2. symbol
3. personification
4. symbol
5. personification

Literary Analysis: Narrative Poetry

Practice, p. 152

1. Hamelin is in Brunswick by Hanover, the Weser River is deep and wide, it washes up on the southern side, the location is a pleasant spot. The poem takes place 500 years ago.
2. The townspeople are plagued by vermin (rats).
3. Student examples should relate to the poem's subject matter and reflect correct usage of the selected form of figurative language.

Assess, p. 153

A 1. B
2. D
3. C
4. D
5. D

B Students should mention figurative language (simile "stabbed like a driven nail") and the rhythm and rhyme of the language.

Vocabulary: Word Roots: *-trans-, -fer-*

Practice, p. 154

(Sentences will differ. Possible responses are shown.)

1. crossing the Atlantic Ocean; We took a transatlantic flight from New York to London.
2. to carry from one place to another; Use a wheelbarrow to transport the plants to the garden.
3. to come together to discuss something; Let's confer at noon to discuss our plans.
4. to give or present something; I'd like to offer my help to you.
5. to carry from one person or place to another; Next year I may transfer to a new school.

Assess, p. 155

(Wording of definitions may vary. Possible responses are shown.)

1. changed the form of
2. to express in a different language
3. consult a source for information
4. a logical assumption based on evidence or reasoning
5. to change position from one place to another

Grammar: Infinitives and Infinitive Phrases

Practice, p. 156

A *Italics* indicate circled portions.

1. Rudolf wanted <u>*to play*</u> *hockey this winter.*
2. Beverly started <u>*to cook*</u> *the peas and carrots.*
3. <u>To err</u> is human, <u>to forgive</u> divine.
4. My dog likes <u>*to swim*</u> *in the lake.*

B 1. Jerry likes <u>to play golf everyday</u>. (phrase serving as the object of the verb *likes*)
2. We went <u>to listen to the opera</u>. (phrase modifying the verb *went*)
3. I like <u>to read stories to my brother</u>. (phrase serving as the object of the verb *like*)

Assess, p. 157

A 1. Her goal, <u>to write a novel</u>, was never realized.

2. The purpose of the class was <u>to teach conservation skills</u>.

3. <u>To achieve the highest grade</u>, the students created a multimedia presentation.

4. Alex and Anna wanted <u>to ride their bikes to the beach</u>.

5. Felix began <u>to paint the house last summer</u>.

B 1. All the campers wanted <u>to swim in the lake</u>. noun

2. The tailor made the dress <u>to fit the princess</u>. adverb

3. The sound vibrations caused the table <u>to shake</u>. adjective

4. Ethan was excited <u>to fish in the lake</u>. adverb

5. The student artists began <u>to paint watercolors</u>. noun

C Student responses should correctly use the infinitives given.

Grammar: Appositives and Appositive Phrases

Practice, p. 158

1. Bonnie, <u>my cousin</u>, lived on a farm. arrow to *Bonnie*

2. <u>The math teacher</u>, Mr. Chang, was my homeroom teacher for the year. arrow to *Mr. Chang*

3. Mark, <u>the pitcher</u>, threw many fast balls during the game. arrow to *Mark*

4. The Garcias, <u>our friends</u>, invited us to the lake to go fishing. arrow to *The Garcias*

5. Ms. Steffa, <u>the school principal</u>, canceled afterschool activities due to the weather. arrow to *Ms. Steffa*

6. Winnie the Pooh, <u>a fictitious character</u>, had many adventures with Christopher Robin. arrow to *Winnie the Pooh*

7. Mollie and Max, <u>golden retrievers</u>, were the winners of the dog show. arrow to *Max and Millie*

8. <u>My cat</u>, Domino, likes to sleep with me. arrow to *Domino*

9. The Racing Rocket, <u>a new thriller rollercoaster</u>, is now open at the park. arrow to *The Racing Rocket*

Assess, p. 159

A 1. Ernesto, <u>my cousin</u>, likes baseball and hockey. circle *Ernesto*

2. A large black cloud, <u>a sign of a thunderstorm</u>, appeared in the sky. circle *cloud*

3. William Shakespeare, <u>a playwright and poet</u>, wrote during the sixteenth and seventeenth centuries. circle *William Shakespeare*

4. Only a few animals, <u>mostly dogs and cats</u>, were found. circle *animals*

5. Pete, <u>my brother's friend</u>, makes the best popcorn over a campfire. circle *Pete*

B Student sentences should use the appositive phrases correctly as well as reflect correct use of punctuation.

Grammar: Verbals

Practice, p. 160

A 1. Karen wore <u>running</u> shoes for the race.

2. Alicia modeled her <u>dancing</u> costume.

3. The <u>bottled</u> water was cold.

4. We arranged a <u>walking</u> tour of the museum.

5. The <u>canned</u> tuna will be on sale.

B 1. The <u>glowing</u> trophy was won by our team.

2. The <u>melted</u> snow made puddles in the street.

3. The <u>winding</u> road led to the park.

4. <u>Disoriented</u>, the hikers returned to the trail.

Assess, p. 161

A 1. <u>Determined</u> campers put their tents up in the rain.

2. The <u>grinning</u> winners of the pie-eating contest sat down.

3. Swimmers, <u>experienced</u> and <u>inexperienced</u>, participated in the meet.

4. <u>Frightened</u> chipmunks ran across the lawn.

5. The picture of a <u>laughing</u> cow appears on cheese.

6. <u>Exhausted</u> children need to go bed early.

7. Successful students set <u>studying</u> time aside.

8. <u>Climbing</u> clothing is available at the store.

B 1. <u>Satisfied</u>, the shopper walked away with the lamp. past

2. A <u>banging</u> sound came from under the hood. present

3. The <u>ground</u> beef was used to make hamburgers. past

4. Deep within the cave, we heard a <u>fluttering</u> sound. present

5. <u>Simplified</u> instructions came with the mixer. past

6. A <u>muffled</u> bark came from the <u>covered</u> basket. past/past

7. <u>Enthused</u>, Billy began to rake the leaves. past

8. <u>Relieved</u>, the mother hugged the lost child. past

Writing: Poem

Practice, p. 162

1. Be sure students complete all of the columns in the chart.
2. Students will need to demonstrate their understanding of the poem's structure when drafting their poems.
3. All poems should have a title.

Assess, p. 163

1. Students should list all of the characteristics of their poem type.
2. Students will need to demonstrate their understanding of the poem's structure when drafting their poems.
3. All poems should reflect an understanding of the poem type and structure, not contain spelling or mechanical errors, and demonstrate an ability to draft a poem.

Writing: Metaphor

Practice, p. 164

A 1. Words are compared to a blast of cold air.
2. Silence is compared to a brick wall.
3. A test is compared to a black cloud.
4. A lake is compared to a mirror.
5. The sun is compared to a golden coin.
6. The stars are compared to diamonds.
7. A room is compared to a peaceful island in a stormy sea.
8. Mist is compared to a cold wet blanket.

B Sample Answers:

The silence was a brick wall between us. It separated us from each other, and we could not seem to cross it.
Overhead, millions of tiny diamonds sparkled in the night sky. I wanted to reach out and take them one by one to make a shining necklace.

Assessment, p. 165

A 1. Fog is compared to a cat.
2. The cat sits looking out over the harbor and city.
3. Details include the haunches of the cat and its moving away.

B Sample Answers:

1. A winter storm is a fierce lion.
2. Its sudden appearance. Its savage roar. Its fierce jaws of ice.
3. The fierce lion strikes suddenly from the north. It roars savagely outside our windows. Its fierce jaws of ice bring down power lines and crush branches on trees.

Writing: Writing for Assessment

Practice, p. 166

1. Choose-identify; discuss-support a generalization with facts and examples.
2. Student details should logically support their position.
3. The main thesis should relate directly to the prompt.
4. Facts, examples, and descriptions should logically support the thesis.
5. Students should write a concluding statement that reinforces the main thesis.

Assess, p. 167

A 1. The opening statement should clearly state the student's position on how the funds should be spent.
2. Examples should logically support the statement.
3. The concluding statement should summarize and reinforce the student's position.

B 1. The opening statement should clearly state the student's position on funding for America's national parks.
2. Examples should logically support the statement.
3. The concluding statement should summarize and reinforce the student's position.

Reading: Paraphrasing

Practice, p. 168

A Possible answers:
1. desire; wish
2. notice; observe
3. brothers
4. People have the same thoughts and feelings all over the world.

B Possible answer: As I sit here alone with my thoughts and dreams, I imagine that there are other people just like me in foreign lands with the same thoughts and dreams, and I feel that they are my brothers.

Assess, p. 169

A Possible answers:
1. echoing
2. bird
3. go down
4 a grassy park or recreational area
5. It lifts the spirits to play outside amid the beauties of nature.

B Possible answer: The bright sun and singing birds make a joyous setting for playing outside until it gets dark and we get tired.

Literary Analysis: Sound Devices

Practice, p. 170
A 1. repetition
2. onomatopoeia
3. alliteration
4. rhyme

B 1. B
2. C

Assess, p. 171
A 6. repetition
7. rhyme
8. alliteration
9. onomatopoeia

B 1. A
2. B
3. A
4. A

Literary Analysis: Rhythm and Rhyme

Practice, p. 172
A 1. I'm Nobody! | Who are you?
2. She was | a child | and I was | a child
3. And I looked at it, | and I thought a bit, | and I looked at my frozen chum;

B Once upon a midnight <u>dreary</u>, while I pondered, weak and <u>weary</u>,

Over many a quaint and curious volume of forgotten <u>lore—</u>

While I nodded, nearly <u>napping</u>, suddenly there came a <u>tapping.</u>

As of some one gently <u>rapping</u>, <u>rapping at my chamber door—</u>

" 'Tis some visitor," I muttered, "<u>tapping at my chamber door—</u>

Only this and nothing <u>more</u>.

Assess, p. 173
A (When) the summer fields are <u>mown</u>,
(When) the birds are fledged and <u>flown</u>,
(And) the dry leaves strew the <u>path</u>;
(With) the falling of the <u>snow</u>,
(With) the cawing of the <u>crow</u>,
Once again the fields we <u>mow</u>
(And) gather in the <u>aftermath</u>.

B 1. It was man | y and man | y a year | ago | / In a king | dom by | the sea.
2. And this | was the rea | son that, long | ago / In this king | dom by | the sea

C 1. Rhythm
2. meter
3. Rhyme

4. feet
5. Vertical lines

Literary Analysis: Comparing Imagery

Practice, p. 174
A 1. rooftops of houses, edge of water, trees in woods
2. wade with naked feet
3. sensation of the water on your feet, roughness of the sand on feet

B 1. Touch
2. sight, sound
3. sight
4. sight
5. sight

Assess, p. 175
A 1. Swimming fish and rocks
2. Function as opposites as one moves and the other is stationary.
3. The sea, fish, rocks, ship

B 1. sight, sound
2. sight
3. sight
4. sight, sound
5. sight
6. sight

Vocabulary: Synonyms

Practice, p. 176
A 1. D
2. H
3. E
4. C
5. A
6. G
7. B
8. F

B (Answers may vary. Possible responses are shown.)
9. asking, inquiring
10. hopeful, wishful
11. sickness, illness
12. uncommon, unusual

Assess, p. 177
A 1. F
2. B
3. H
4. A
5. E
6. C

408 Reading Kit Answers

© Pearson Education, Inc., publishing as Pearson Prentice Hall.

7. G

8. D

B (Answers may vary. Possible responses are shown.)

9. promising, vowing

10. unfriendly, unkind

11. slimness, thinness

12. rebox, recrate

Grammar: Independent and Subordinate Clauses

Practice, p. 178

A 1. My book, which has many pictures, has little text.

2. That cat, which is mine, is an Abyssinian.

3. When cats prowl at night, their eyes adjust to the dark.

4. Although wild cats hunt at night, they prefer dusk or dawn.

5. Whereas Angora cats have long hair, Siamese cats have short hair.

6. Cats, which vary in size, also have many different colorings.

7. Cats may shrill loudly when they are hungry.

8. Most lions in Africa live in national parks, where they are protected.

B Sample answers

1. The house has many windows that let in the light.

2. Many people eat vegetables because they are healthy.

3. Some athletes prefer swimming, although some prefer running.

Assess, p. 179

A 1. Although she was in charge, she was not bossy.

2. Laura was in charge because she was an excellent camper.

3. Before we started, we checked our backpacks.

4. After we ate, we put out the fire.

5. We set up our tents when we arrived there.

6. Before an hour had passed, the stars came out.

7. Although breakfast was good, dinner was better.

8. Dan skis well, although he is slow.

9. If the sun shines, we will have a picnic.

10. Cats purr when they are happy.

B 1. clause

2. subordinate

3. independent, subordinate

4. independent

5. subordinate

Grammar: Sentence Structure

Practice, p. 180

A 1. simple

2. compound

3. simple

4. compound

5. complex

B Sample answers

1. The student teacher liked to write poetry. (simple)

2. Although he was a poet, Lewis Carroll also wrote novels. (complex)

Assess, p. 181

A 1. simple

2. simple

3. complex

4. compound

5. simple

6. compound

7. complex

8. simple

B Sample Answers

1. Although she made her own clothing, Joan wanted to buy a dress for the dance. (complex)

2. It was raining when Josh got up, but he went to the pool anyway. (compound)

3. He went to the picnic in the car. (simple)

4. The chairs and table arrived and the delivery workers brought them in the house. (compound)

Grammar: Fragments and Run-On Sentences

Practice, p. 182

Sample Answers

1. The class arrived early this morning.

2. Correct

3. We didn't go swimming because they warned us not to.

4. My sister has a horse she has been riding a long time. His name is Ben.

5. Correct

6. Tom opened all his presents after his birthday meal.

Assess, p. 183

A 1. S 2. R 3. F 4. S 5. R

B Sample Answers

1. Sam spent time working in Paris as a cook.

2. For her next project at school, Alice reported on the solar system.

3. Work on the kitchen went fast once the cabinets arrived.

4. They do not run well for long distances.

5. Mozart had severe hardships and disappointments, but his music is cheerful and vigorous.

6. His father taught him carpentry. He never attended a class.

7. Kelly writes stories. She does not write music.

Spelling: Words with Prefixes and Suffixes

Practice, p. 184

A 1. <u>mis</u>spell

2. canceled

3. fam<u>ous</u>

4. <u>un</u>necessary

B 1. reenlist

2. unnecessary

3. happiness

4. correct

Assess, p. 185

A 1. suspenseful

2. happiness

3. occurred

B 1. postdated

2. unnecessary

3. reenlist

4. misspell

C 1. C

2. B

3. C

Writing: Poem

Practice, p. 186

1. Students should write a four line poem using alliteration.

2. Student poems should reflect an understanding of the use of alliteration. A pattern of consistent repetitive sounds should be evident throughout the work.

3. Student responses should relate to the subject of the poem.

4. Students should show evidence of having reviewed the poem.

Assess, p. 187

A 1. A

2. B

3. A

B Student poems should reflect an understanding of the use of alliteration. A pattern of consistent repetitive sounds should be evident throughout the work.

1. Student responses should relate to the subject of the poem.

2. Circled responses should demonstrate an understanding of alliteration.

Writing: Paraphrase of a Poem

Practice, p. 188

Sample Answer: The moon seemed to be pouting. The moon thought the sun should not be there during the night. She (the moon) thinks the sun is very rude to be there during her time.

Assess, p. 189

Sample Answers:

1. trotting—jogging; scarcely—not, barely

2. "Do you want to go home now?" the Carpenter asked the oysters. But they did not answer because they had been eaten by the Walrus and the Carpenter.

3. The carpenter asked the oysters if they wanted to go home. They did not answer because they had all been eaten.

Writing: Persuasive Essay

Practice, p. 190

Sample Answers:

1. homework limits

2. Homework should be limited to two hours per night.

3. Too much homework makes it difficult to participate in after-school activities. It also limits family time.

4. Each class is taught by a different teacher. Teachers do not know what all the rest of a student's teachers are assigning for homework. To solve this, teachers in each subject area could be given specific nights on which they can assign homework.

5. Some people might say that it would be impossible to limit homework because teachers do not know what other teachers are assigning. To solve this, I suggest that teachers in each subject be assigned specific nights on which they are allowed to assign homework.

Assess, p. 191

Sample Answers:

1. all schools should have uniforms; parents should not limit their children's time playing video games; young people should tell an adult if they see other young people drinking or doing drugs

2. (Topic: Parents should not limit video game time.) Students who play video games often have very good concentration skills. They are also usually very good at solving problems and puzzles. They have great fine motor skills and hand-eye coordination.

3. Argument: Video games cause young people to become violent. Response: This is very rare. For most young people, it lets them take out any bad feelings on the game and not in real life. Argument: Video games keep young people from making friends. Response: Video game players make friends with other video game fans.

4. Parents should not limit their children's time playing video games. As long as kids finish their homework and chores, video games are a great way to spend their time. Video games help young people learn to concentrate for a very long time. Video game players also learn to solve problems. Finally, they have great hand-eye coordination.

Unit 5

Reading: Setting a Purpose for Reading

Practice, p. 192
1. C
2. B
3. D
4. B

Assess, p. 193
1. B
2. C
3. A

Reading: Adjust Reading Rate

Practice, p. 194
1. F; You would read a sports magazine for enjoyment, and probably quickly.
2. F; You would probably read your favorite poem at a comfortable rate, and you might reread parts that mean the most to you.
3. T; You would read carefully and slowly when studying for a test to retain information.
4. T; You would read a fantasy novel for enjoyment at whatever rate is comfortable for you.

Assess, p. 195
1. B
2. D
3. B
4. D
5. B

Literary Analysis: Dialogue

Practice, p. 196
1. A
2. C
3. A
4. B

Assess, p. 197
1. B
2. B
3. A
4. C

Literary Analysis: Stage Directions

Practice, p. 198
1. B
2. C
3. A

Assess, p. 199
A **Characters on Stage:** older man
Movement of Character: walks by tracks; wipes sweat; jumps back; stumbles; readies camera
Description of Lighting: sunny and warm
Description of Sounds: birds chirping; train whistle; train sounds
Other Special Effects: train smoke
B Sample Answers:
1. father returns home after a trip with gifts for kids; A family won a prize.
   A. excited children run out of the house—door slams open
   B. car races up driveway (in a hurry) with honking horn
   C. man gets out of car with presents and balloons

Literary Analysis: Comparing Characters

Practice, p. 200
A 1. generous
2. sneaky
3. funny
4. brave
5. smart
6. daring
B 1. excited
2. calm
3. serious
4. shy
5. friendly

1. **A.** red hair; freckles

   B. brown hair, sunburned face

2. **A.** joker or funny

   B. forgetful or generous

3. **A.** watches sister; feeds family dog

   B. mows lawn; takes out trash

4. **A. & B.** Sample answers: neighbors, friends, biking, or basketball

Vocabulary: Suffixes *-ment, -tion*

Practice, p. 202

(Sentences will differ. Possible responses are shown.)

1. **New Word:** instruction **Sentence:** Her instruction was very clear, and I learned a lot.

2. **New Word:** encampment **Sentence:** We slept very soundly in our forest encampment.

3. **New Word:** distraction **Sentence:** The constant barking was a terrible distraction.

4. **New Word:** establishment **Sentence:** Fifty new members have joined since the establishment of our club in 2004.

Assess, p. 203

(Sentences will differ. Possible responses are shown.)

1. **New Word:** illustration **Sentence:** I'll use an illustration of different types of birds.

2. **New Word:** statement **Sentence:** His statement concerned the condition of his ship.

3. **New Word:** enchantment **Sentence:** The enchantment began with a beautiful song about teeth.

4. **New Word:** argument **Sentence:** Their noisy argument continued for over an hour.

5. **New Word:** digestion **Sentence:** Yes, rest will help the digestion of a big meal.

6. **New Word:** agreement **Sentence:** After a long argument, they finally reached an agreement.

7. **New Word:** completion **Sentence:** Upon completion of this worksheet, let's go for a swim.

Grammar: Interjections

Practice, p. 204

A 1. Ouch

2. Wow

3. Yuck, Ugh

4. Yikes

5. Uh

6. Oh, Wow

7. Whew

B 1. Aw,

2. Wow!

3. Ouch!

4. Whew,

5. Darn,

6. Ugh! Gee,

7. Hey,

Assess, p. 205

A 1. Wow

2. Yuck

3. Yikes

4. Hey

5. Oops

6. Boy

7. Hmm

B Sample answers

1. Yuck, this broccoli tastes horrible.

2. Hey, I'm over here.

3. Wow, that car sure is fast!

4. Hmm, I wonder what he means by that.

5. Oops, I dropped the butter.

6. Whew, I sure am glad that's over.

7. Boy, that was a long walk.

Grammar: Double Negatives

Practice, p. 206

A 1. any; 2. anything; 3. any; 4. anything; 5. any; 6. anybody; 7. any

B 1. The poor man has no shoes.
   The poor man doesn't have any shoes.

2. We are going nowhere this summer.
   We aren't going anywhere this summer.

3. Why will you have nothing to do with him?
   Why won't you have anything to do with him?

4. Joan never reads anything but books about horses.
   Joan reads nothing but books about horses.

Assess, p. 207

A 1. will; 2. ever; 3. could; 4. any; 5. anything; 6. don't; 7. ever

B 1. Do nothing until you receive further instructions.
   Don't do anything until you receive further instructions.

2. There is no one on our team who plays as well as James.
   There isn't anyone on our team who plays as well as James.

3. Bill can't find any of his original drafts of the story.
   Bill can find none of his original drafts of the story.

4. They won't allow anyone in until 7:45 P.M.
   They will allow no one in until 7:45 P.M.

Grammar: Word Usage

Practice, p. 208

A 1. effect; 2. accept; 3. except; 4. affect;
5. accept; 6. effect; 7. except

B 1. affect; 2. affect; 3. except; 4. effect; 5. accept

Assess, p. 209

A 1. accept; 2. effect; 3. affect; 4. except;
5. accept; 6. effects; 7. except

B Sample Answers
1. correct
2. except
3. correct
4. affect
5. accept

Writing: Friendly Letter

Practice, p. 210

A 1. B
2. C
3. A

B Friendly letters will vary. Students should show
an understanding of the five parts of a friendly
letter with a clear purpose in the body of the
letter.

Assess, p. 211

A 1. A
2. D
3. C
4. D

B Friendly letters will vary. Students should show
an understanding of the five parts of a friendly
letter with a clear purpose in the body of the
letter.

Writing: Tribute

Practice, p. 212

1. Students should pick an appropriate person
   to offer a tribute to.
2. Students should describe what that person
   did.
3. Students should offer three adjectives to
   describe that person.
4. Students should describe why this person is
   worthy of a tribute.

Assess, p. 213

Students' tributes should include most of the
elements that were reviewed in the Practice page
using the information provided.

Writing: Multimedia Report

Practice, p. 214

1. A; students' responses should include the
   ideas that "Types of Whales" is a focused
   topic, and it has many print and nonprint
   sources, including photos, video, and audio.
2. Responses will vary but should introduce the
   topic of chocolate.
3. D
4. Responses will vary but will probably include
   ideas about using video, music, photos, and
   even hands-on props for a multimedia
   presentation for a very young audience.

Assess, p. 215

Sample Answers

1. Students should pick an appropriate topic,
   such as: Dolphins.
2. Students should suggest a variety of sources
   for print media, for example: I would use
   articles from nature magazines and
   encyclopedias for print media.
3. Students should suggest a variety of
   reasonable sources for nonprint media, for
   example: I would use photos and film clips
   from documentaries, and also audio clips of
   dolphins making sounds. There are many
   photos available on dolphins, too.
4. Students should relate a reasonable
   prediction of the response their report will
   receive.
5. Students should write a two-sentence
   introduction to a multimedia report.

Reading: Summarize

Practice, p. 216

1. B
2. C
3. D

Assess, p. 217

1. The Willow Grove botanical garden has rare
   purple roses.
2. Student's answers might include the details
   that gardeners are not allowed to cut the
   purple roses; the roses are so valuable that
   they can be sold at the fundraising auction
   for the hospital.
3. Students' summaries should include the
   main ideas and brief recounting of details:
   The Willow Grove botanical garden has rare
   purple roses that are very valuable, and
   many other varieties of roses, too. The
   botanical garden donates bouquets of roses
   to the hospital, and one purple rose bush
   every year to the auction.

Reading: Close Reading for Applications

Practice, p. 218
    1. C; 2. B; 3. C

Assess, p. 219
    1. D; 2. C; 3. D; 4. A

Literary Analysis: Character's Motives

Practice, p. 220
A 1. hope
    2. anger
    3. fear

B Sample Answers
    1. B; The tears in Vicki's eyes suggest that she feels bad for the dog.
    2. C; The fact that they keep trying despite their failures shows they are determined to come up with a solution.

Assess, p. 221
    1. C, 2. B, 3. A, 4. A

Literary Analysis: Comparing Dramatic Speeches

Practice, p. 222
A 1. c

B 2. **optimistic:** Speech 1, Character: debate club member, Example: "I just know all our hard work will pay off."; **unreliable:** Speech 2, Character: Miles, Example: Then why have you missed so many meetings? And why are you never prepared when you do show up?; **honest:** Speech 2, Character: Emily, Example: Frankly, Miles, it's because of you.

Assess, p. 223
Speech 1: Type: dialogue, Main Characters: Chrissy, Jamal, Description: Chrissy is critical and likes her privacy; Jamal tries to see the good in people, How Learned: Through their conversation; Chrissy calls Mrs. Healy nosy and a busybody; Jamal thinks she's friendly.

Speech 2: Type: monologue, Main Characters: the speaker, Description: open-minded, appreciative, How Learned: through her thoughts and feelings; She understands how some might be turned off by inquisitive neighbors but also appreciates how such people can benefit the neighborhood.

Vocabulary: Suffixes -ize and -yze

Practice, p. 224
(Sentences will differ. Possible responses are shown.)
    1. **New Word:** theorize **Sentence:** I theorize that there are several more planets to be discovered.
    2. **New Word:** paralyze **Sentence:** Why did the accident paralyze the horse?
    3. **New Word:** familiarize **Sentence:** This book will familiarize you with several wildflowers.
    4. **New Word:** energize **Sentence:** Running should energize you.

Assess, p. 225
(Sentences will differ. Possible responses are shown.)
    1. **New Word:** characterize **Sentence:** I would characterize him as a proud and honest man.
    2. **New Word:** analyze **Sentence:** No, I would analyze that poem quite differently.
    3. **New Word:** Americanize **Sentence:** I would Americanize it by adding ketchup.
    4. **New Word:** memorize **Sentence:** No, it's easy for me to memorize songs.
    5. **New Word:** categorize **Sentence:** I would categorize them as large mammals.
    6. **New Word:** initialize **Sentence:** Yes, they will initialize it with a large W.

Grammar: Sentence Functions and Endmarks

Practice, p. 226
A 1. What are you doing this afternoon?
    2. I'm cleaning my room and vacuuming the rug.
    3. How long will it take you?
    4. It's really a mess this time.
    5. Well, hurry up!
    6. It may take me all afternoon.

B 1. I; Is that a bear over there in the park?
    2. D; That's a black bear beyond the evergreens.
    3. E; Oh, how friendly he looks!
    4. Im; Don't go near him or you may be sorry.
    5. D; He may not be so friendly up close.
    6. Im; Please take a picture of him for our album.

Assess, p. 227
A 1. I wanted you to go to the movies with me.
    2. I'd like to, but I can't finish doing my chores in time.
    3. Let me come over and help you.
    4. I couldn't ask you to do that.
    5. I'll come right over on my bike.
    6. Do you mean it?

7. Of course I do!

8. I'll see you soon.

B 1. I; How does the homing pigeon find its way home?

2. D; I read an interesting magazine article about pigeons.

3. Im; Read this article if you want to learn about them.

4. I; Did you know that pigeons can see special light rays?

5. D; These light rays are invisible to humans.

6. D; Pigeons use their vision to find the sun's position.

7. E; How remarkable that pigeons can do this!

8. Im; Imagine the world from a pigeon's-eye view.

9. E; How different it must look!

Grammar: Subject-Verb Argreement

Practice, p. 228

1. live; 2. are; 3. likes; 4. take; 5. feeds; 6. stray; 7. are; 8. want; 9. object; 10. have; 11. are; 12. has; 13. are; 14. know

Assess, p. 229

A 1. have; 2. leads; 3. were; 4. are; 5. are; 6. live; 7. take; 8. has; 9. is; 10. are

B 1. picks; 2. tastes; 3. cooks; 4. are; 5. has; 6. are; 7. are; 8. drive; 9. take; 10. have

Spelling: Plurals

Practice, p. 230

A 1. knife

2. country

3. box

4. disk

B 1. Add *s* to the noun.

2. If a noun ends in an *o* that follows a vowel, then add *s*.

3. Add *es* to nouns that end in *s*, *sh*, *ch*, or *x*.

4. If the final *o* of a noun follows a consonant, add *es*.

5. If a noun ends in a *y* that follows a consonant, form the plural by changing the *y* to *i* and adding *es*.

6. Irregular plural. Some nouns have the same spelling in both singular and plural.

Assess, p. 231

1. C

2. A

3. D

4. B

5. C

6. C

Writing: Report

Practice, p. 232

1. Students may choose either C or D because they are very familiar activities that they experience every day.

2. For C, students may include details such as whether they buy or bring their lunch, how many kids eat together, how noisy it is, why they chose to buy or bring (money, diet, choice), the time and length of lunch period, and what they might change about the experience. For D, details might include the length of their commute, type of transportation, what friends or relatives they travel with, length of time they spend commuting, and how they use that time. Recommendations for change should also be included.

Assess, p. 233

Students' recommendations should be based on how effectively they do their homework. Details in the report should point directly to its recommendations.

Writing: Cause-and-Effect Essay

Practice, p. 234

Sample Answers:

1. Cause: Not Washing Your Hands

2. Some of the effects of not washing your hands are catching a cold, spreading germs, and/or getting an infection.

3. I can go to the library or browse medical web sites for more information to support my topic.

4. My audience could learn the benefits of good hygiene.

Assess, p. 235

1–4. Students should supply an appropriate topic for a cause-and-effect essay, with one cause and three effects.

5. Students should state what they hope their audience will learn from the essay.

Unit 6

Reading: Cause and Effect

Practice, p. 236

A 1. B; 2. C; 3. A

B 1. <u>Jack missed the school bus</u> because <u>he overslept</u>.

2. <u>Traffic was terrible</u>, so <u>we were two hours late getting home</u>.

3. <u>Rachel felt unhappy</u> because <u>she was unable to find a summer job.</u>

4. <u>Ice covered the road,</u> so <u>traffic moved slowly.</u>

5. <u>Kathy couldn't ride her bike</u> because <u>it had a flat tire.</u>

C Cause: likes to show off   Effect: drives over the speed limit

Cause: drives too fast   Effect: damages car; gets speeding ticket

Cause: gets speeding ticket   Effect: has to pay fine; couldn't drive car for month

Assess, p. 237

A 1. <u>Because of the rain,</u> <u>our basement flooded.</u>

2. <u>Jake broke his leg;</u> therefore, <u>he couldn't play in the game</u> and <u>had to use crutches to walk.</u>

3. As a result of last night's <u>power outage,</u> <u>we ate a cold dinner by candlelight.</u>

4. <u>Jane forgot to put the top on the grasshopper's box;</u> consequently, <u>the insect escaped.</u>

5. Since <u>it has not rained in several days</u> and <u>because it has been cold,</u> <u>the new seedlings have died.</u>

6. <u>Joe's dad left his car's headlights on</u> last night; <u>so the car won't start.</u>

7. The <u>farmland meant everything to the Hutchinsons</u> because <u>it had been in the family for generations.</u>

8. <u>Rosemary overslept this morning,</u> and as a result, <u>she didn't have time to eat breakfast</u> and <u>was late for work.</u>

B Answers will vary.

Reading: Skim and Scan

Practice, p. 238

(Sample answers follow T or F indication.)

1. F; I would scan or skim a table of contents in a textbook to find a particular chapter.

2. F; I would definitely skim headings to see what topics were covered in a chapter.

3. F; Captions of photos and graphs are always worth scanning.

4. T

5. T

6. F; Headings give main ideas and key points in a textbook, so I would look at headings when looking for a main idea.

7. T

Assess, p. 239

Students should indicate appropriate skimming and scanning strategies: they might check the table of contents for the location of Chapter Three; they might skim the headings within the chapter looking

for "taxation without representation"; they might look for a map that would show the colonies; they might look in a glossary or look at photos to see if they can find "lobsterback," the British redcoat soldier; they might skim paragraphs looking for key words. Some combination of these strategies would be needed to pass the open book quiz.

Literary Analysis: Myth

Practice, p. 240

1. B; 2. C; 3. B

Assess, p. 241

1. D

2. C

3. Apollo and Zeus. Apollo causes the sun to move across the sky, and Zeus can hurl thunderbolts.

4. Too much confidence can be dangerous, especially when you don't have the necessary skills.

Literary Analysis: Legend

Practice, p. 242

2. larger-than-life human; details about the culture

3. larger-than-life human; fantastic elements

Assess, p. 243

1. C, 2. D, 3. D, 4. A

Literary Analysis: Epic Conventions

Practice, p. 244

1. D; 2. B

Assess, p. 245

A 1. C; 2. C

B 1. Yes; long adventure; wins battle

2. No; ordinary people; everyday event

Vocabulary: Denotation and Connotation

Practice, p. 246

1. **Denotation:** had a low price **Connotation:** positive

2. **Denotation:** had a low price **Connotation:** neutral

3. **Denotation:** had a low price **Connotation:** negative

Assess, p. 247

1. **Denotation:** a rainy event **Connotation:** neutral

2. **Denotation:** a rainy event **Connotation:** negative

3. **Denotation:** a rainy event **Connotation:** positive

4. **Denotation:** of light weight **Connotation:** negative

5. **Denotation:** of light weight **Connotation:** positive

6. **Denotation:** of light weight **Connotation:** neutral

Grammar: Colon

Practice, p. 248

A 1. My favorite sports are the following: baseball, basketball, soccer, and tennis.

2. Four states border Mexico: California, Arizona, New Mexico, and Texas.

3. The box had the following: rocks, marbles, shoes, and rope.

4. Add these things to your list: bread, eggs, milk, and flour.

5. This is what I have to do on Sunday: clean my room, baby-sit for my brother, and finish my homework.

6. Sam is afraid of these jungle animals: tigers, leopards, and snakes.

B Answers will vary.

C 1. We have studied the following kinds of punctuation marks: commas, colons, and apostrophes.

2. Correct

3. We have two excellent players this year: Tom and Mike.

4. Correct

Assess, p. 249

1. Four team sports are popular in U.S. schools: basketball, baseball, football, and soccer.

2. The day after Thanksgiving is a holiday in these states: Florida, Maine, Minnesota, Nebraska, and Washington.

3. The basic unit consists of three rooms: a living room, bedroom, and kitchen.

4. Maryanne chose three different poets to study: Dickinson, Frost, and Sandburg.

5. In this wallet are my life's savings: six dollar bills, eight quarters, and two nickels.

6. Their birthdays were all in the summer: June 27, July 11, and August 9.

7. The salad contains three ingredients: lettuce, tomatoes, and mushrooms.

8. My father always grows a variety of vegetables: carrots, squash, tomatoes, and cucumbers.

9. Campers need the following items: a sleeping bag, tent, warm clothing, and sturdy shoes.

10. We have the following trees on our property: maple, elm, and oak.

11. Bees do things such as the following: sing, sting, and fly away.

12. I have two favorite seasons: spring and fall.

13. We have practice on the following days: May 18, May 20, and May 21.

14. I had to choose a book about one of these topics: the Civil War, the Industrial Revolution, or immigration.

15. The first three United States presidents were the following: George Washington, John Adams, and Thomas Jefferson.

16. I met the following people at the party: Gary, Patty, and James.

17. The following roads will be closed by today: Dover, Webster, and Bell.

Grammar: Commas

Practice, p. 250

A 1. Jan, Dot, Steve, and Corey are coming to the party.

2. I've called the guests, bought the food, and warned the neighbors.

3. I think this will be a loud, enjoyable, and exciting party.

4. By the way, can you bring plates?

5. Sarah walked, ran, and even rode a bike to get here.

B 1. After we eat, we will do the dishes.

2. With very little money, she left home to spend a day in the city.

3. After he finished school, he went to visit his father at work.

4. To win the state championship, the team practiced day and night.

5. Whenever you are ready, we can leave.

C 1. You were away having a good time, and I was here bored and lonely.

2. Mars is closer, but Jupiter appears brighter.

3. The hours ticked away, but the phone never rang.

4. I enjoy watching football, but I like baseball better.

5. It was a superbly written book, and I could not put it down.

Assess, p. 251

A 1. Jerry tried out for the lead, but Tom got the part.

2. Sandy ran up the block, across the park, and around the school.

3. The storm caused great damage and washed away several bridges. [Correct]

4. Last Saturday was windy, cold, and rainy.

5. I stopped by to pick you up, but you had already left.

6. We arrived early and stayed late. [Correct]

7. My shoes are not under my bed, in the closet, or under the couch.

8. If it does not rain tomorrow, the roads will be jammed.

9. Jackie and Katie will be roommates next year. [Correct]

10. Firs, spruces, and pines are evergreen trees.

B 1. Spring came, and the birds flew north.

2. I can hand in a written report on spiders, or I can give an oral report.

3. They had been working very hard, but they didn't seem especially tired.

4. Usually we study in the morning, and we go swimming in the afternoon.

Grammar: Revising Incorrect Use of Commas

Practice, p. 252

A 1. The campers were hot and tired, for they had been hiking all day.

2. The doctor examined the patient carefully, but she did not say a word.

3. Kevin is not very heavy but is the best football player on the team. [Correct]

4. An Arabian stallion is a fast, beautiful horse.

5. The long, dark pathway led to a grim, ruined house.

6. Jack hit a line drive and dashed for first base. [Correct]

7. Elephants are lazy, friendly, and good-natured.

8. Everyone wondered who had been in the house, what he had wanted, and where he had gone.

9. Cathy likes tennis and golf but doesn't like softball. [Correct]

10. We had eaten everything in the refrigerator, but we were still hungry.

B Val was almost ready to give up, but she finallyˣ spotted a light in the distance. She had been lost, in the woods for hours, yet she had kept moving. The day had started out beautifully, and it had seemed like a good idea to go for a hike. Valerie was a personˣ who always tried to plan ahead. She had put some provisions in a backpack, for she wanted to be prepared for a hike of several hours. She had not counted on being out, for so long. Since she used up her supplies hours ago, now she was hungryˣ and thirsty. The distant light was a signal that all would be well, and Valerie hurried toward it.

Assess, p. 253

A 1. Bike riding, brisk walking, and swimming are good forms of exercise.

2. The victims of the hurricane were stunned, for they had lost everything.

3. Crabs and lobsters are both shellfish. [Correct]

4. The quiet, obedient dog is a pleasure to be around.

5. The pilot boarded the plane, checked her instruments, and prepared for takeoff.

6. The tornado took a heavy toll in lives and property. [Correct]

7. Susan wanted to explore the cave, but her parents had forbidden it.

8. He and his wife skied in the Alps and enjoyed it very much. [Correct]

9. We had lessons in swimming, canoeing, and archery.

10. The radio announcer warned of the storm, but no one paid any attention.

B 1. Mowing a lawn on such a hot, hazy, humid day was no fun.

2. Sandy folded the clean laundry, and I placed it in a basket.

3. The teacher repeated the directions, but I was still confused.

4. We found seaweed in the water, on the sand, and under the rocks.

5. The writer opened her book and started to read one of her stories to the audience. [Correct]

6. The doctor recommended plenty of liquids, extra rest, and a light diet.

7. You can use this free ticket for yourself, or you can give it to a friend.

8. Several tired hikers straggled back to camp. [Correct]

9. Dad has several old, valuable stamps in his collection.

10. I eat balanced meals, take vitamins, and get enough sleep.

Writing: Myth

Practice, p. 254

A 1. C, 2. D, 3. A, 4. B

B 1. Students should think of a workable topic for a myth, preferably an idea based on a natural phenomenon.

2. Students should offer two characters for their myths; they may use proper names or common nouns, e.g., "the sea god," and "a sailor."

3. Students should offer two adjectives that reasonably apply to each of their chosen characters.

Assess, p. 255

Sample Answers

1. Main characters: Rascal, Luna; Traits: Rascal, mischievous; Luna, eager

2. Students should add details that describe such things as neatly combed hair, fine clothing or accessories, and so on. Sample answer: He wore a long red cape with delicate gold braiding, and his beard was neatly trimmed.

3. Sample answer: Sparks flew from his fingertips.

4. Student responses should reflect the idea that Rascal has mischief on his mind. Sample answer: Rascal plays a cruel trick on the villagers.

5. Details: evening fire, cool colorful flames, trailing moon; Phenomenon: why fire is hot, or why the moon sits high up in the sky; Sample answer: Fire is hot so that people approaching it will be warned of its danger.

Writing: Description

Practice, p. 256

A Details will vary.

B Details will vary but should follow the guidelines provided.

C Paragraphs will vary but should include the guidelines in activity B.

Assess, p. 257

A 1. sight
   2. sound
   3. touch
   4. touch
   5. sight
   6. sound
   7. sight
   8. taste
   9. touch
   10. taste

B Paragraphs will vary but should follow the guidelines in the directions.

Writing: Business Letter

Practice, page 258

1. B
2. C; This sentence is appropriate because its tone is polite, and it includes supporting details.
3. C

Assess, p. 259

1. Sir:
2. Students' answers should state the point that the shoes were faulty, and might include a description of what was wrong.
3. Students' answers should state the point that the customer wants his or her money refunded.

4. Students' answers should support their statement; they should explain why a refund is fair in this case.
5. Sincerely, *or* Respectfully,
6. Student should sign here.
7. Student should print his or her name here.

Reading: Compare and Contrast

Practice, p. 260

1. Cousin Christine and Cousin Sophie were both afraid of burglars entering their homes at night.
2. Cousin Christine piled her belongings outside her bedroom because she was more afraid of being bothered than losing her belongings. Cousin Sophie claimed that she scared off the burglars at night by piling all the shoes in the house by her bed to throw them down the hallway.

Assess, p. 261

A Sentences will vary but should use words and phrases that compare and contrast.

B Answers will vary, but students should write at least six similarities and/or differences.

Literary Analysis: Cultural Context

Practice, p. 262

1. C
2. C
3. A
4. Sample response: He says that the trip is always difficult, a reminder that travel over great distance was much slower than it is now. An ocean trip probably took many weeks and could be very dangerous as well as uncomfortable.

Assess, p. 263

1. A
2. C
3. B
4. Sample response: The author is from a world in which people have been flying by means of their own bodies for some time, instead of in airplanes. Her world is more advanced technologically than ours, which she seems to find backward. In her society, people can travel to other worlds and disguise themselves to blend in.

Literary Analysis: Folk Tale

Practice, p. 264

1. C
2. D

3. A

4. Sample response: The similarities are mostly in the plots. Both the folk tale and "Hansel and Gretel" are about siblings lost in the woods who find a house to eat and then kill an evil figure who plans to cook one of them.

Assess, p. 265

1. A; 2. B; 3. D; 4. C

Literary Analysis: Tone

Practice, p. 266

A 1. Informative
2. humorous
3. depressed
4. dreamy
5. angry

B Sample answer:
Tone: depressed, unhappy

Assess, p. 267

A 1. C; 2. D; 3. A; 4. B; 5. F; 6. E; 7. F

B Sample answers:
1. nervous, anxious, scary
2. excited, enthusiastic
3. depressed
4. scary, mysterious

Vocabulary: Idioms

Practice, p. 268

Sample answers:
1. Let me give you some good advice about how to do well on tests.
2. After school, I like to be with my friends.
3. I think that story isn't accurate.
4. I was exhausted after the game.
5. Some people enjoyed the new television show, but I thought it was terrible.
6. Whom do you think I met today?

Vocabulary: Idioms

Assess, p. 269

Sample answers:
1. What seems to be Mr. Smith's problem?
2. Solving that problem was easy.
3. Spectators sometimes have to lower their heads so they won't get hit by a baseball during the game.

4. Let me present all my thoughts and then let's discuss them.
5. His rude answer made me very angry.
6. Could you loan me a few dollars?
7. What are your ideas?
8. Are you serious, or are you trying to fool me?
9. Have a great time on your vacation.
10. Can you keep my secret or will you tell it to someone?

Grammar: Capitalization

Practice, p. 270

A 1. My
2. My, You
3. My, Syracuse University
4. Olga, German
5. Let's, Kate
6. Aunt Dora, Jefferson High School
7. Mayor Bailey, Governor Frey

B 1. Sarah's, Would
2. My
3. On, Africa, Rita
4. Officer Patricia Cabot
5. When, Harriet, What
6. My, Uncle Chris, United States
7. Mom, Jackie, I've

Assess, p. 271

A 1. When, I
2. The, Cathy Jordan
3. My, University, Wisconsin, September
4. She, Thursday, Friday, Mr. Stevens
5. In, I, Spanish, Italian
6. The Mohave Desert, California

B 1. We waited for the inspector. The atmosphere was tense. Soon the inspector arrived.
2. He said, "The case is over. We have found the thief."
3. "It's not me," Harry said.
4. "Relax, Harry," the inspector said, "because you're innocent."
5. The inspector had a note. Everyone listened eagerly.
6. "Dear Sir," he read. "Max stole the jewels. He buried them in the yard. Sincerely yours, Pat the Rat."
7. "Impossible!" Kay cried. "My dog is a good dog and is not a thief."

Grammar: Abbreviations

Practice, p. 272

A 1. Mr. Charles Cunningham
2. 197 Maple Ave.
3. Dr. Frances Thompson
4. Thurs., Sept. 13
5. 6:45 P.M., Wed., May 9
6. D. H. Lawrence
7. Mon., 7:30 A.M.
8. St. Louis, MO.
9. Mr. James S. Watson, Sr.
10. Providence, RI

B 1. F; 2. G; 3. J; 4. A; 5. H; 6. I; 7. B; 8. C; 9. D; 10. E

Assess, p. 273

A 1. Thurs., Oct. 15, 7:30 P.M.: babysit for Mrs. Morris
2. Soccer practice: Mon. through Fri., 9 A.M. to 1 P.M.
3. Girl Scout meeting: Orchard St., Wed., 8:00 P.M.
4. 5:00 P.M.: appointment with Dr. Hollings
5. Band rehearsal: Tues., 9:30 A.M.

B 1. Jr.; 2. km.; 3. Blvd.; 4. Md. or MD; 5. ft.

Grammar: Correct Use of Pronoun Case

Practice, p. 274

1. I; 2. her; 3. they; 4. He; 5. me; 6. them; 7. they; 8. her 9. he; 10. I; 11. me; 12. him; 13. her; 14. him; 15. I

Assess, p. 275

A 1. I; 2. I; 3. I; 4. she; 5. I; 6. she; 7. I; 8. him; 9. We; 10. he

B 1. She; 2. her; 3. them; 4. me; 5. I; 6. me

Spelling: Unstressed Syllables

Practice, p. 276

A. 1. 3; 2. 4; 3. 4; 4. 3; 5. 3

B. The food they served us in that <u>restraunt</u> was awful. It tasted like it came from a <u>labratory.</u> Our whole <u>famly</u> agreed that we would never go back there. This was <u>extrordinary,</u> because we hardly ever agree on anything.
1. restaurant; 2. laboratory; 3. family; 4. extraordinary

Assess, p. 277

A 1. C; 2. A; 3. A; 4. B

B 1. C; 2. C; 3. D; 4. A

Writing: Plot Summary

Practice, p. 278

1. Patience and virtue are rewarded.
2. The prince found Cinderella and made her princess.
3. No, although some individual words and phrases can be questioned.

Assess, p. 279

A 1. A
2. C
3. B

B Paragraphs will vary but should follow the guidelines in the checklist.

Writing: Review

Practice, p. 280

1. Responses will vary.
2. Students should explain their reasons rather than simply describing their responses.

Assess, p. 281

1. Responses will vary.
2. Students should explain their reasons rather than simply describing their responses.
3. Students' explanations should relate one way in which their writing experience led to an enhanced understanding or appreciation of their chosen poem.

Writing: Research Report

Practice, p. 282

A Narrowed topics will vary.
B Research questions will vary.

Assess, p. 283

A 1. almanac
2. encyclopedia
3. atlas
4. *Readers' Guide*

B 1. <u>atlas</u>
2. <u>encyclopedia</u>
3. <u>*Readers' Guide*</u>
4. <u>nonprint media</u>
5. <u>book of quotations</u>
6. <u>almanac</u>